KV-388-710

FROUDE AND CARLYLE

LONGMANS, GREEN AND CO. LTD.

39 PATERNOSTER ROW, LONDON, E.C.4
6 OLD COURT HOUSE STREET, CALCUTTA
53 NICOL ROAD, BOMBAY
MOUNT ROAD, MADRAS

LONGMANS, GREEN AND CO.

55 FIFTH AVENUE, NEW YORK
221 EAST 20TH STREET, CHICAGO
TREMONT TEMPLE, BOSTON
128–132 UNIVERSITY AVENUE, TORONTO

FROUDE & CARLYLE

A STUDY OF
THE FROUDE-CARLYLE CONTROVERSY

BY

WALDO H. DUNN

PROFESSOR OF ENGLISH IN THE COLLEGE
OF WOOSTER, U.S.A.

WITH 2 PLATES

LONGMANS, GREEN AND CO.
LONDON ◆ NEW YORK ◆ TORONTO
1930

A1438
920

Made in Great Britain. All rights reserved

TO

RICHARD STEELE DOUGLAS
MARY MATEER DOUGLAS

ALWAYS MY CHARITABLE
READERS

PREFACE

In 1916 I ventured a first statement about the Froude-Carlyle controversy.[1] Mr. Thomas Seccombe's hearty approval of my work encouraged me to continue the investigation. Of necessity I had to consider the whole of Froude's relations with Carlyle, and this volume is the result. I have endeavoured to assemble here, once for all, the essence of the abundant literature which has grown out of the controversy. I have not hesitated to repeat where I have felt that clarity demanded repetition. On the other hand, I have presented only a small portion of the material upon which this volume is based. If I have not herein mentioned a matter that has been called in question by Froude's enemies, it must not be assumed that I have failed to investigate it. There is a limit to the size of books.

I regret that Mr. Alexander Carlyle would not permit me to examine the Carlyle papers in his possession. When I asked permission to collate the documents around which the controversy centres he said that he would be glad to collate for me such portions as I cared to submit for that purpose. In reply I said : 'I cannot submit passages for collation by another. What I publish must be based on material which I have seen with my own eyes and transcribed with my own hand. Only thus can I guarantee it.'

[1] See my *English Biography*, pp. 168–179.

Miss Margaret Froude and Mr. Ashley Froude, however, have assisted me in every way within their power. They have put into my hands everything in their possession which has any bearing on the controversy. I must have wearied them greatly at times, both in person and by letter, as I plied them with questions. Notwithstanding, they have been uniformly kind throughout, and my warmest thanks can be small return for their patient and courteous assistance.

Because of Mr. Alexander Carlyle's attitude I have been compelled to rely upon his published versions of documents. It may be taken for granted, I think, that he has omitted nothing favourable to his side of the controversy. We may feel sure, then, that he has made the most effective use of the material which he has in hand so far as it counts against Froude. I claim, therefore, that my findings are reasonably definitive. If, however, any new evidence comes to light, I shall welcome it, whatever its bearings may be.

To James Anthony Froude, Carlyle gave by will the manuscript of the 'Letters and Memorials of Jane Welsh Carlyle,' 'with whatever other fartherances and elucidations may be possible,' from other personal documents. From the great mass of material thus placed in Froude's hands I quote by the kind permission of his legal representatives and his publishers, Longmans, Green & Company. To the Longmans I am also under deep obligations for replies to my many questions and for the care with which they have produced this book.

Sir James Crichton-Browne and Mr. David Wilson have generously given permission to quote from their books. Through the kindness of the Houghton Mifflin Company I am enabled to use the correspondence of Charles Eliot Norton. Mr. Arthur Severn and Mr. Alexander Wedderburn have kindly permitted the use of letters from, to, and about John Ruskin ; and Mr. Wedderburn has consented to my quoting from the Library Edition of Ruskin's 'Works,' edited by himself and Sir Edward T. Cook.

With my colleague, Mr. Howard F. Lowry, I shall always be happy to associate memories of my work upon this book. He gathered material, he read several drafts of the manuscript, he scrutinised my conclusions, he helped with the proof-reading. For invaluable information, as well as much patient and unwearied verification of facts, I am indebted to Mr. James B. Rye, whose admiration for Mr. Froude goes back to the days when, as a student at Oxford, he attended the lectures of the Regius Professor of Modern History. To Mr. Norwood Young I am grateful for giving me the benefit of his opinion as to the claims of Mary Carlyle. To Mr. Karl Young, Professor of English at Yale University, I owe thanks for a reading of my complete manuscript and for helpful suggestions. To Horace N. Mateer, M.D., my colleague and friend for many years, I am under obligation for reading a portion of the manuscript and for advice upon matters beyond my own province. To Miss Katharine Bricker I am obliged for assistance in procuring books of reference.

Mrs. Daisy V. Lowry, Mr. Clayton K. Howard, and Miss Mildred Mendenhall most generously assisted in preparing the manuscript for publication. My daughters Dorothy and Lorna helped to verify the quotations, make the index, and read the proofs. Other obligations are acknowledged in footnotes.

Dr. Charles F. Wishart, President of the College of Wooster, has followed my work with cordial and loyal interest. To him, and through him, to the Board of Trustees, I wish to express my warmest thanks for encouragement and aid.

WALDO H. DUNN.

WOOSTER, September 10, 1929.

CONTENTS

CONTENTS

LIST OF PLATES

SOURCES CITED BY ABBREVIATION

All other works are referred to by full title.

'Reminiscences,' by Thomas Carlyle. Edited by James Anthony Froude. In two volumes. 1881. Referred to as *Reminiscences*, Froude edition.

'Thomas Carlyle: A History of the First Forty Years of his Life, 1795–1835,' by James Anthony Froude. In two volumes. 1882. Referred to as *Thomas Carlyle*, 1 and 2.

'Letters and Memorials of Jane Welsh Carlyle. Prepared for Publication by Thomas Carlyle.' Edited by James Anthony Froude. In three volumes. 1883. Referred to as *Letters and Memorials*.

'Thomas Carlyle: A History of his Life in London, 1834–1881,' by James Anthony Froude. In two volumes. 1884. Referred to as *Thomas Carlyle*, 3 and 4.

'Early Letters of Thomas Carlyle.' Edited by Charles Eliot Norton. In two volumes. 1886. Referred to as *Early Letters of Carlyle*.

'Reminiscences,' by Thomas Carlyle. Edited by Charles Eliot Norton. In two volumes. 1887. Referred to as *Reminiscences*, Norton edition.

'Letters of Thomas Carlyle.' Edited by Charles Eliot Norton. In two volumes. 1888. Referred to as *Letters of Carlyle*.

'The Table-Talk of Shirley,' by Sir John Skelton. 1895. Referred to as *Shirley*.

'New Letters and Memorials of Jane Welsh Carlyle.' Annotated by Thomas Carlyle and edited by Alexander Carlyle, with an Introduction by Sir James Crichton-Browne. In two volumes. 1903. Referred to as *New Letters and Memorials*.

'My Relations with Carlyle,' by James Anthony Froude. 1903. Referred to as *Relations*.

'The Nemesis of Froude.' A Rejoinder to J. A. Froude's *My Relations with Carlyle*. By Sir James Crichton-Browne and Alexander Carlyle. 1903. Referred to as *Nemesis*. The English edition is the one cited. An American edition of the same date has different paging.

SOURCES CITED BY ABBREVIATION

'New Letters of Thomas Carlyle.' Edited by Alexander Carlyle. In two volumes. 1904. Referred to as *New Letters of Carlyle*.

'Letters of John Ruskin to Charles Eliot Norton.' In two volumes. 1904. Referred to as *Ruskin-Norton Letters*.

'Moncure Daniel Conway: Autobiography, Memories, and Experiences.' In two volumes. 1904. Referred to as *Autobiography*.

'The Love Letters of Thomas Carlyle and Jane Welsh.' Edited by Alexander Carlyle. In two volumes. 1909. Referred to as *Love Letters*.

'The M.P. for Russia: Reminiscences and Correspondence of Madame Olga Novikoff.' Edited by W. T. Stead. In two volumes. 1909. Referred to as *Novikoff*.

'Letters of Charles Eliot Norton.' With Biographical Comment by his daughter Sara Norton and M. A. De Wolfe Howe. In two volumes. 1913. Referred o as *Norton Letters*.

'Jane Welsh Carlyle: Letters to her Family.' Edited by Leonard Huxley. 1924. Referred to as *Jane Welsh Carlyle Letters*.

'Carlyle till Marriage (1795–1826),' by David Wilson. 1923.

'Carlyle to "The French Revolution" (1826–1837),' by David Wilson. 1924.

'Carlyle on Cromwell and Others (1837–1848),' by David Wilson. 1925.

'Carlyle at his Zenith (1848–1853),' by David Wilson. 1927.

The four volumes preceding are referred to as *Carlyle*, 1, 2, 3, and 4.

CONTROVERSIÆ PERSONÆ

The names of those most prominent in the controversy are listed below. The connection of all others is made sufficiently clear in the text.

ALEXANDER CARLYLE (1842–), son of Carlyle's brother Alexander (1797–1876), who emigrated to Canada in 1843. Went to Great Britain in July 1879, and married his cousin Mary Aitken, August 21, 1879. Has edited several volumes of correspondence of Thomas Carlyle and Jane Welsh Carlyle.

JOHN CARLYLE (1801–1879), brother of Thomas Carlyle ; physician ; translator of Dante's *Inferno.* 'I wish him to be regarded as my second self, as my surviving self,' run the words of Thomas Carlyle's will, a wish frustrated by John's death.

MARY CARLYLE (1848–1895), born Mary Aitken, daughter of Thomas Carlyle's sister Jean, who married James Aitken. She became her uncle's housekeeper and amanuensis in 1868. Married her cousin Alexander Carlyle, August 21, 1879.

THOMAS CARLYLE (1795–1881), about whose commission to James Anthony Froude and Froude's fulfilment of it the controversy centres.

MONCURE CONWAY (1832–1907), American clergyman. Was minister of South Place Chapel in London, 1864–1897, and frequented the society of Carlyle. Was one of the first to publish a brief biography of Carlyle in 1881.

Sir JAMES CRICHTON-BROWNE (1840–), Scottish physician of Crindau, Dumfries, Scotland. He knew Carlyle personally. Engaged in the controversy in 1903 on behalf of Alexander Carlyle.

EDWARD FITZGERALD (1809–1883), the well-known translator of *The Rubáiyát* of Omar Khayyám ; a personal friend of Thomas Carlyle, whom he aided in preparing *Cromwell.*

JOHN FORSTER (1812–1876), an intimate and valued friend of Thomas Carlyle, by whom he was appointed one of the executors of his will.

ASHLEY FROUDE (1863–), son of James Anthony Froude, and with his sister Margaret executor of his father's will. With Margaret Froude supervised the publication of *My Relations with Carlyle.*

CONTROVERSIÆ PERSONÆ

James Anthony Froude (1818–1894), about whom as literary executor and biographer of Thomas Carlyle the controversy centres.

Margaret Froude (1850–), daughter of James Anthony Froude, and with her brother Ashley executor of her father's will. With Ashley Froude supervised the publication of *My Relations with Carlyle*.

Richard Garnett (1835–1906), author of *Thomas Carlyle* in 'Great Writers' Series.

Geraldine Jewsbury (1812–1880), authoress, friend of Thomas Carlyle and Jane Welsh Carlyle. In a letter to Mrs. Russell, July 13, 1854, Mrs. Carlyle refers to Geraldine as 'the most intimate friend I have in the world.' See *Letters and Memorials of Jane Welsh Carlyle*, ii. 246, and *Selections from the Letters of Geraldine Jewsbury to Jane Welsh*, edited by Mrs. Alexander Ireland.

William E. H. Lecky (1838–1903), historian. Published hostile review of Froude's *English in Ireland* in *Macmillan's Magazine*, June 1874. Is also hostile to Froude in the *History of England in the Eighteenth Century* (1878–1890).

David Masson (1822–1907), Professor of Rhetoric and English Literature in the University of Edinburgh, 1865–1895; Historiographer Royal of Scotland, 1893–1907.

John Nichol (1833–1894), Regius Professor of English Literature in the University of Glasgow, 1862–1889. His *Carlyle* in the 'English Men of Letters' Series is called 'the fruit of a life's intellectual and moral sympathy' by A. W. Ward in the *Dictionary of National Biography*.

Charles Eliot Norton (1827–1908), Professor of the History of Art in Harvard University, 1875–1898, and translator of Dante's *Divina Commedia*. Had a limited personal acquaintance with Thomas Carlyle.

Margaret Oliphant (1828–1897), author of the *Life of Edward Irving* and many other volumes. She sharply criticised Froude's handling of Carlyle's papers. She was doubtless offended because she was not selected to have some part in the work, particularly in commemorating Mrs. Carlyle. Froude said that her animosity towards him was of long standing.

Herbert Paul (1853–), author of the *Life of Froude* which refutes the attacks upon Froude as historian.

John Ruskin (1819–1900), was for many years an intimate friend of Thomas Carlyle and Jane Welsh Carlyle. Mrs. Carlyle once said: 'No one managed Carlyle so well as Ruskin; it was quite beautiful to see him.' See *Anne Gilchrist*, p. 82, and the Library edition of Ruskin's *Works*, xviii. p. xlvii.

John Skelton (1831–1897), Scottish advocate, historian, and man of letters. Author of *Maitland of Lethington and the Scotland of Mary Stuart*, *Mary Stuart*, and *The Table-Talk of Shirley*.

CONTROVERSIÆ PERSONÆ

Sir James Stephen (1829–1894), Judge of the Queen's Bench Division, 1879–1891. With James Anthony Froude an executor of the will of Thomas Carlyle.

David Wilson (1864–), Scottish barrister. Indian Civil Service, 1886–1911. 'I went to London first in 1883 and never saw Carlyle. So I could only study him as he had studied Burns and Goethe, Frederick and Cromwell,' says Wilson in his *Carlyle*, I. p. xi.

'But as for man, his conflict is continual with the spirit of contradiction, that is without and within ; with the evil spirit (or call it, with the weak, most necessitous, pitiable spirit), that is in others and in himself. His walk, like all walking (say the mechanicians), is a series of *falls*. To paint man's life is to represent these things. Let them be represented, fitly, with dignity and measure ; but above all, let them be represented. No tragedy of *Hamlet* with the part of Hamlet omitted by particular desire ! No ghost of a biography, let the Damocles' sword of Respectability (which, after all, is but a pasteboard one) threaten as it will ! '—THOMAS CARLYLE on 'Sir Walter Scott' in *London and Westminster Review*, 1838.

'Every man who has played a distinguished part in life, and has largely influenced either the fortunes or the opinions of his contemporaries, becomes the property of the public. We desire to know, and we have a right to know, the inner history of the person who has obtained our confidence. And the oblivion and obscurity which is permitted to those whose actions have affected only themselves or their personal circle, is refused to the larger natures which have been the guides or the representatives of their age. When the life of an eminent man is written, he is brought back from the grave for a rehearsal of the ultimate judgment upon him.'—JAMES ANTHONY FROUDE on 'Lord Macaulay' in *Fraser's Magazine*, 1876.

'Mr. Froude . . . forbore from defending himself, though the materials for defence were in his hands, partly because he looked on his assailants with a somewhat over-indolent contempt, partly . . . because of his tenderness to the memory of the man whom he was accused of so wantonly vilifying.'—WILLIAM H. MALLOCK on 'The Secret of Carlyle's Life' in the *Fortnightly Review*, 1903.

FROUDE AND CARLYLE

A STUDY OF THE FROUDE-CARLYLE CONTROVERSY

CHAPTER I

INTRODUCTORY

FEW tasks are harder than the attempt to revise or alter an opinion of long standing. The difficulty is increased when the opinion has been advanced and supported with zealous partisanship, and allowed to circulate without organised opposition. What has been for a long time promulgated comes at last to be accepted. Not often does the public take the trouble or the time necessary to disclose the origin of an opinion which has been strongly supported and widely disseminated. A habit of mind persists.

In the literature of biography the controversy associated with James Anthony Froude's 'Thomas Carlyle' has settled into an opinion hard, fast, and persistent. In general, the opinion is that Froude's biography of Carlyle is not only false as to fact but deliberately malignant in purpose. Froude is charged with having manipulated his materials cunningly in order to cast obloquy upon his subject. The public has been given to understand that at almost every point the statements of Froude are questionable. David Wilson goes so far as to suggest that the number of pages in the Carlyle biography should be multiplied by an estimated number of errors on one page and the product taken as indicative of the worthlessness of Froude's work. Historians of English literature have carried on the traditional opinion. It is seldom, indeed, that Froude's volumes on Carlyle are mentioned in a history of English literature apart from a statement that his work is to be regarded with suspicion.

It was quite by accident that I first became interested in this controversy. At an early age I was attracted to the personality and the writings of Thomas Carlyle. Very soon, of course, I turned to Froude's account of Carlyle's life, and read it with delight that I cannot easily describe. When I first became acquainted with the biography I was unaware of any controversy about it, and read it without partisan feeling. After reading it, I felt a still greater interest in Carlyle as a man and respect for his accomplishment in literature in the face of all obstacles. With Walt Whitman I felt that the biography was inspiring. I was entirely innocent of any notion that the whole work was the artful attempt of a treacherous disciple to malign the memory of his master. The charges against Froude surprised me.

I set out at once to discover the truth. My study has now extended over a quarter of a century. I have examined all of the published material and as many of the unpublished documents as I have been permitted to see. I began, as I say, with no feeling for Froude one way or the other, except admiration for his literary performance. My enthusiasm was all for Carlyle. The result of my investigations has increased my respect for Froude, and in no way lessened my opinion of Carlyle. Carlyle remains for me essentially what he is represented to be in Froude's biography.

The following pages present the results of my

study of the origin and progress of the controversy in regard to Froude's fulfilment of his duties as literary executor and biographer of Carlyle. I have attempted to present the material so as to enable anyone to follow the evidence for himself. I have tried to be fair to both sides. I do not hesitate to affirm, however, that my verdict is given in favour of Froude. Knowing most of the difficulties under which biographers labour, I do not maintain that he is faultless. What I do wish to emphasise is that Froude was in a better position than any other person to portray the real Carlyle, and that, with all of its faults, his portrayal remains the best work on Carlyle's life in print. Clerical errors may be corrected, typographical errors may be eliminated, knowledge concealed from Froude may be supplied, gaps in Froude's record may be filled, the whole range of Carlyle literature published since Froude's death may be put under requisition; in the face of all this revision, the general features of the portrait painted by Froude remain unchanged. To borrow a sculptor's figure, Froude has portrayed his subject in the round, and the result cannot easily be set aside by any lesser hand.

As I followed my studies I came to a realisation of the difficulties under which Froude had laboured for many years. I think it is doubtful whether any other man of letters in Great Britain of equal ability has been the object of such bitter misrepresentation and such organised opposition as has Froude. Briefly, this opposition and misrepresentation began when he turned his back upon the Oxford Movement, resigned his deacon's orders in the Church of England, and surrendered his fellowship at Oxford. Let no one unfamiliar with the bitterness attendant upon religious controversy from 1830 to 1890 venture to gainsay the organised clerical opposition to Froude. The publication of 'The Nemesis of Faith' started the outcry. When, in order to earn a livelihood for himself, after the Church had made it impossible for him to act as rector of a school in Tasmania, Froude turned to writing the 'History of England,' his earlier volumes were assailed as being only a continuation of his attack upon the Church. Both the Roman and the Established Churches were arrayed against the author, and the running fire of criticism continued until the last volume of the 'History' ceased to be of immediate interest. Careful readers will recall that a paragraph in Charles Kingsley's review of the first volume of the 'History' in *Macmillan's Magazine* led to the famous controversy with Cardinal Newman, which resulted in the publication of the 'Apologia pro Vita Sua.' That one incident is proof of the dynamite latent in the subject-matter which Froude was handling.

Very early in Froude's career as a writer of history, Edward Augustus Freeman sought to bring discredit upon his work. Freeman and Froude were temperamentally incompatible. Freeman evidently resented Froude's entrance upon historical writing; at any rate, he conducted in the pages of the *Saturday Review* and the *Contemporary Review* a systematic campaign of disparagement of Froude as an historian. He professed to be a disinterested and impersonal seeker after truth, and disclaimed any personal animosity towards Froude. Since the publication of Herbert Paul's 'Life of Froude' in 1905 not much has been heard of Freeman's disinterestedness. Any reader who will take the time to examine the fifth chapter of Paul's book, the chapter entitled 'Froude and Freeman,' will turn from its perusal with a new sense of the conditions which Froude had to face. Incidentally, too, he will have gained a new conception of the fairness and impartiality of some historians. He may even be inspired to go on to a study of the charges against Froude originated by

Edward Wakefield, and transmitted without investigation by Fisher, Langlois, Seignobos, and James Ford Rhodes. There are few more interesting stories than the one started by Wakefield to the effect that Adelaide, Australia, is built on an eminence, and that no river runs through it. In the light of such knowledge one becomes wary of accepting charges against Froude's accuracy without careful investigation. All this, to be sure, belongs to a consideration of Froude as historian ; it cannot, however, be disregarded in a consideration of Froude as biographer, for the reason that the charges of inaccuracy against Froude as historian are used to buttress the attacks made upon his accuracy as biographer.

The opposition of ecclesiastics and historians was sufficiently formidable. To that must be added the enmity towards Froude of the Manchester School of Political Economy, of most Oxonians, of the Irish Nationalists, of the Liberal Party, of the Negroes, of the Little Englanders, of the opponents of Carlyle during Carlyle's lifetime, and after Carlyle's death of the fanatical admirers of Carlyle. Surely such an array is sufficient to make any one man tremble. It was Froude's portion in life to please no one faction. Perhaps no better testimony could be offered to his ability to see all sides of a question than the fact that he saw enough and said enough on both sides of almost every subject which he treated to earn the ill-will of the adherents of both sides.

Many people question the value of an investigation into the facts behind this controversy. No one, they say, can possibly be interested at the present in personal controversies of a half-century ago. Were the issues involved matters simply of personal controversy the case would be different. The truth is that the integrity of one of England's most famous historians and biographers is involved. If we are to believe the charges brought against Froude, then we must be prepared to concede that little confidence can be placed in either his portrayal of Carlyle, or in his editions of the ‘ Reminiscences ’ and the ‘ Letters and Memorials of Jane Welsh Carlyle.’ It seems to me that a matter touching the honesty and good faith of such a man as James Anthony Froude is not a matter to be dismissed lightly.

I began this investigation to satisfy my own curiosity. As I complete it I feel sufficiently rewarded in a knowledge of what seems to me a reasonable approach to the truth. I offer my findings to the public with the conviction that all fair-minded people will be glad to know just how matters stand between Thomas Carlyle and James Anthony Froude. I trust that I have submitted enough evidence to make it for ever impossible, so far as this controversy is concerned, to substitute unsupported statements for truth.

CHAPTER II

THE CONTROVERSY IN BRIEF

WHAT is known as the Froude-Carlyle controversy may be summarised in little space, and it is doubtless wise to begin with such a summary in order that the general reader may follow the narrative with the greatest degree of profit. It is the claim of James Anthony Froude that in June 1871 Carlyle asked him to undertake the task of supervising the publication of his own and Mrs. Carlyle's private papers ; that in 1873 he made a second assignment of papers to him, and at that time charged him with the task of writing his biography. When Carlyle died his will revealed that he had given to Froude the manuscripts now known as the 'Letters and Memorials of Jane Welsh Carlyle,' turned over to him whatever other materials were needed to elucidate them, and left to his discretion the time of publication and the matter of preparing a biography.

Froude, acting upon what he claims were Carlyle's oral instructions to him, instructions which, in his opinion, the will embodies and supports, published the 'Reminiscences' within a month after Carlyle's death. As early at least as 1873, Mary, Carlyle's niece and amanuensis, became cognisant of the fact that Carlyle was entrusting valuable material to Froude. The evidence leads one to think that she began at once to remonstrate with her uncle and to do what she could to have him guarantee that

Froude would return the papers to her when he had finished his task. Carlyle was not in the habit of being dictated to, and he endeavoured to assure Mary that eventually the papers would be returned to her. She, however, was not content to let the matter rest. She continued to urge her uncle until he finally told Froude that when he had completed his task he should give the material to Mary. The evidence indicates that Carlyle was trying to quiet Mary without interfering with the commission which he had entrusted to Froude. Mary continued to be a disturbing factor during the remainder of her uncle's life. She married her cousin, Alexander Carlyle, August 21, 1879, and the two turned their attention to possible profits from the proposed publications. Her story of what passed between herself and Froude is not entirely consistent.

As yet the public knew little of the relations between Froude and the Carlyles. On May 4, 1881, Mary sent a communication to the London *Times* and the London *Daily Telegraph* in which she accused Froude of bad faith, charging that he had published the 'Reminiscences' against her uncle's wishes. This letter was the formal beginning of the controversy whose echoes have not yet subsided.

Mary's next move was an attempt to get the materials out of Froude's hands, or at least to make it impossible for him to write the biography. She maintained that her uncle had made a gift of 'the papers' to her in 1875. A long dispute followed. At one time Froude was so irritated that he published a letter in *The Times* saying that he would return the papers to Mary at once. Sir James Stephen, co-executor with Froude of Carlyle's will, immediately refused to agree to Froude's suggestion, on the ground that the papers were not Froude's to return, but the property of the executors.

In the face of all obstacles and criticism Froude,

ably supported by Sir James Stephen, completed the full task committed to him by Carlyle. In all, he published nine volumes about the Carlyles—volumes of reminiscence, correspondence, biography. When he had finished the work he returned all the manuscripts to Mary Carlyle, except those which had been specifically willed to him, and obtained her receipt for them. He did not do what he might easily have done—remove all notations which bore witness to the vacillations of Carlyle's mind. With a lack of guile which gives evidence of either great confidence in his own integrity of purpose or an almost silly unwisdom he placed in the hands of Mary Carlyle and her successors the material upon which he had been labouring for more than twelve years.

After the appearance of the last volumes of the 'Thomas Carlyle,' October 6, 1884, a new turn was given to the controversy by the publication from 1886 to 1888, under the editorship of Charles Eliot Norton, of a series of seven volumes of Carlyle material, the intent of which was to reflect upon Froude's work. The controversy then gradually subsided until 1903, when it was revived by the publication on the part of Alexander Carlyle and Sir James Crichton-Browne of the 'New Letters and Memorials of Jane Welsh Carlyle.' A full discussion of the details of the controversy here briefly outlined forms the subject-matter of the chapters which follow.

CHAPTER III

HOW FROUDE BECAME INVOLVED

FROUDE first met Carlyle one evening in the middle of June 1849, when James Spedding accompanied him to Cheyne Row. Froude was then just thirty-one; Carlyle was in his fifty-fourth year. Froude, living at Plas Gwynant in Wales and engaged upon the first volume of the 'History of England,' found it necessary to make frequent trips to London to consult historical documents. After the introduction he called frequently on the Carlyles and was made welcome. The friendship advanced to the point where Froude felt justified in submitting to Carlyle the proofs in pamphlet form of the first two chapters of the 'History,' which Carlyle read and annotated carefully. Carlyle's final notes on the proof are dated September 27, 1855. All of the evidence points to the fact that Carlyle was interested in Froude and eager to promote his success as an historian.

So matters stood between the two until 1860. 'In the autumn of that year, however, London became my home,' writes Froude. 'Late one afternoon, in the middle of the winter, Carlyle called on me, and said that he wished to see more of me—wished me in fact to be his companion, so far as I could, in his daily rides or walks. Ride with him I could not, having no horse; but the walks were most welcome—and from that date, for twenty years, up to his own death, except when either or both of us were out of town, I never ceased to see him twice or three times a week, and to have two or three hours of conversation with him.'[1] In 1860 Froude was in his forty-third, Carlyle in his sixty-fifth year.

Both Carlyle and his wife liked Froude, and invited him frequently to the little gatherings for which the Cheyne Row home was famous. Such contact gave him, of course, unusual opportunity to know the Carlyles at close range. Then, on April 21, 1866, while her husband was lingering in Scotland after his Rectorial address at the University of Edinburgh, came the sudden death of Mrs. Carlyle. Froude was one of her last invited guests. She had asked him to a tea-party, set, as it turned out, for the very day of her death. When the news reached Froude, he and Geraldine Jewsbury hastened to St. George's Hospital, whither the body had been conveyed; and later, at Cheyne Row, he conferred with John Forster and the Rev. Gerald Blunt about the best means of communicating the news to Carlyle and preventing an inquest upon Mrs. Carlyle's body.

The story of Carlyle's passionate grief is well known. For a long time he was as a man stunned, caring to see no one except Ruskin and Froude. As the weeks passed he leaned more and more upon Froude, and found in him solace and support. 'For about fifteen years,' wrote Sir James Stephen, 'I was the intimate friend and constant companion of both of you, and never in my life did I see any one man so much devoted to any other as you were to him during the whole of that period of time. The most affectionate son could not have acted better to the most venerated father. You cared for him, soothed him, protected him as a guide might protect a weak old man down a steep and painful path.'[2]

During the next five years the problem of disposing

[1] *Thomas Carlyle*, 4. pp. 254–255.

[2] In a letter to Froude of December 9, 1886, published in *Relations*, p. 62.

of his own and his wife's private papers continued to harass him. To increase his difficulties, he soon came to a realisation that whether he wished it or not a biography of himself was sure to be written. He learned, indeed, that several people were only waiting for his death in order to publish something about him. It is not surprising that under these circumstances he should turn to Froude. One day between the middle and the end of June 1871, Carlyle brought in person to Froude's home a large parcel of papers. These he put into Froude's hands, told him that the materials were his simply and absolutely as his own, without reference to any other person or persons, and that Froude should do with them as he pleased after Carlyle's death. The materials included a transcript of Carlyle's sketch of his wife, two fragmentary accounts of her family and herself, a collection of Mrs. Carlyle's letters, an attempt at a preface, with notes, commentaries, and introductory explanations.

Carlyle told Froude that he himself could do no more with the work, could form no opinion about publication; wished, in fact, never to hear of the matter again. 'I must judge. I must publish it, the whole, or part—or else destroy it all, if I thought that this would be the wiser thing to do. He said nothing of any limit of time. I was to wait only till he was dead, and he was then in constant expectation of his end. Of himself he desired that no biography should be written, and that this Memoir, if any, should be the authorised record of him. So extraordinary a mark of confidence touched me deeply, but the responsibility was not to be hastily accepted. I was then going into the country for the summer. I said that I would take the MS. with me, and would either write to him or would give him an answer when we met in the autumn.' [1]

[1] Froude, *Thomas Carlyle*, 4. p. 409.

When Froude examined the material he discovered that he was confronted with a more difficult task than he had surmised. In brief, the question was whether or not he should take the responsibility for revealing the story of the relations existing between Carlyle and his wife. 'He had here built together, at once a memorial of the genius which had been sacrificed to himself, and of those faults in himself which, though they were faults merely of an irritable temperament, and though he extravagantly exaggerated them, had saddened her married life. . . . He regarded it evidently as an expiation of his own conduct, all that he had now to offer, and something which removed the shadow between himself and her memory. The question before me was whether I was to say that the atonement ought not to be completed, and that the bravest action which I had ever heard of should be left unexecuted, or whether I was to bear the reproach, if the letters were given to the world, of having uncovered the errors of the best friend that I had ever had. Carlyle himself could not direct the publication, from a feeling, I suppose, of delicacy, and dread of ostentation.'[1] As the summer went on Carlyle grew more and more eager to know Froude's decision, longing much, as he wrote, September 6, 1871, 'with a tremulous, deep and almost painful feeling,' about the fate of the Jane Welsh Carlyle Memoir. 'Be prepared to tell me, with all your candour, the *pros* and *contras* there.'[2]

When the two met again after the summer vacation the whole matter was gone over in 'fullest confidence.' Froude told Carlyle that, as far as he could then form an opinion, the letters might be

[1] Froude, *Thomas Carlyle*, 4. p. 410.

[2] See Paul, *Life of Froude*, p. 294, *note* 2. Had Alexander Carlyle and Sir James Crichton-Browne been aware in 1903 of the existence of this letter with its proof that Carlyle had submitted the documents to Froude in 1871 they would probably not have been so emphatic in *The Nemesis of Froude*. Paul's *Life of Froude* was not published until 1905.

published, provided that the sketch of Mrs. Carlyle should precede their publication. Froude's thought was that the publication of the sketch would prepare the way for a correct understanding of the letters. To this arrangement Carlyle assented. Froude asserts that he required and received direct permission to print the sketch. Then followed a discussion in regard to the time of publication. On the last page of the sketch Carlyle had placed a pencil-note indicating in its first form that the manuscript should not be published until twenty years after his death. Later he erased the phrase 'after my death.' Froude pointed out that he was then in his fifty-fourth year, that he could not count on living twenty years longer, and that Mrs. Carlyle's letters, if published at all, were to be published by him. In the preceding June Carlyle had said only that publication of the letters was to wait until his death. He now agreed that ten years would be a sufficient time—ten years from the date of the conversation.

On these conditions Froude accepted the charge, 'but still only hypothetically.' Carlyle told him that if he should find himself in difficulty he might consult John Forster and John Carlyle. Froude sent the materials to Forster, who read them, but gave no expression of opinion in regard to publication; he merely said that he would talk to Carlyle and tell him that unless he made Froude's position perfectly clear in his will, trouble would certainly arise. Nothing more passed between Forster and Froude in regard to the matter.

As time went on, and it became clear to Carlyle that willing or unwilling he would be made the subject of biography, he reached the conclusion that 'if he was to figure before the world at all after his death he preferred that there should be an authentic portrait of him.' At the close of 1873, therefore, he sent to Froude a vast mass of material—'his own and his wife's private papers, journals, correspondence, reminiscences, and other fragments, a collection overwhelming from its abundance.' In substance he said to Froude : 'Take them, and do what you can with them. All I can say to you is, Burn freely. If you have any affection for me, the more you burn the better.' In short, Carlyle charged Froude with the task of writing his biography, and from 1873 onward to the time of his death did all that he could to forward the preparation of the work.

That Froude was acting under commission of Carlyle prior to 1874 is proved by a letter hitherto unpublished. It is dated from 5 Cheyne Row, April 10, 1874. The original, in Mary's handwriting, is signed by Carlyle. Mrs. Froude had but recently died. Carlyle, after a deeply sympathetic reference to Froude's grief, passes on to the subject so close to his own heart. 'The little bit of work you are at present engaged on,' he writes, 'is naturally above all others interesting to me : that also is according to all human calculation a thing you will soon have to do ; and surely it is wise to be thinking of that withal while it is called To-day.' Froude's 'English in Ireland' had been published earlier in the year ; Carlyle speaks of it in this letter as having been already reviewed in the London *Times* and the *Glasgow Herald.* Having given up the thought of writing on Charles V, Froude was now, at Carlyle's especial request, about to give up the editorship of *Fraser's Magazine*, in order to devote his time to Carlyle. 'The little bit of work' so supremely important to Carlyle was, of course, the editorial and biographical task which he had entrusted to Froude, and about which only a few months before he had embodied directions in his will. This letter likewise supports Froude's statement that at the time Carlyle was looking forward to early death. And yet Froude's enemies maintain that he had no writing in support of his commission. In view of the letter just quoted, that of September 26, 1871, previously quoted, one of September 23, 1879, to be given presently, and in harmony with Mary's allegations that she furnished Froude with materials to be used expressly for her uncle's biography, we may conclude without hesitation that Froude's commission was well known and accepted. Mary's statement that in 1877, after some communications between Carlyle and Froude, her uncle asked her to send to Froude such papers as would be useful in preparing the biography, does not in any way preclude the fact of previous communications about the matter.[1] It is to be taken for granted that many such communications, both oral and written, passed between subject and biographer.

A threefold task was now confronting Froude: the oversight of the publication of the sketch of Mrs. Carlyle, the publication of her letters, and the preparation of Carlyle's biography. During the next seven years Froude was diligently engaged over the material. 'I continued to work at his papers, to copy for myself the most important of his manuscripts, since I could trust no other to do it for me, and I put off my final decision till Carlyle himself should be gone and I could think more calmly over my responsibilities and of the manner in which I was to act. I anticipated as not unlikely the resentment of relations, but Carlyle had selected me apparently because I was not a relation and would be free from influences of a private kind.'[2] It has perhaps escaped the attention of most readers that Froude had completed the first draft of Carlyle's biography as far as p. 356 of the second volume by June 27, 1880.[3] In other words, about half of the 'Thomas Carlyle' was completed seven months before Carlyle's death. I find myself wondering whether Froude ever read any of the manuscript to Carlyle, and to what

[1] *Nemesis*, p. 138. [2] *Relations*, p. 27. [3] *Thomas Carlyle*, 2. p. 356.

extent Carlyle gave direction to the task as it grew under Froude's hands. We shall probably never know.

Carlyle died on the morning of February 5, 1881. When his will was read on February 21 the following passage in regard to the disposition of his manuscripts became public :

'My Manuscript entitled "Letters and Memorials of Jane Welsh Carlyle" is to me naturally, in my now bereaved state, of endless value, though of what value to others I cannot in the least clearly judge ; and indeed for the last four years am imperatively forbidden to write farther on it, or even to look farther into it. Of that Manuscript, my kind, considerate and ever-faithful friend, James Anthony Froude (as he has lovingly promised me) takes precious charge in my stead ; to him therefore I give it with whatever other fartherences and elucidations may be possible ; and I solemnly request of him to do his best and wisest in the matter, as I feel assured he will. There is incidentally a quantity of Autobiographic Record in my Notes to this Manuscript ; but except as subsidiary, and elucidative of the Text I put no value on such : express Biography of me I had really rather that there should be none. James Anthony Froude, John Forster and my Brother John, will make earnest survey of the Manuscript and its subsidiaries there or elsewhere, in respect to this as well as to its other bearings ; their united utmost candour and impartiality (taking always James Anthony Froude's practicality along with it) will evidently furnish a better judgment than mine can be. The Manuscript is by no means ready for publication ; nay, the questions, How, When (after what delay, seven, ten years) it, or any portion of it, should be published, are still dark to me ; but on all such points James Anthony Froude's practical summing up and decision is to be taken as mine.'

The will is dated February 6, 1873; the codicil was added a little less than six years later, on November 8, 1878. Carlyle's last legal utterance makes Froude his surviving self so far as his private papers and their bearings are concerned. One other fact stands out prominently. John Forster, true to the word he gave Froude, influenced Carlyle to make Froude's position legally clear. Carlyle lost no time in expressing his wishes unequivocally. So far as the will is concerned all matters relating to the publication of manuscripts and the preparation of a biography were in Froude's hands. By the codicil of November 8, 1878, Carlyle in addition appointed Froude one of the executors of his will. Froude himself always considered the words of the will the strongest defence of his own course of action.

In conclusion, then, it is clear that Carlyle died knowing that he had committed to Froude both orally and by will private papers concerned with the most intimate details of his own and Mrs. Carlyle's life. He died knowing that Froude intended to publish much of this material in a time order agreed upon by both. He died knowing that he had commissioned Froude to write his biography, and in full knowledge of the fact that at least half of the narrative had been composed. He had gone about the whole matter deliberately. He had been intimately acquainted with Froude for more than twenty years when he first entrusted him with a portion of the material. As he was in the habit of reading all that Froude published, he had accurate knowledge of the manner and spirit in which Froude dealt with history and biography. After 1871 his confidence in Froude increased, and he grew impatiently eager to know that Froude was making progress on the work entrusted to him. It will become evident in the following pages that Carlyle's increasing confidence in Froude aroused the sharp suspicion of Mary and Alexander

Carlyle. It is certain that Carlyle left Froude commissioned personally and legally to represent him before the world, and died content to believe that his disciple, friend, and intimate companion of more than thirty years would do his wisest and best to speak of him as he was, to extenuate nothing, nor set down aught in malice. For any man to win the confidence of Carlyle in such a matter was a mark of high distinction.

CHAPTER IV

FROUDE UNDERTAKES THE COMMISSION

It was pretty generally known in the intimate circle of friends of both Carlyle and Froude that Froude had been for a long time occupying himself with a study of Carlyle's private papers. Just how far he had gone was known, of course, to only a few. The two volumes of the 'Reminiscences' appeared March 5, 1881, in the preface to which Froude made the following statements in regard to his task :

'In the summer of 1871 Mr. Carlyle placed in my hands a collection of MSS. of which he desired me to take charge, and to publish, should I think fit to do so, after he was gone. They consisted of letters written by his wife to himself and to other friends during the period of her married life, with the "rudiments" of a preface of his own, giving an account of her family, her childhood, and their own experience together, from their first acquaintance till her death. They were married in 1826 ; Mrs. Carlyle died suddenly in 1866. Between these two periods Carlyle's active literary life was comprised ; and he thought it unnecessary that more than these letters contained should be made known, or attempted to be made known, about himself or his personal history. The essential part of his life was in his works, which those who chose could read. The private part of it was a matter in which the world had no concern. Enough would be found, told by one who knew him better than anyone else knew him, to satisfy such curiosity as there might be. His object was rather to leave a monument to a singularly gifted woman, who, had she so pleased, might have made a name for herself, and for his sake had voluntarily sacrificed ambition and fortune.

'The letters had been partially prepared for the press by short separate introductions and explanatory notes. But Carlyle warned me that before they were published they would require anxious revision. Written with the unreserve of confidential communications, they contained anecdotes, allusions, reflections, expressions of opinion and feeling, which were intended obviously for no eye save that of the person to whom they were addressed. He believed at the time I speak of, that his own life was near its end, and seeing the difficulty in which I might be placed, he left me at last with discretion to destroy the whole of them, should I find the task of discriminating too intricate a problem.

'The expectation of an early end was perhaps suggested by the wish for it. He could no longer write. His right hand was disabled. His temperament did not suit with dictation, and he was impatient of an existence which he could no longer turn to any useful purpose. He lingered on, however, year after year, and it gradually became known to him that his wishes would not protect him from biographers, and that an account of his life would certainly be tried, perhaps by more than one person. A true description of it he did not believe that any one could give, not even his closest friend ; but there might be degrees of falsity ; and since a biography of some kind there was to be, he decided at last to extend his original commission to me, and to make over to me all his private papers, journals, notebooks, letters, and unfinished or neglected writings.

'Being a person of most methodical habits, he

had preserved every letter which he had ever received of not entirely trifling import. His mother, his wife, his brothers, and many of his friends had kept as carefully every letter from himself. The most remarkable of his contemporaries had been among his correspondents—English, French, Italian, German, and American. Goethe had recognised his genius, and had written to him often, advising and encouraging. His own and Mrs. Carlyle's journals were records of their most secret thoughts. All these Mr. Carlyle, scarcely remembering what they contained, but with characteristic fearlessness, gave me leave to use as I might please.

'Material of such a character makes my duty in one respect an easy one. I have not to relate Mr. Carlyle's history, or describe his character. He is his own biographer, and paints his own portrait. But another difficulty arises from the extent of the resources thrown open to me. His own letters are as full of matter as the richest of his published works. His friends were not common men, and in writing to him they wrote their best. Of the many thousand letters in my possession, there is hardly one which, either on its special merits or through its connection with something which concerned him, does not deserve to be printed. Selection is indispensable ; a middle way must be struck between too much and too little. I have been guided largely, however, by Carlyle's personal directions to me, and such a way will, I trust, be discovered.

'Meanwhile, on examining the miscellaneous MSS. I found among them various sketches and reminiscences, one written in a notebook fifty years ago on hearing in London of his father's death ; another of Edward Irving ; another of Lord Jeffrey ; others (these brief and slight), of Southey and Wordsworth. In addition there was a long narrative, or fragments of a narrative, designed as material for the introduction to Mrs. Carlyle's letters. These letters would now have to be rearranged with his own ; and an introduction, under the shape which had been intended for it, would be no longer necessary. The "Reminiscences" appeared to me to be far too valuable to be broken up and employed in any composition of my own, and I told Mr. Carlyle that I thought they ought to be printed with the requisite omissions immediately after his own death. He agreed with me that it should be so, and at one time it was proposed that the type should be set up while he was still alive, and could himself revise what he had written. He found, however, that the effort would be too much for him, and the reader has here before him Mr. Carlyle's own handiwork, but without his last touches, not edited by himself, not corrected by himself, perhaps most of it not intended for publication, and written down merely as an occupation, for his own private satisfaction.

'The Introductory Fragments were written immediately after his wife's death ; the account of Irving belongs to the autumn and winter which followed. So singular was his condition at this time, that he was afterwards unconscious what he had done ; and when ten years later I found the Irving MS. and asked him about it, he did not know to what I was alluding. The sketch of Jeffrey was written immediately after. Some parts of the introduction I have reserved for the biography, into which they will most conveniently fall ; the rest, from the point where they form a consecutive story, I have printed with only a few occasional reservations. "Southey" and "Wordsworth," being merely detached notes of a few personal recollections, I have attached as an appendix.

'Nothing more remains to be said about these papers, save to repeat, for clearness' sake, that they are published with Mr. Carlyle's consent but without his supervision. The detailed responsibility is therefore entirely my own. . . .'

The foregoing explanations help us to understand how the 'Reminiscences' could be published a month after Carlyle's death. For almost ten years the subject-matter had been upon Froude's mind. Passages from Froude's contemporary correspondence enable us to verify his published statements in regard to his commission from Carlyle, as well as to follow the progress of the task as it shaped itself under his hands. We can almost look on with him as he went about his work. That the publication of the 'Reminiscences' was only an incident in the progress of the greater task of writing Carlyle's biography is now clear. For several years Froude had leisurely studied and arranged the material which Carlyle had placed in his hands, and copied such portions as he wished to incorporate in the biography. By the end of 1879 he had the composition of the life well under way. 'I am hard at work on Carlyle's Life,' he wrote to John Skelton on March 19, 1880.

The following letters [1] addressed by Froude to Madame Olga Novikoff enable us to follow his work :

'April 11th, 1880—I am writing quietly at Carlyle's "Life," and I hope I may live to complete it. He and Byron will alone be remembered five centuries hence of all our modern men of *genius* ! ! !—wonderful genius ! These two have been real men ; the rest will be found to be but the notes of broken banks, worth as much as the paper on which the promise to pay is written. But against the promise will be written "No effects."'

'April 15th, 1880—For myself, I am busy with Carlyle's "Life," with which he is impatient to know that I am making progress. He himself grows weaker and weaker. But he has still a great reserve of strength, and may last for longer than he wishes.

[1] As given in *Novikoff*, ii. 323–325.

As soon as he is gone I mean (if I survive him) to leave this foolish idiotic London and take a house among the Scotch mountains, where at least I shall hear no more nonsense.'

'January 1881—I have had an interesting letter about "Cæsar" from Paris, from Comte de Vitzthum. Do you know him? He wants me to do Augustus. But it cannot be. Carlyle's "Life" must be my next, most likely my last work in this world.'

'September 30th, 1881—Carlyle's women friends expected me to paint for them the foolish idol which their own foolish minds had made of him, and are furious at me because I could not and would not gratify them. The "Reminiscences" will be like Boswell's "Life of Johnson." All the world howled for a year or two at poor Boswell, and then found that he had given them the best biography in the English language.'

'On December 23, 1880,' writes Sir John Skelton, 'Froude informed me that he had begun to print Carlyle's "Reminiscences." He had allowed me to read the earlier sketches some years previously, and I had been delighted by their idiomatic force and freshness. The pictures of that old homely Scottish life were, it seemed to me, racy of the soil. Now he asked me to revise them as they went through the press, with reference more particularly to various Scotch names and idioms in the early sheets.' [1] December 26, 1880, Froude wrote to Skelton: 'I send a few more sheets. I have marked one or two words specially, which seem to me doubtful. Carlyle himself is not in a condition to be asked questions. I fear the end cannot now be very distant.' [2]

Froude's comments upon the reception of the 'Reminiscences' are revealing.[3] April 7, 1881, he

[1] In *Shirley*, p. 172.

[2] *Shirley*, p. 173.

[3] The three following quotations from Froude's letters to Skelton are taken from *Shirley*, pp. 175, 176, and 177. Edmund Gosse, after long reflection, gave the following opinion: 'It has always seemed to me that Froude . . . was unfairly treated in the controversies of 1881.' See Gosse's *Books on the Table*, p. 304. The volume was published in May 1921.

wrote thus to his friend Skelton : ‘ I am more surprised than I should have been at the reception of the “ Reminiscences.” It is Carlyle himself—the same Carlyle precisely that I have known for thirty years ; and it seemed to me that my duty was to represent him (or let him represent himself) as near the truth as possible. To me in no one of his writings does he appear under a more beautiful aspect ; and so, I am still convinced, will all mankind eventually think. I cut out everything which could *injure* anybody. To have cut out his general estimates of men and things would have turned the book into a *caput mortuum*.’ Again, on June 17, 1881, he wrote : ‘ The storm which broke over me has pretty well passed. You were wise and kind in taking no notice of it. In a year or two every one whose opinion is worth having will be grateful for having a true Carlyle before them, and not a mutilated and incredible one.’ And on the 11th of the following September he wrote once more : ‘ Burton gone—Stanley gone—Carlyle gone—all in this last year. I care not how soon I follow, if I may only live to finish Carlyle’s Life. I have had a most hearty letter from the one surviving brother in Annandale.’

After the ‘ Reminiscences ’ were in print Froude returned to Mary Carlyle the manuscripts of the work, and girded himself for the remainder of his labour. It was to be no holiday task. He had been under no delusions as to the difficulty of the task laid upon him by Carlyle, but he was not prepared for the kind of attack which was made upon him by one portion of Carlyle’s own family. It will be necessary to investigate the origin and nature of that attack with much care.

CHAPTER V

MARY CARLYLE ATTACKS FROUDE

When the 'Reminiscences' appeared Froude himself had little notion of the difficulties into which the work was to bring him. Beyond the facts which he gave in the preface not much was known by the public of the relations existing between Carlyle and his editor. In sponsoring the volumes Froude was acting upon the deliberate thought of years, and definitely setting himself to the fulfilment of Carlyle's commission. He had not, however, been permitted to enjoy 'the quiet and still air of delightful studies.' Certain forces had been gathering which for a time bade fair to put an end to his hope of completing the task.

Young Alexander, son of Carlyle's brother Alexander, came from Canada to London in July 1879, and on August 21 following, married his cousin, Mary Aitken, who had been for about eleven years companion and amanuensis to her uncle. The marriage provided her with an ally and an adviser. At least as early as 1877 Mary had begun to look askance upon the freedom with which Carlyle was entrusting materials for the biography to Froude, and thereafter continued to insist that her uncle should impress upon Froude the necessity of returning the papers to her when he had finished with them. So far as I know, the first direct application of Mary to Froude for the return of anything was in February

1878. On February 17 or 27, 1878, Froude, in a letter to his daughter Margaret, wrote : 'A terrible job waits for you when you come back. The little girl [1] wants four or five letters to Carlyle out of the enormous box full in the closet. There are 10,000 there, at least. I have been, and am, too busy to begin the search. It is out of all reason to expect such a thing.' Throughout 1879 and 1880 Mary continued to press upon Carlyle and Froude her desire to have the papers when the biography was completed.

It was in 1877, according to Mary, that Carlyle, after 'some communications' with Froude in regard to a biography, asked her to send Froude 'such of the papers' as in her opinion would be useful for that purpose. She asserts that her uncle told her distinctly that she was to have 'the papers all back again,' and that Froude so understood. She maintains that, after a conversation with Froude on February 16, 1880, she became apprehensive lest Froude should not return them.

'After Mr. Froude . . . had left, it occurred to me to make sure there should be no mistake about the return of the papers to me. I therefore said to my uncle I was sorry I had sent so many of the papers to Mr. Froude and wondered if Mr. Froude understood they were to be all returned to me. My uncle replied, "Froude perfectly understands that, for I have often said so to him." I expressed a wish that my uncle would speak to Mr. Froude again on the subject so as to prevent any misapprehension, which he promised to do. Mr. Froude used to come to our house twice a week, Tuesdays and Fridays, to walk and latterly to drive out with my uncle. On the Tuesday following the Sunday upon which the

[1] 'The little girl'; that is, Mary Aitken, later the wife of Alexander Carlyle. She was called 'the little girl' by members of the Froude family from the time that she first came to London to live with her uncle.

above mentioned conversation took place my uncle drove out with Mr. Froude in a hansom cab. After the drive and after Mr. Froude had left, my uncle said to me, "Froude perfectly understands the papers are yours and will return them all to you. He has promised to do so."

'In February 1880 Mr. Froude again spoke of returning Mr. Alexander Carlyle's letters. This to me revived my fear lest he might not return the others. I therefore again raised the subject with my uncle in February 1880. He said to me, "Froude understands beyond any kind of doubt that they are yours—it is no use bothering him again." But I persisted, and he promised me to speak to Mr. Froude about it again for the purpose of insuring that the papers should be returned to me as soon as Mr. Froude had done with them.

'Mr. Froude's letter to me of 10th February 1880, which I showed to my uncle, satisfied both my uncle and myself that no further question would be raised on the subject. "That I was to have," as Mr. Froude there said, "the entire collection when he had done with it," appeared to me all I wanted.' [1]

While Mary was thus striving for the return of 'the papers,' communications of the utmost importance were passing between Froude and Carlyle; and it should be borne in mind that at this time Mary was writing most of Carlyle's letters to dictation. Sometime in September 1879 Mary, at her uncle's request, informed Froude that Carlyle wished him to go forward with the work which had been entrusted to him. The substance of the letter may be inferred from Froude's reply of September 23.[2]

'I conclude from what your niece said in her last letter,' he wrote, 'that you are again in London. We return ourselves in three weeks. She implies that you wish me to proceed at once with the task

[1] *Nemesis*, pp. 138–140. [2] *Ibid.*, pp. 85–86.

which you have imposed on me. So, of course, I will do so. I began it two years ago, but I found so many injunctions attached to the letters by yourself that there was nothing to be done until long after you had yourself gone.'

According to Alexander Carlyle the biography was 'the task' in question. He seems to forget that his identification of the biography as the task 'imposed upon' Froude nullifies his later assertion that it is impossible to say whether the work of becoming Carlyle's biographer was thrust upon Froude, or whether he diligently sought it.[1] The likelihood is that the phrase refers to the whole task, editorial as well as biographical. At any rate it is clear that Mary and Alexander accepted the correspondence as evidence of Carlyle's commission to proceed at once with the work about which Mary had been so long concerned. Subsequent events reveal what emotions the letters evoked in the minds of both. They bestirred themselves immediately, and appear to have had some communications with Froude in regard to financial arrangements.

Mary avows that 'the monetary value of the papers' was first discussed with Froude 'shortly after' September 23, 1879. 'I considered the papers referred to as very precious,' she says, 'but I never thought of them as valuable in point of money until, as presently mentioned, Mr. Froude arranged with me to hold the proceeds of the "Reminiscences" for me.' It is difficult to determine from Mary's somewhat confused statements whether or not the phrase 'shortly after' means November 20, 1879. If so, she evidently intends to have it understood that between September 23 and November 20 she never

[1] *Nemesis*, p. 115. Froude always maintained that Carlyle requested him to do the work. See the important contemporary statements in *Letters of Edward FitzGerald to Fanny Kemble*, pp. 243–244, *note*; Hector Macpherson's *Thomas Carlyle*, pp. 136–137; and Sir Arthur Hardinge's *Life of Henry Howard Molyneux Herbert Fourth Earl of Carnarvon*, iii. 311.

thought of value 'in point of money.' Once more I quote from her statement:

'On the 20th of November 1879 my husband and I dined with Mr. Froude at his residence, Mr. Froude's son, Mr. Ashley Froude, and his daughter, Miss Margaret Froude, being present. On this occasion Mr. Froude distinctly stated that he would hold the whole proceeds of the "Reminiscences" for me. This promise was frequently repeated by Mr. Froude, who, on one occasion, a month before my uncle's death, in the presence of my husband, added, "The book was written by your uncle, not by me, and therefore there would be no propriety in my receiving the money for it. But of course it will be different with the biography, which I shall write myself." My husband and I both assented to this, and looked upon it as settled. My uncle was informed of this arrangement on the 20th of November 1879, by myself and my husband, and subsequently by Mr. Froude, and expressed his approval of it as natural and proper, so that we regarded it as a settled thing.

'After this arrangement had been made, and possibly to some extent influenced by it, I sent Mr. Froude, for use and return to me, further papers which my uncle had given me, especially the letters of my uncle, Thomas Carlyle, to his brother, Dr. John Carlyle, a very large collection of which, extending over sixty years, were returned to my uncle, Thomas Carlyle, by Dr. Carlyle's executor a few months after the death of Dr. Carlyle in September 1879. These my uncle, Thomas Carlyle, gave me for my own as soon as he received them, and I, at his wish, lent them to Mr. Froude, relying on his promise to restore all the papers to me when used for the purpose of the biography.' [1]

It is clear that during the remainder of Carlyle's life Mary was uneasy about his relations with Froude.

[1] *Nemesis*, p. 141.

When Carlyle died on February 5, 1881, she was free to act on her own initiative, and even before the will was read on the following 21st of February she had entered into controversy with Froude. The immediate occasion of difference was the question of dividing the proceeds from the prospective publication of the 'Reminiscences.' It is alleged that on February 14, 1881, Mary heard from Froude, whether by letter or conversation is not stated, that the publishers had paid him £650 for the forthcoming edition of the 'Reminiscences,' of which he proposed to give her £300. She complained, when first is not stated, that such was not the arrangement come to on November 20, 1879. At that date, she said, Froude had promised her the whole of the 'Reminiscences,' which, however, did not then include the memoir of Mrs. Carlyle, admittedly Froude's property. On the strength of the alleged promise she refused to accept any share of the proceeds less than the whole.[1]

Eventually, on February 21, Sir James Stephen, in the presence of Mary and Alexander and Mr. Ouvry, a solicitor who had witnessed Carlyle's will, made a memorandum which embodied Mary's understanding of the facts relating to Carlyle's papers. The version which follows is that printed by Alexander Carlyle in 'The Nemesis of Froude.' It differs at three minor points—two of them certainly typographical errors—from the version given in 'My Relations with Carlyle.'

'*Memorandum.*

'1. Papers relating to the late Mrs. Carlyle bequeathed to Mr. Froude by the will of Mr. Carlyle. These papers Mrs. A. Carlyle considers to be Mr. Froude's absolutely.

[1] *Nemesis*, pp. 102–103.

'2. The papers relating to Mr. Carlyle's father, Mr. Irving and Lord Jeffrey, intended to be published under the title of "Reminiscences," Mrs. A. Carlyle also understands to have been given to Mr. Froude after the death of Mr. Forster, though she does not know what may have passed between Mr. Carlyle and Mr. Froude on the subject. She, however, says that Mr. Froude sometime ago promised to give her the whole of the proceeds of the "Reminiscences" when published, and that she informed her uncle of this intention, and that he approved of it, and under these circumstances she declines to receive any share of the proceeds less than the whole.

'3. The papers relating to Mr. Carlyle and intended to serve as materials for his biography. These papers Mrs. A. Carlyle understands to have been given to Mr. Froude so that the property in them passed to him. She also understands that Mr. Carlyle intended that any profit to be derived from the book, for which they were to be materials, was to go to Mr. Froude, and she has no wish to interfere in any way with Mr. Froude's discretion as to the use to be made of these papers. On the other hand, Mrs. A. Carlyle considers that Mr. Froude ought not to burn or otherwise destroy any of these papers, but to return them to her (Mrs. A. Carlyle) after the biography for which they are to be used as materials is published.

'J. F. STEPHEN.'

The 'Reminiscences,' as we have seen, appeared on March 5, 1881. Those who were hostile to Froude immediately began to criticise. On April 7 Froude wrote to his daughter Margaret: 'The Carlyle storm is beginning, I believe, but I think the promoters will have but a limited success. The *Scotsman* has been violent, but this I have no doubt at all is David Masson's work. He wanted to have the thing to do, and will therefore do his utmost to raise a prejudice against me.' On May 3 Froude returned to Mary the notebook which contained the sketch of Jane Welsh Carlyle. He returned it just as it was, with the old prohibition of 1866 still attached. On May 4 Mary sent the following communication to *The Times* and the *Daily Telegraph*, which was published in the issues of May 5 :

'The last half of the manuscript of the article in Mr. Carlyle's "Reminiscences" headed "Jane Welsh Carlyle" came into my hands yesterday (sent to me by Mr. Froude). At the end of this MS., I find the following words in my uncle's handwriting :

'"I still mainly mean to burn this book before my own departure ; but feel that I shall always have a kind of grudge to do it, and an indolent excuse, 'Not yet ; wait, any day that can be done !' and that it is possible the thing may be left behind me legible to inter[est]ed survivors,—friends only, I will hope and with worthy curiosity, not unworthy !

'"In which event I solemnly forbid them, each and all, to publish this bit of writing as it stands here ; and warn them that without fit editing no part of it should be printed (nor so far as I can order, shall ever be) ;—and that the 'fit editing' of perhaps nine-tenths of it will, after I am gone, have become impossible. T. C. (Saty, 28 July 1866)."

'Mr. Froude explains that these very clear directions were cancelled by subsequent oral communications to him by Mr. Carlyle. Mr. Froude's words are : "My own conviction is that he wished it to be published, though he would not himself order it." I was aware of the existence of this manuscript notebook, and many times during the nearly thirteen years I was his constant companion heard my uncle speak of it. I was led to form an opinion entirely different from Mr. Froude's as to his wishes regarding it; and was astounded when I learned by chance that it was in print.'

To this letter Froude hastened to make the following reply:

'Mrs. Alexander Carlyle's letter requires an answer from me, which I would have been gladly spared the necessity of writing. The memoir to which Mrs. Carlyle refers was written in 1866, and at the end of it were the words which she quoted. Subsequently this memoir, with a large number of other papers referring to his late wife, was transcribed by Mr. Carlyle's direction, and the whole collection was placed in my hands with a personal request that I would take charge of it, and would do with it whatever might seem best to me after he was gone.

'The request itself was wholly unexpected. A "discretion" of so delicate a kind could not be welcomed. I said that I would look the papers over, and would then reply. After examining them, I came to the conclusion that the greater part of the "Memoir" ought to be published as it was. If this was first done, I could undertake to edit the rest; otherwise I must decline the responsibility. I cannot give my reasons without entering on a subject on which it is better to be silent. It is enough that I immediately told Mr. Carlyle what I thought. He replied that he left the decision to me. He himself was unable to judge. It was understood that certain parts would be omitted. The only condition that he made was that the publication should be deferred till ten years from that time. This was in 1871.

'In his will dated two years later Mr. Carlyle confirmed the discretionary authority which he had given to me, with express reference to these papers. My opinion, he said, was to be accepted as his own. Never since that time has he said one word to me to imply a desire to guide or influence my opinion in any way. I repeat that a permission to publish the

"Memoir" was the condition under which alone I could have undertaken the charge Carlyle laid upon me. I did not seek this charge. I did not like it. I accepted it only out of my personal regard for himself. Mrs. Carlyle will remember that two years ago I offered to surrender it into her hands. My task is difficult enough as it stands. I shall be sorry if the difficulty is increased by a demand for further explanations, which I shall be very reluctant to give.'

With the publication of the foregoing letters Froude's position became unpleasant and difficult. He was compelled to assume the defensive. Whatever confidence he had hitherto reposed in Mary Carlyle was now gone. He finally recognised that she was determined to do all within her power to defeat the expressly declared legal intention of Carlyle that on all points having to do with publication 'James Anthony Froude's practical summing up and decision' was to be taken as his own. Already she had made clear that in her opinion Carlyle's own choice of literary executor was unwise, and that Froude was disqualified to carry out her uncle's wishes. The manner of her attack shocked him. To the day of his death he felt that he had deserved better treatment at the hands of Carlyle's niece. Painful and difficult as was his position, he realised that repining could not better it. Indeed, as Mary became more aggressive, he had little leisure for repining. The interchange of letters between the solicitors representing the two sides of the controversy continued until October 1881. Then, in the words of Alexander Carlyle, it became evident that Froude 'was determined to go on with his "Life of Carlyle."' The law was clearly on the side of Carlyle's biographer. The remainder of his task, however, was to be disturbed by constant turmoil.

CHAPTER VI

FROUDE FULFILS THE COMMISSION

FROM May until October 1881 Mary strove to prevent Froude from completing the biography of Carlyle by attempts to establish a claim upon the materials. In a communication to *The Times* of May 7 she suggested that he should surrender them immediately. On May 9 Froude replied: 'The remaining papers [that is, the materials upon which the 'Thomas Carlyle' is based], which I was directed to return to Mrs. Alexander Carlyle as soon as I had done with them, I will restore at once to any responsible person whom she will empower to receive them from me.' Alexander Carlyle maintains that on the following day Mary's solicitor applied for the papers, but Froude refused to give them up.[1] Much has been made by Froude's enemies of his refusal to surrender the papers after his positive statement in *The Times*. 'The fact remains,' assert Alexander Carlyle and Sir James Crichton-Browne, 'that Froude deliberately broke his deliberate promise. The humiliating position in which he thus placed himself does not seem to have been improved by the excuses of his friends.'[2] Such assertions seem to me to be founded upon an incomplete and unsympathetic

[1] *Nemesis*, p. 91.

[2] *Ibid.*, p. 93. On May 9, 1881, *The Times* in an editorial expressed a hope that 'no terrorism should fetter his [Froude's] judgment in the future.' See the editorial among the illustrative documents on pp. 292–296 of this volume.

knowledge of the conditions under which the offer was made.

It must be borne in mind that in proposing to return the papers Froude had no intention at that time of forgoing the preparation of Carlyle's biography. 'My offer to return them *at once*,' he wrote, 'was made in a moment of irritation at the unworthy treatment which I had received from Mrs. Carlyle. I conceived, however, at that time that the long labour which I had undergone over these papers would enable me to write the biography without further use of them. Mrs. Carlyle had disclaimed any wish to interfere with me in the use which I might make of the materials which I had already selected, and I was unwilling to remain in any relations to Mrs. Carlyle whatever. *I withdraw that letter and that offer. The greater part of the biography is written.* The first part of it will be published in the spring. Mr. Carlyle's family, his surviving brothers and sisters, have earnestly protested against my abandoning the trust which Mr. Carlyle himself committed to me, and I mean to fulfil it unless I am otherwise ordered by a court of law.' [1]

Sir James Stephen has made the clearest statement in regard to Froude's refusal to surrender the papers immediately. 'It was a mere statement of your intention,' wrote Stephen to Froude, 'and was at the most a voluntary promise, founded on no consideration, made in a moment of irritation, and which did not in any degree alter Mrs. Alexander Carlyle's position. If a man made an unqualified promise to leave all his property to another, he would, I think, be entitled to withdraw it at any time before it had affected the plans in life of the person to whom it was made. To have given up the papers

[1] From Froude's letter of October 12, 1881, to Sir James Stephen, now published for the first time among the illustrative documents in this volume on pp. 296–298.

would have been to waste the labour of seven or eight years of your life, and to fail in carrying out the wish of Mr. Carlyle, that you should write his life, and your promise to him to do so. Quite apart from this a further question arose. You discovered soon after writing the letter of May 9 that you had no right to give the papers up without my consent. We were advised by counsel, on May 13, 1881, and upon a case which embodied your statement of the facts, that the papers in question belonged not to you personally but to Mr. Carlyle's executors, and that Mr. Carlyle's direction to give them up to Mrs. Alexander Carlyle when you had done with them was "an attempted verbal testamentary disposition, which has no legal authority." You could not therefore have given them up without my consent, and I never gave, or would have given, it.'[1]

The legal proceedings of the summer of 1881 will be examined in the next chapter. It is enough to say here that neither Froude nor his co-executor Sir James Stephen ever deviated from their original position. Nor did Froude allow distractions to interfere with his work. 'I went on with my task,' he wrote, 'and I finished in the best way that I could, amidst threatened lawsuits, lawyers' letters pressing for the papers, feeling throughout that I was handling burning coals and under a hailstorm of unfavourable criticism, which under the circumstances was perfectly natural. I was keeping back the essential part of the story which had governed my own action, and the world, not knowing the full truth, considered that I made too much of trifles which need not have been spoken of at all.'[2]

Froude was fortunate in being associated with Sir James Stephen, who took most of the legal burden upon himself. On August 19, 1881, Froude wrote to

[1] See the illustrative documents in this volume on pp. 312–331.
[2] *Relations*, pp. 36–37.

his daughter Margaret: 'You do not say if you have heard from Stephen. I begin to think that I should prefer the question going before a court that the whole story may be known and all difficulties authoritatively adjusted. But I left him power to arrange as he pleased.' And about the same time he wrote to Olga Novikoff:

'I am living under conditions which try friendship, and yours has proved itself real. Those whom I trusted have fallen from me. Those of whom I know nothing have come forward to help me; and what is it all about? Mine is the true confidence in Carlyle. I look on him as one of those great men who will be lights in the world a hundred years hence: one who must be known as he was. Known in all particulars. And there has been no great man of letters whose history, as a whole, will stand a sterner scrutiny. Goethe's "Autobiography" was a shock to foolish idolaters, yet who would part with it? In wise men's eyes it detracts nothing from Goethe. Yet Goethe tells things of himself a thousand times worse than the worst which can be known of Carlyle. Had I been a friend of Rousseau, and if he had trusted me with the "Confessions," so strong is my belief that a man who has powerfully influenced his age should be shown in his true personality, that I believe I should have published it: though I positively *loathe* the aspect of Rousseau which his "Confessions" reveal.

'I don't know what will come of it all. The whole question is now in lawyers' hands. If the law will relieve me of my trust I shall make no objection. If it confirms Carlyle's disposition, I shall go through with what I have undertaken, and however things go, I shall be eternally obliged to the few who have not turned their backs on me.' [1]

The foregoing letters strongly confirm the account which Froude wrote from memory in Cuba in 1887.

[1] *Novikoff*, ii. 328–329.

'I, for my own part, was now anxious that a court of law should be appealed to. I should see my way as executor, and in my own capacity I should be delivered out of complications which threatened to choke me. Either the papers would be declared to belong to me, or to belong to the executors, or to belong to Mary Carlyle. If they belonged to me or to the executors, I could go on peaceably with my work, so far as I could have peace at all amidst the world's outcries. If to her, I should be delivered altogether from further trouble about the matter. I should have lost ten years of labour and anxiety, but I was ready to sacrifice anything to escape out of a situation which was intolerable. . . . I had more than once resolved to throw the work up and go no farther, but I had promised Carlyle to write his "Life," and I did not like to have my commission wrenched out of my hands by pretensions which had not been proved to have a foundation. A court of law would settle all that. The intricacies of the situation would be disentangled under cross-examination, and we should all know where we stood. If Mary Carlyle did not press her own claim, I wished to appeal myself to the Court of Chancery to interpret Carlyle's will and determine our several rights and duties. I was overruled by my brother-executor, who was unwilling that Carlyle's name should be soiled in a lawsuit. I have no doubt that on the whole Sir James Stephen was right in this. I had myself been worried into too great impatience. At any rate, I submitted to his opinion.' [1]

The summer of 1881 was not, however, without encouragement for Froude. One source of gratification to him was a letter from a sister and a brother of Carlyle.[2] Its importance can scarcely be overrated.

[1] *Relations*, pp. 69–70.

[2] For reference to the attitude of Janet Carlyle Hanning, Carlyle's youngest sister, see *Life and Letters of George Jacob Holyoake*, ii. 126–127. I reprint the the material on pp. 358–360 of this volume.

The straightforward expressions of Carlyle's honest and simple-hearted kinsfolk reveal the truth. James Carlyle and Mary Austin were fully aware of their brother's opinion of Froude. They knew also what Carlyle's 'express wishes' in regard to a biography were. The exact text of the letter follows :

Newlands Cottage,
Ecclefechan, N.B.
August 8, 1881.

'JAS. A. FROUDE, Esqre.,
'London.

'DEAR SIR,—We have heard that it is possible you may decline altogether to write a Life of our late Brother Thomas.

'Knowing the great esteem and regard entertained for you by Thos. Carlyle and having respect to his express wishes we should view such a conclusion with great regret. And we take this method of assuring you of our perfect trust in you ; and particularly of our non-participation in the vexatious dispute now going on.

'We are now advanced in years and less than ever capable of grasping difficult statements and forming opinions upon them ; and therefore also resolve to leave the Executry in the hands of the Executors, in whom we have the most implicit confidence, without any interference on our part.

'And we are, Dear Sir,
'Yours respectfully,
'JAMES CARLYLE,
'MARY CARLYLE AUSTIN.'

To Margaret, on August 29, Froude wrote : 'Write at once to James Carlyle and thank him for his letter, and tell him that I will write myself on my return. . . . I shall now be able to do the Carlyle life satisfactorily and shall let the terrible letters of Mrs. Carlyle hang on.'

As he toiled over the manuscript of the biography he occasionally relieved himself by writing to friends. 'It has occurred to me that Goethe's representatives may have a voice in the matter,' he wrote to Max Müller, December 8, 1881. 'I do not know who they are, or what is usual in Germany in such cases. So much ill will has been shown me in the case of other letters that I walk as if on hot ashes, and often curse the day when I undertook the business. I had intended when I finished my "English History" to set myself quietly down to Charles the Fifth, and spend the rest of my life over him. I might have been half through by this time, and the world all in good humour with me. My ill stars were uppermost when I laid this aside. There are objections to every course which I can follow. The arguments for and against were so many and so strong that Carlyle himself could not decide what was to be done, and left it to me. He could see all sides of the question. Other people will see one, or one more strongly than another, whatever it may be; and therefore, do what I will, a great many would blame me. What have I done that I should be in such a strait? But I am sixty-four years old, and shall soon be beyond it all.'

Again, on January 16, 1882, he wrote to Max Müller: 'I hear from Scotland that the personal admiration of Carlyle grows daily there "in spite of the 'Reminiscences'"!! What would they have known of him without it? The world wanted an idol which they could completely worship. They were astonished and exasperated to find a prickly reality of flesh and blood. I fear that in my work [the 'Thomas Carlyle' then in preparation] there is too much of the idol.'

Under such circumstances Froude completed the first two volumes of the biography, which cover the first forty years of Carlyle's life. They were published

March 30, 1882. In a preface of sixteen pages, every word of which should be read by those who wish to understand the facts, Froude explained the genesis of the biography and the principles which he had followed in writing it.

He began by saying that Carlyle had expressed a desire in his will that no biography of him should be written. He explained that in 1871 Carlyle had placed in his hands the annotated letters of Mrs. Carlyle to be published or not as Froude should decide. Carlyle, he said, intended the collection of letters to form 'a monument to a character of extreme beauty,' and at the same time to 'tell the public as much about himself as it could reasonably expect to learn.'

'Two years later, however, soon after he had made his will, Carlyle discovered that, whether he wished it or not, a life, or perhaps various lives, of himself would certainly appear when he was gone. . . . Carlyle knew that he could not escape. Since a "Life" of him there would certainly be, he wished it to be as authentic as possible. Besides the memoir of Mrs. Carlyle, he had written several others, mainly autobiographical, not distinctly to be printed, but with no fixed purpose that they should not be printed. These, with his journals and the whole of his correspondence, he made over to me, with unfettered discretion to use in any way that I might think good.' [1]

An examination of the documents brought Froude face to face with the dilemma which confronts almost every biographer. 'In the papers thus in my possession,' he wrote, 'Carlyle's history, external and spiritual, lay out before me as in a map. By recasting the entire material, by selecting chosen passages out of his own and his wife's letters, by exhibiting the fair and beautiful side of the story only,

[1] *Thomas Carlyle*, I. pp. vi–vii.

it would have been easy, without suppressing a single material point, to draw a picture of a faultless character. . . . But it would have been a portrait without individuality—an ideal, or, in other words, an "idol," to be worshipped one day and thrown away the next. Least of all men could such idealising be ventured with Carlyle, to whom untruth of any kind was abominable. If he was to be known at all, he chose to be known as he was, with his angularities, his sharp speeches, his special peculiarities, meritorious or unmeritorious, precisely as they had actually been. He has himself laid down the conditions under which a biographer must do his work if he would do it honestly, without the fear of man before him; and in dealing with Carlyle's own memory I have felt myself bound to conform to his own rule.'

At this point Froude quotes the passage in defence of John Gibson Lockhart from Carlyle's review of Lockhart's 'Life of Sir Walter Scott.' Froude always felt, and I feel, that hostile critics of Froude's 'Carlyle' have never taken sufficiently into consideration the full import of Carlyle's statements in this review. In a later chapter I shall revert to Carlyle's notions of biography as set forth in his estimate of Lockhart's work. In the preface Froude makes no further comment on the passage than the remark that he considered the principles there laid down to be strictly obligatory upon himself in writing the biography.

A preliminary examination of the material revealed to Froude that he could not write the life of Carlyle without careful selection from all the documents—particularly from Carlyle's own autobiographical sketches and the collection of Mrs. Carlyle's letters—which had been placed in his hands. He shrank from the task of taking the materials apart and constructing a narrative of his own. 'Mr. Forster and John Carlyle having both died,' says

Froude, ' the responsibility was left entirely to myself. A few weeks before Mr. Carlyle's death, he asked me what I meant to do. I told him that I proposed to publish the memoirs as soon as he was gone—those which form the two volumes of the " Reminiscences." Afterwards I said that I would publish the letters about which I knew him to be most anxious. He gave his full assent, merely adding that he trusted everything to me. The memoirs, he thought, had better appear immediately on his departure. He expected that people would then be talking about him, and that it would be well for them to have something authentic to guide them.[1] These points being determined, the remainder of my task became simplified. Mrs. Carlyle's letters are a better history of the London life of herself and her husband than could be written either by me or by anyone. The connecting narrative is Carlyle's own, and to meddle with his work would be to spoil it. It was thus left to me to supply an account of his early life in Scotland, the greater part of which I had written while he was alive, and which is contained in the present volumes. The publication of the letters will follow at no distant period. Afterwards, if I live to do it, I shall add a brief account of his last years, when I was in constant intercourse with him.'

With such prefatory statements the two volumes of ' Thomas Carlyle ' went before the public. On the surface they are uncontroversial ; they contain no reference to the disputes with Mary Carlyle ; the entire text is restrained and dignified. The hasty publication of the letter in *The Times* offering to return the materials had taught Froude a lesson. However much thereafter he chafed under circum-

[1] This is the explanation of the early publication of the *Reminiscences*. That Carlyle was right in wishing to give the public something authentic is proved by the number of sketches, biographies, etc., which appeared as rapidly as they could be compiled. Moncure Conway was one of the first to publish a sketch of Carlyle.

stances in private, in public he gave no sign of the indignation under which he was labouring.

When the volumes were almost ready for publication Froude announced the fact to his friend John Skelton in a letter dated February 17, 1882, from which a few sentences may be quoted as indicative of Froude's state of mind. 'Carlyle's "Life"—the Scotch part of it—will be out in three weeks or a month,' he wrote. 'I shall perhaps go abroad till the tongues have done wagging. . . . The end will be that C. will stand higher than ever, and will be loved more than ever. When a man's faults are not such as dishonour him, we are all the nearer to him because of them, and because we feel the common pulse of humanity in him.' [1] Skelton, it seems, was somewhat slow in expressing his opinion of the volumes, but when he did, his verdict gave Froude great pleasure. 'I did not write,' he informed Skelton on June 15, 1882, 'partly because . . . I could not tell from your silence whether you did not share in the feeling of disappointment of Carlyle's "Life," which Tulloch and Boyd led me to suppose is general in Scotland. Judge then if your letter has not given me pleasure. What motive could I have in writing as I have done except to do what I believe Carlyle to have wished? It would have been idle folly to have kept anything back.' [2]

A year later came the third instalment of materials as Froude had promised in the preface to 'Thomas Carlyle.' The three volumes of the 'Letters and Memorials of Jane Welsh Carlyle' were published April 2, 1883. The title-page announced that the material was 'prepared for publication by Thomas Carlyle' and 'edited by James Anthony Froude.' Again there was no inclusion of controversial matter; only the following preface, dated February 28, 1883, appeared over Froude's name:

[1] *Shirley*, p. 178. [2] *Ibid.*, pp. 178–179.

'The letters which form these volumes were placed in my hands by Mr. Carlyle in 1871. They are annotated throughout by himself. The few additional observations occasionally required are marked with my initials.

'I have not thought it necessary to give an introductory narrative of Mrs. Carlyle's previous history, the whole of it being already related in my account of the "first forty years" of her husband's life. To this I must ask the reader who wishes for information to be so good as to refer.

'Mr. Carlyle did not order the publication of these letters, though he anxiously desired it. He left the decision to Mr. Forster, Mr. John Carlyle, and myself. Mr. Forster and Mr. John Carlyle having both died in Mr. Carlyle's lifetime, the responsibility fell entirely upon me. Mr. Carlyle asked me, a few months before his end, what I meant to do. I told him that, when the "Reminiscences" had been published, I had decided that the letters might and should be published also.

'Mr. Carlyle requested in his will that my judgment in the matter should be accepted as his own.'

Froude sent the three volumes to Carlyle's brother James, and received the following letter in acknowledgment:

Newlands Cottage,
Ecclefechan, N.B.
April 28, 1883.

'J. A. Froude, Esqre.,
'London.

'Dear Sir,—My father desires me to thank you for the three volumes of "Letters and Memorials" which came quite duly. He (father) enjoys them much: being better able to recall the events and circumstances referred to than he can remember what has transpired a few days ago.

'Again thanking you for your kind and prompt attention, I am,

'Yours faithfully,

'JAMES CARLYLE, Junior.'

While the sheets of the 'Letters and Memorials' were passing through the press Froude was busy over the last volumes of the biography, and was finding the task no easier as he drew near the end. 'The rest of my working life, short or long, must be given to Carlyle,' he wrote to John Skelton, December 10, 1882. 'I believe no biographer had ever a more difficult or troublesome task bequeathed him.' [1] Like other things, however, agreeable or disagreeable, the long task came to an end, and on October 6, 1884, the remaining volumes of 'Thomas Carlyle,' the last of the series of nine, were published. The first volume opens with seven pages of introductory matter. There is no reference to Mary Carlyle, no mention of the disagreeable controversy in which Froude had been involved, yet everyone who was cognisant of the facts knew that in those pages Froude was putting on record the difficulties which had confronted him, the spirit in which he had wrought, and the motives which had actuated him.

'Reluctantly, and only when he found that his wishes would not and could not be respected, Carlyle requested me [wrote Froude] to undertake the task which he had . . . described as hopeless; and placed materials in my hands which would make the creation of a true likeness of him, if still difficult, yet no longer as impossible as he had declared it to be. Higher confidence was never placed by any man in another. I had not sought it, but I did not refuse to accept it. I felt myself only more strictly bound than men in such circumstances usually are, to discharge the duty which I knew to be expected from me.

[1] *Shirley*, pp. 179–180.

Had I considered my own comfort or my own interest, I should have sifted out or passed lightly over the delicate features in the story. It would have been as easy as it would have been agreeable for me to construct a picture, with every detail strictly accurate, of an almost perfect character. An account so written would have been read with immediate pleasure. Carlyle would have been admired and applauded, and the biographer, if he had not shared in the praise, would at least have escaped censure.

'Had I taken the course which the "natural man" would have recommended, I should have given no faithful account of Carlyle. I should have created a "delusion and a hallucination" of the precise kind which he who was the truest of men most deprecated and dreaded ; and I should have done it not innocently and in ignorance, but with deliberate insincerity, after my attention had been specially directed by his own generous openness to the points which I should have left unnoticed. I should have been unjust first to myself—for I should have failed in what I knew to be my duty as a biographer. I should have been unjust secondly to the public.

'Lastly, I should have been unjust to Carlyle himself and to everyone who believed and has believed in him. To have been reticent would have implied that there was something to hide, and, taking Carlyle all in all, there never was a man—I at least never knew of one—whose conduct in life would better bear the fiercest light which can be thrown upon it. . . . Tender-hearted and affectionate he was beyond all men whom I have ever known. His faults, which in his late remorse he exaggerated, as men of noblest natures are most apt to do, his impatience, his irritability, his singular melancholy, which made him at times distressing as a companion, were the effects of temperament first, and of a peculiarly sensitive organisation ; and secondly of absorption in his work and of his determination to do that work as well as it could possibly be done. . . . His life was not a happy one, and there were features in it for which, as he looked back, he bitterly reproached himself. But there are many, perhaps the majority of us, who sin deeper every day of their lives in these very points in which Carlyle sinned, and without Carlyle's excuses, who do not know that they have anything to repent of. The more completely it is understood, the more his character will be seen to answer to his intellectual teaching. The one is the counterpart of the other. There was no falsehood and there was no concealment in him. The same true nature showed itself in his life and in his words. He acted as he spoke from his heart, and those who have admired his writings will equally admire himself when they see him in his actual likeness.

'I, for myself, concluded, though not till after long hesitation, that there should be no reserve, and therefore I have practised none. I have published his own autobiographical fragments. I have published an account of his early years from his letters and journals. I have published the letters and memorials of his wife which describe (from one aspect) his life in London as long as she remained with him. I supposed for a time that if to these I added my personal recollections of him, my task would be sufficiently accomplished; but I have thought it better on longer consideration to complete his biography as I began it. He himself quotes a saying of Goethe that on the lives of remarkable men ink and paper should least be spared. I must leave no materials unused to complete the portrait which I attempt to draw.'

At the very end of the biography Froude referred once more to the conditions under which he had accepted the trust. In describing Carlyle's last days he said: 'He was still fairly cheerful, and tried, though with diminished eagerness, to take an interest in public affairs. He even thought for a moment of taking a personal part in the preparation of his memoirs. . . . It was suggested[1] that he might revise the sheets personally, and that the book might appear in his lifetime as edited by himself. He turned the proposal over in his mind, and considered that perhaps he might try. On reflection, however, he found the effort would be too much for him. He gave it up, and left everything as before to me, to do what I thought proper.'

'At this time [continues Froude] there had been no mention and no purpose of including in the intended volume the memoir of Mrs. Carlyle. This was part of his separate bequest to me, and I was then engaged, as I have already said, in incorporating both memoir and letters in the history of his early life. I think a year must have elapsed after this before the subject was mentioned between us again. At length, however, one day about three months before his death, he asked me very solemnly, and in a tone of the saddest anxiety, what I proposed to do about "the letters and memorials." I was sorry—for a fresh evidence at so late a date of his wish that the letters should be published as he had left them would take away my discretion, and I could no longer treat them as I had begun to do. But he was so sorrowful and earnest—though still giving no positive order—that I could make no objection. I promised him that the letters should appear with such reservations as might be indispensable. The letters implied the memoir, for it had been agreed upon from the first between us that, if Mrs. Carlyle's letters were published, his memoir of her must be published also. I decided, therefore, that the memoir should be added to the volume of reminiscences ; the

[1] Froude himself made the suggestion.

letters to follow at an early date. I briefly told him this. He was entirely satisfied, and never spoke about it again.

'I have said enough already of Carlyle's reason for preparing these papers, of his bequest of them to me, and of the embarrassment into which I was thrown by it. The arguments on either side were weighty, and ten years of consideration had not made it more easy to choose between them. My final conclusion may have been right or wrong, but the influence which turned the balance was Carlyle's persevering wish, and my own conviction that it was a wish supremely honourable to him.' [1]

A letter from Carlyle's sister Mary (Mrs. James Austin) by the hand of her daughter Jane strongly confirms Froude's assertion of Carlyle's trust in him. It will no doubt surprise those who have looked upon Froude only in the light of the accusations brought against him by his enemies to find that after the fulfilment of his trust Carlyle's sister was still on friendly terms with the betrayer of her brother's confidence, and desirous of having one of his photographs! This is the letter:

The Gill,
Annan, N.B.,
October 20, 1884.

'J. A. FROUDE, Esq.

'DEAR SIR,—My mother wishes me to acknowledge receipt of the last two volumes of my Uncle's life, and to thank you very much for your kindness. From what we have seen we think the last two volumes will be the most pleasant to read. We are very glad—for your sake—that your task is finished—a task that has not been, I am afraid, easy or agreeable to you; only, my Uncle at all times placed implicit confidence in you, and that confidence has not, I am sure, in any way been abused. He always spoke of you as his best and truest friend.

[1] *Thomas Carlyle*, 4. pp. 465–467.

'If it is not too much to ask, my mother would feel very much pleased by your giving her a photograph of yourself. She would have written herself, only she has been confined to her bedroom for some time with a broken arm.

'I am,

'Yours very sincerely,

'JANE C. AUSTIN.'

So far as Froude wished and hoped he was now through with the Carlyle matter. Mary had exerted herself to the utmost to prevent him from fulfilling the express wishes of Carlyle as set forth in his will. We are not left in doubt as to her object. 'It was to prevent him from writing the "Life" that Mrs. Alexander Carlyle had striven, but she was advised that, having lent him the papers for that specific purpose, she could not insist on their return until that purpose was accomplished, and that Froude was not legally bound by his unconditional offer to return them at once, if he chose to stand confessed a promise-breaker in the sight of all men. She was therefore obliged helplessly to wait and watch with grief and indignation what she regarded as the profanation of her uncle's memory.'[1] Such were the words of Mary's spokesmen in 1903. An examination into the justice of her claims follows.

[1] *Nemesis*, p. 157.

CHAPTER VII

MARY CARLYLE'S CLAIMS

MARY urged her ownership of the materials upon which the biography of Carlyle is based on the ground that her uncle had made an oral gift of the papers to her in 1875, as here explained :

'In June 1875 my uncle Thomas Carlyle bought seven £1000 1873 5 per cent. Russian bonds from our next-door neighbour, Mr. Laisné, a stockbroker. On the 30th of June 1875 these bonds were delivered to him, and as I sat writing in the dining-room at Cheyne Row after breakfast my uncle altogether unexpectedly brought me one of these bonds and gave it to me as a present. He said that he had in addition to this provision for me left me by his will £500. He also told me that he had left to his brother John (my uncle Dr. John Carlyle, who was then staying with us at Cheyne Row) all the things in the house as they stood, but that he now gave these same things to me instead, which arrangement he had explained to his brother John who would also speak of it to me. He also said specifically that he gave me also his papers and his wife's jewellery. He said, " I give you the papers and all the jewels of your aunt." He at the same time gave into my possession the keys of these papers and his wife's jewels, which keys I had never up till that time used except on occasions when they were lent to me by him for some specific purpose. My uncle John A. Carlyle the same day spoke of this gift of a thousand pounds. He spoke of it as being in his opinion a small provision, but he added, "Your uncle has also given you all the things in the house which he has bequeathed to me by his will. I quite approve of his doing so and I renounce all claim upon them."'[1]

It is necessary to consider the meaning of the words 'papers' and 'things,' and what Carlyle's remarks meant at the time to himself and to his niece. Notice that Mary makes a clear distinction between 'things' and 'papers.' She says that her uncle gave her the things in the house as they stood and also the papers. Notice also that John Carlyle, in speaking to his niece, does not mention the papers, which, equally with the things, had been bequeathed to him. If he had supposed that the papers passed also to Mary, he would scarcely have failed to mention them. He understood that beyond the £1000 bond the only provision for Mary was 'the things' in the house, and with regard to that provision he would have spoken quite differently if he had supposed that it was an immediate transfer of property. In that case he would not have referred to his prospective rights under Carlyle's will, which were not waivable by him, for they had not matured. The claim which he renounced was a provision after Carlyle's death. He understood that Carlyle's oral gift was intended to take effect after Carlyle's death.

Mary's statement continues:

'In 1877, after some communications between my uncle and Mr. Froude as to a biography of my uncle, my uncle asked me to send Mr. Froude such of the papers as I thought would be useful for that purpose, but told me distinctly that he had taken care I should have them all back again. I was then, as always, anxious to carry out every wish of my uncle, and I accordingly sent almost all the papers I had, but I

[1] *Nemesis*, p. 136.

might have retained all if I had desired. I left the selection to Mr. Froude of my own free will and without my uncle's knowledge.' [1]

Mary contended that 'papers' meant all papers except private accounts and those specifically bequeathed to Froude—namely, the letters and memorials and the sketch of Mrs. Carlyle—which were already in his possession. She maintained that none of the papers for the biography were sent to Froude before 1877. On that supposition the collection in the house when Carlyle spoke to her in 1875 must have been very large, some thousands of letters with all the original manuscripts of Carlyle's writings. That view is untenable, as the evidence already given is conclusive that the documents about Mrs. Carlyle were sent to Froude in 1871. The papers sent in 1873, which Mrs. Froude saw before her death on February 12, 1874, must therefore have been the materials for the biography.[2]

The kind of material that remained in Cheyne Row in 1875 is shown by Mary's further statement. She says that she gave to Mr. Allingham for publication a translation from Goethe and an account of a tour in the Netherlands. To Mr. Anstruther she gave a paper on a new method of roughing horses and another unimportant paper. She framed and hung in her room two letters from Thackeray and a poem of Goethe, and put a paper of her uncle's into her scrap-book. She cut out and gave away autographs, and presented a portion of the manuscript of 'Frederick' to Mrs. Lecky. Carlyle saw and approved.

[1] *Nemesis*, p. 138.

[2] On March 15, 1884, Froude wrote to Skelton: 'In two months, if I continue able to work, I shall have written the last line of a business which has been a perplexity and worry to me for the last fourteen years.' And on May 16, 1884, he wrote: 'You will be glad to hear that yesterday I *finished* the MS. of Carlyle.' See *Shirley*, pp. 183 and 185. These statements are in harmony with Froude's assertions that the first materials came into his hands in 1871.

Corroborative evidence was available. Mr. Allingham and Mr. Anstruther supported Mary's statements as to her gifts to them. Alexander Carlyle said that Mary had told him that Carlyle 'had given her his manuscripts.' Mr. Friedmann said that once when he was driving with Carlyle, Carlyle had informed him that Goethe's letters belonged to his niece. Madame Venturi asserted that Mary had told her 'in Carlyle's presence and hearing' that he had given her all 'his letters and papers.'

Notwithstanding Mary's exercise of rights of proprietorship over some minor pieces of her uncle's papers, it is permissible to doubt whether either she or Carlyle in 1875 considered that the property in all of Carlyle's papers, or even in the papers then in Cheyne Row, had passed from him to her so completely that, as she said in 1881, she might have refused to send any of them to Froude. If such were the fact, she might, against Carlyle's wish and protest, have given them to a rival biographer of her own selection; she might have burned or sold or published them; she might even have declined to allow Carlyle to look at his wife's letters. There is ground for Sir James Stephen's belief that when the conversation took place in 1875 neither Carlyle nor his niece supposed that it had the effect then and there of transferring the complete ownership of all Carlyle's papers to Mary.

The most reasonable explanation is that, forgetting his remarks to Froude about burning, remarks which were nothing more than affectation, Carlyle intended that, with the exception of those which he had willed to Froude, his papers should, after his death and when Froude had finished with them, remain in the family. When in 1875 he said to his niece 'they are yours,' he meant 'they will be yours after my death.' As an earnest of his intention he gave Mary the keys of the receptacles which contained the least important papers still in the house. He wished her to have immediate control over them and to save him bother about them. If inquiries were made about those minor papers, Mary was to deal with them. It was second nature with Carlyle to avoid decisions and put the responsibility on others.

Carlyle's shrinking from decisions helps to explain his reticence towards Froude. In 1881 Mary said that her uncle had told her early in 1879 that Froude perfectly understood that the papers were to be returned to her when done with, " for I have often said so to him." A remark of Froude's to Mary caused her, however, to feel that he did not understand, a circumstance which leads to the conclusion that Carlyle had perhaps not spoken clearly to Froude. At Mary's request Carlyle then did speak. In February 1879 he told Froude in a casual way to return the papers to Mary when he had finished with them. According to Froude's deliberate statement that was the first warning he received.

Carlyle said nothing to Froude in 1879, or at any time, about the conversation with Mary in 1875, partly from a constitutional Scottish reticence, partly because he considered the arrangement of 1875 as included in and explained by his talk with Froude in February 1879. In June 1875 he told Mary that after his death the papers were to be hers. In February 1879, at her request, he told Froude. The contention that the papers belonged to Mary since June 1875 cannot be sustained, for in that case Carlyle would have had no right to direct Froude about them. It is clear that he considered them as still his own property. If he had already given them to Mary, the natural thing would have been to say to Froude : 'I have given all my papers to my niece. They are her property, are lent to you by her, and must be returned to her when you have done with them.'

Instead, he spoke as the one to whom the papers belonged. The result was that Froude, who of all men should have received early information, was not told until February 1879 that the papers were not his to burn if he thought fit, and did not hear of the alleged gift of 1875 until several months after Carlyle's death.

With regard to the 'things' which Mary said her uncle had given her, corroborative evidence was also produced. Mrs. Jean Carlyle Aitken, Mary's mother, said that she had been told by her brother John that the things in the house which were left to him were to be Mary's. Miss Ann Aitken, Mary's sister, was told by John, 'Your uncle has left all the things in his house to me, but they are Mary's.' Again one observes that John said nothing about papers.[1] There is abundant evidence that Carlyle's remark to Mary in 1875 did not mean that the 'things' in the house which had been bequeathed by will to John—that is to say, the 'furniture, plate, linen, china, books, prints, pictures, and other effects therein'—belonged thenceforth to her. Mary never exercised any rights of proprietorship over these effects, but Carlyle himself continued to do so.

By the codicil to his will, dated November 8, 1878, Carlyle appointed John Carlyle, Froude, and Sir James Stephen executors, John Forster, a former executor, having died in February 1876. The writing table which by his will he had given to Mary he now gave to Sir James Stephen. To Mary he gave a screen; to other beneficiaries, pictures and books. He revoked the gift to John of his lease of the house in Cheyne Row, and of the furniture, plate, linen, china, books, prints, and pictures. Instead, he now gave John only a life interest in the house and effects, which after John's death were to go to Mary absolutely. Obviously he regarded the house and its

[1] *Nemesis*, pp. 143–144.

contents as still his own, or at least to be dealt with as he pleased. After his death they were valued for probate duty and included in his estate. Mary's claim in 1881 that they had been given to her in 1875 must have been due to a misunderstanding of the same nature as that about the papers. Her claim to the 'things' weakens her claim to the 'papers,' which rests upon the same conversation and similar corroboration. The conclusion is unavoidable that both Carlyle and his niece understood that the papers belonged to her only after his death, subject to Froude's prior right of publication.

The assertions of Mary in 1881 mean that after June 1875 the whole contents of the house at Cheyne Row, all papers and all removable objects, belonged to her. Accordingly, she might at once in Carlyle's lifetime have burned all his manuscripts, leaving no materials for a biography; she might have hawked about his wife's letters; she might have disposed of everything in the house—Carlyle's writing-desk, even his bed—leaving him nothing but the bare walls. Carlyle was no King Lear to put himself into such a position. He kept a firm grip on financial matters. 'My uncle always drew his own cheques,' asserts Mary.[1] It is impossible to believe that either Carlyle or Mary understood the remarks of 1875 to confer such absolute and immediate rights upon her.

Mary's claim upon the documents soon became complicated with her claim upon the proceeds from the 'Reminiscences.' This latter claim arose out of a misunderstanding in regard to a proposed 'immense sum' which Moncure Conway told Froude that Harper & Brothers would pay for an American edition of the work. This large sum Froude promised to Mary Carlyle. 'It appeared afterwards,' he wrote, 'that she had misunderstood me, so far that she thought I was speaking of all the profits, English

[1] *Nemesis*, p. 135.

as well as American.'[1] Eventually the Harper offer came to nothing. Conway's covert handling of the negotiations bungled the whole matter and involved Froude in difficulties with both Harpers and Scribners, the rival American publishers. The affair was characteristic of Conway, whose versions of matters having to do with Froude and Carlyle cannot be trusted. The same kind of mistaken zeal had previously, by his own confession, involved him in serious difficulty with the government of the United States.[2]

Alexander and Mary Carlyle dined with the Froudes on November 20, 1879. Then it was that Froude voluntarily proposed to give Mary returns from an American edition of the 'Reminiscences.' Margaret Froude and Ashley Froude, children of the biographer, were both present. Miss Froude's recollection as expressed to me in July 1925 is that 'at this dinner, as once before in my hearing, my father urged the propriety of the arrangement about the American profits on the ground that the money would in that case belong to the Carlyles and not to him. He said it was fairer that Mary should have a reward for her trouble in copying so many of her uncle's manuscripts; but she answered both times that she had no right, and her uncle wished the money to be

[1] *Relations*, pp. 65–66. The whole proposal is explained by Froude in *Relations*, pp. 64–70.

[2] On June 10, 1863, 'on behalf of the leading anti-slavery men in America,' Conway addressed a letter to J. M. Mason, who was then representing the Confederate States of America in Great Britain, proposing that the Confederacy emancipate the slaves. He represented that in the event of emancipation the abolitionists and anti-slavery leaders of the North by the immediate withdrawal of every kind of support would force a cessation of war. Mason's prompt publication of the letter in the London *Times* put Conway in an uncomfortable position. 'And here I am ready to confess,' he wrote to *The Times* on June 22, 'that my inexperience in diplomatic and political affairs has led me to make a proposition, the form of which is objectionable. . . . I inferred hastily and improperly that the right to declare the object of the abolitionists in the war justified me in sending the proposition to Mr. Mason personally. . . . I shall hope that the apparent disloyalty of it, of which I was unconscious, will be condoned by the country I meant to serve.' Those who care to read more of Conway's mistaken zeal will find a full version in his *Autobiography*, i. 412–432. He had seemingly learned little by 1879 about the conduct of important negotiations.

my father's. Both my brother and I could swear to her words, " I have no right," and he is positive as to this particular occasion for a particular reason. He was only a schoolboy, and neither knew nor cared about the " Reminiscences "—had never heard of Harpers' offer—but he regretted hearing my father press money—Harpers' immense sum—on Mary, when he knew that money was at the time wanted for a yacht we were building at Salcombe. He heard my father say to Mary, " All that will be yours," and her answer came as so great a relief that he did not forget it—" No, I have no right. Uncle wishes you to have it." What is certain is that neither Carlyle talking to my father, nor Mary talking to me during the fifteen months of constant communication that followed, ever hinted such a thing. I was sorry for her. It seemed hard that she should have worked for so many years and yet should only share equally with all the many other nephews and nieces, as by Carlyle's will it was arranged. I remember speaking to her often of what seemed to me an injustice. She never gave me reason to think she had any further provision.' The testimony of Ashley Froude, with whom also I conferred in July 1925, corroborates that of his sister.

John Carlyle died September 15, 1879. The bequest to him of papers and the life interest in the house and furniture lapsed. When Carlyle died on February 5, 1881, the leasehold house and the furniture became the property of Mary. The papers which had been bequeathed to John, passed *prima facie* to the executors on behalf of the residuary legatees: namely, Carlyle's brother James, his sisters Mary Austin, Jean Aitken, and Janet Hanning, and the children of his brother Alexander. The question at once arose whether Carlyle's remark to Froude that he was to send the papers to Mary when he had done with them gave her the immediate property in them. Oral dispositions must be strongly supported by corroborative evidence if they are to nullify the terms of a will.

In order to come to an understanding, Sir James Stephen drew up on February 21, 1881, in the presence of Mary Carlyle and her husband and of Mr. Ouvry, a solicitor then acting for both parties, a memorandum which was read and accepted by all present as a correct statement. A copy was sent to Mary the same day. The terms of this memorandum have been given previously.[1] It is only necessary to repeat here that in regard to the materials for Carlyle's biography Mary agreed that her understanding was that they had been given to Froude 'so that the property in them passed to him.' Mary protested afterwards that she had not understood the meaning of the last words, and said that she had told Sir James Stephen that these papers had been sent to Froude not by her uncle but by herself.[2]

When Froude in his letter to *The Times* of May 9, 1881, offered to return the papers at once, Sir James Stephen, as we have seen, demurred. To decide the questions at issue the opinion of counsel, Mr. Vaughan Hawkins, was obtained. A case was then prepared for counsel on behalf of Mary, a draft of which was sent to Sir James Stephen. It contained no reference to the oral gift of 1875.[3] The revised case in which the conversation of 1875 was at last put forward was sent to Stephen on June 28, 1881. Stephen's reply to the solicitors acting for Mary is now published in full for the first time. Only the last paragraphs appear in 'The Nemesis of Froude.' [4]

[1] See pp. 32–33.

[2] See the whole of Mary's case as set forth in *Nemesis*, pp. 127–157.

[3] In justice to Mary's side of the case I must refer to the contention of her supporters that the first draft was incomplete, as explained in *Nemesis*, p. 148. It is difficult to believe, however, that so important a fact as that of the oral gift of 1875 should have been omitted from the preliminary statement of the case.

[4] On p. 149.

32 De Vere Gardens, W.
July 5, 1881.

'GENTLEMEN,—I have now considered the case which you submitted to me a few days ago. It has not weakened, but confirmed the opinion I expressed in my last letter to you. The only part of the statements you have put into the form of proofs which appears to me to be of much importance is Mrs. Carlyle's account of the gift which she says her uncle made to her of the papers in June 1875.

'I cannot trust the accuracy of her recollection, for many reasons, some of which I will mention :

'(1) The statement referred to was not mentioned in the first edition of the case which you sent me. Mrs. Carlyle must therefore have recollected it for the first time about six years after she says it was made.

'(2) Her present view is inconsistent with and contradictory to the statement which she made to me on 21st February, of which I made a memorandum at the time. Whatever Mrs. Carlyle may say, I should be prepared to testify in any court of justice that one principal subject of our conversation on that occasion was to ascertain as far as we could who was the legal owner of the papers deposited with Mr. Froude. It seemed to me that if they were not his they must have passed to the executors, as John Carlyle had died. I positively assert that Mrs. Carlyle did then tell me that she understood they were given to Mr. Froude so as to pass the property to him, and that she did not say or even hint that they were ever given to her, and that she said nothing which led me to doubt that they were given to Mr. Froude by Mr. Carlyle's order or authority, though I think she did say (I cannot recollect the words) that they were given by her hands.

'(3) I had a long conversation with Mrs. Carlyle at my house on 27th February 1881, as the result of which she signed a letter of that date, a copy of which is set out in the case. This conversation proceeded throughout on the supposition that the papers were Mr. Froude's, and that his promise to give her the proceeds of the "Reminiscences" was a voluntary promise, the only question as to which was as to its extent.

'I cannot recollect the whole of a conversation which lasted perhaps half or three-quarters of an hour, but I distinctly remember impressing upon Mrs. Carlyle the point that as there was no consideration for it, the promise was only morally and not legally binding, and I suggested to her that as it was a generous act in him to make her a present of a large sum of money, it was ungracious in her to insist upon his promise being fulfilled according to her recollection of its terms. The result was that she at last appeared to assent to my view, and signed the letter I referred to. She never even hinted to me on this occasion that the papers were hers. Had she done so, I should never have argued with her as I did.

'(4) Mrs. Carlyle's recollection of the alleged conversation of 1875 cannot be accurate, or if it is, Mr. Carlyle cannot have intended to give to her a present property in the papers; according to her report of it the furniture was given to her as much as the letters.

'Indeed, the gift was more emphatic, as it was referred to, as she says, by both her uncles. The furniture, however, did not then pass to her. It was bequeathed to her by the codicil of 1878, three years afterwards, and was valued for probate at Mr. Carlyle's death as part of his estate. A writing table which formed part of the furniture was specifically bequeathed to me by the codicil of 1878. If Mrs. Carlyle's account was correct, this was a bequest of property belonging to her. When Mr. Carlyle asked me to be his executor (which I suppose must have been in 1878) he asked me to choose something as a present, telling me not to choose certain pictures, as he meant to give them to other friends. I chose the writing table in question, but Mrs. Carlyle's name was not mentioned in connection with the subject.

'I could make further remarks upon the subject, but these are enough to explain the view which I take upon it. As to the rest of your letter it is of course a question entirely for you, whether you will or will not take counsel's opinion on the matter. If you do, I hope you will add this letter to the case.

'I must however inform you that I have quite determined that I will not take the responsibility of deciding between the claims which are or may be set up to these papers by Mrs. Carlyle, the residuary legatees, and Mr. Froude in his personal capacity. If the question cannot be amicably arranged I shall refuse to act except under the direction of the Court. I think such an arrangement most desirable, and I suggested its terms in my last letter to you. I have given the reasons why I cannot accept Mrs. Carlyle's account of her uncle's gift to her. I see no reason to disbelieve Mr. Froude's statement as to the authority given him to burn the letters and papers. It certainly is inconsistent with Mrs. Carlyle's view of what passed, but for the reasons already given, this does not appear to me to be an objection to it. No doubt the language of Mr. Froude's letters to *The Times* favours Mrs. Carlyle's claim, but what he wrote in 1881 cannot alter the legal effect of things said and done years before, and it must be remembered that he has always admitted that Mr. Carlyle desired him to return all the papers to Mrs. Carlyle when he had done with them. On the other hand, he has the papers, and *prima facie* they are his.

'The claim of the executors on behalf of the estate is free from the difficulty which always attends claims founded on recollections of conversations to which there is only one living witness, and which took place (if at all) several years before the claim is decided; but our claim is open to this remark: Its enforcement would do no good to anyone, and would certainly defeat Mr. Carlyle's intentions both by depriving Mrs. Carlyle of the profits of the "Reminiscences," and by hampering Mr. Froude (to an extent which depends on the determination of an entirely new and very doubtful point of law) in making use of the papers for biographical purposes.

'The result is that in every view of the case a settlement appears advisable, and I earnestly recommend the parties concerned to adopt either the terms which I proposed in my last letter, or some modification of them. I should be much surprised if Mr. Cozens-Hardy, or any other independent person whose opinion may be taken on the subject, did not recognise the force of these observations.

'I am, Gentlemen,

'Your obedient servant,

'J. F. STEPHEN.

'Messrs. S. M. & J. J. BENSON.'

As to the case presented on behalf of Mary, Mr. Herbert H. Cozens-Hardy, afterwards Lord Justice of Appeal, advised:

'*Prima facie* the right to the manuscript letters and family papers vests in the executors of the late Thomas Carlyle. I think, however, that there is good ground for contending that the ownership of these documents is not vested in the executors, but is vested in Mrs. Alexander Carlyle, to whom they were given by her uncle in June 1875. It appears . . . that what took place amounted to an *immediate present gift*, as distinguished from an intention to give, and moreover that the fact of such a gift was repeatedly acknowledged by Mr. Carlyle in a manner which will supply the corroboration which is necessary to support Mrs.

Alexander Carlyle's claim. This being so, I think that Mrs. Carlyle is entitled to claim the documents from Mr. Froude or from the executors. In saying this, I do not of course intend to say that Mr. Froude may not use for the purpose of the biography the letters which were lent to him by Mrs. Carlyle for that express purpose.' [1]

On the one hand we have the opinion of Mr. Vaughan Hawkins and Sir James Stephen, Judge of The Queen's Bench Division; on the other, that of a future Lord Justice of Appeal. Until a case has been presented in court and argued fully by counsel on both sides we cannot assume that we know what the decision of a judge will be. It is to be regretted that the case was not taken into court. A legal decision would have solved all difficulties. As matters stood, in the end a settlement was reached. Mary received the profits of the 'Reminiscences,' less a sum of £300, which went to Froude. Froude completed the biography and received the profits. He returned all of Carlyle's papers when he had done with them, except those which were admittedly his private property. In view of the attacks made against him, it seems necessary to say what would be otherwise superfluous, that his conduct throughout was that of a man of honour. Indeed, it may be added that it was generous and magnanimous.

If Froude had known the treatment he was to receive he would, of course, have returned the papers at once to Carlyle, and declined to have anything to do with them. 'No one would undertake so dangerous a task on such conditions,' are his own words.[2] In his West Indian journal he wrote on March 8, 1887: 'Had I known that after I had done my best the persons into whose hands the papers were to pass were to be at liberty to vilify me and what I might do, I would have had nothing to do with it,

[1] *Nemesis*, p. 147.

[2] *Relations*, p. 28.

nor would anyone in such a situation.' Froude was not in need of subjects to write about.

The mistake he made throughout the whole affair was to rely upon conversations. The intentions of Carlyle on all points should have been made clear in writing. Froude realised this when it was too late. 'I was content, most incautiously,' he wrote, 'with a promise that Mary Carlyle would do nothing without consulting me and without my consent. . . . I see now—I saw it before, but I was unwilling to worry him [Carlyle]—that I ought to have insisted on receiving from him in writing his own distinct directions. If they were not satisfactory to me I could then have declined to go on.' [1] Any business man could have foreseen that with Carlyle's hesitations and vacillations and the differences between his oral directions and his written instructions, disputes and difficulties were bound to arise.

Who can doubt that Carlyle's written directions would have been to the effect that nothing was to be done with the papers after their return to Mary without Froude's consent? For Carlyle's opinion of Froude was not that of those who assert that they know Froude better than Carlyle knew him ; that the great painter of portraits remained, after years of close intimacy, foolishly ignorant of his friend's true character. Such an assertion is similar to that of those who declare they know better than Froude what Carlyle said to him. In an unpublished letter to John Skelton, dated May 25, 1881, Froude speaks with justifiable contempt of the 'absurdity of supposing that I, being in constant and confidential communication with Carlyle, did not know his wishes, and that when he left me full discretionary power he did not mean me to use it.'

[1] *Relations*, pp. 28–29.

CHAPTER VIII

CHARLES ELIOT NORTON TAKES A HAND

NOTHING perhaps did more to injure Froude's reputation as editor and biographer than the part taken in the controversy by Charles Eliot Norton. Alexander Carlyle has always pointed to him as the most serviceable convert to Mary's cause. As a professor at Harvard University, a careful student of Dante, and an intimate friend of Emerson, Lowell, Ruskin, and many other distinguished literary men, Norton had won a reputation for discretion, dignity, and integrity. One cannot pass lightly over anything with which he was connected. No specific study, I believe, has ever before been made of his alliance with Mary Carlyle against Froude. Since the publication in 1904 of the Ruskin-Norton correspondence and of the 'Letters of Charles Eliot Norton' in 1913 such a study is now made possible, and one can understand and evaluate more accurately than heretofore Norton's part in the controversy.

Norton's acquaintance with Carlyle began in March 1869 when Carlyle was in his seventy-fourth year. According to Norton their mutual friendship continued throughout the rest of Carlyle's life. It was likewise in 1869 that he first came to know Mary. Norton was immediately impressed by 'the extravagance, the wilfulness, and the recklessness of Carlyle.' In a letter of June 7, 1869, to Miss E. C. Cleveland, he wrote: 'Emerson and Ruskin are the only distinguished living men of whom Carlyle spoke—in all the talk I ever had with him—with entire freedom from sarcasm or depreciation, with something like real tenderness.' He felt, though, that when proper allowances were made for 'the court-jester of the century' there remained 'a vast balance of what is strong, masculine, and tender in his nature.' Norton did not yet feel, however, that his judgments were sure. 'I have not seen him enough to speak confidently of him,' he told Miss Cleveland.[1]

Norton spent the winter of 1872–1873 in London, and took advantage of every opportunity to be with Carlyle. 'I think the chief pleasure of my stay in London this year has been the frequent walks and talks I have had with Carlyle,' he wrote to George William Curtis, December 27, 1872. 'I see him often enough to have grown familiar in some sort with him, and sincerely attached to him. He is, though seventy-seven years old, in excellent health, and vigorous for his years. Age has tempered whatever once may have been hard in him.'[2] I estimate that in all Norton was in London about ten months after his first introduction to Carlyle. From the very first he concluded that the key to the interpretation of Carlyle's character was a proper understanding of his peculiar humour.

Late in 1873 Emerson gave the letters which Carlyle had written him to Norton for such disposition as he saw fit. With commendable thoughtfulness and courtesy Norton informed Carlyle of Emerson's action, and asked what his own wishes were. The reply, dated January 24, 1874, is characteristic and revealing. Two points in it stand out clearly : first, Carlyle's request that if Froude should ever want to consult the letters he should get 'a just response' ; and second, the growing conviction on Carlyle's part that he could not escape biography.

[1] *Norton Letters*, i. 332–339.

[2] *Ibid.*, i. 420.

The letter confirms Froude's account of Carlyle's commission to him, and emphasises the purpose expressed in Carlyle's will.

'Understand then at once [wrote Carlyle] that I entirely agree with Emerson in his disposal of these letters, and have or can have no feeling on the subject, but that if he was going to do anything at all with the stuff he could not in the world have found anybody better to take charge of it than yourself. Accept it therefore, I pray you ; lock it by in some drawer till I have vanished ; and then do with it what to your own just mind shall seem best. If my brother, Dr. Carlyle in Dumfries, or Froude, who are appointed executors, should ever want it, they will know that it is in your keeping, and will get a just response upon it on application. And that is all I have to say on this small matter,—which I confess grows smaller and smaller to me every day, and every year, for the last forty ; the wish rising stronger and stronger in me, were it possible, not to have any Biography at all in a kind of world like this, but rather to lie purely silent in the Land of Silence ; intimating to all kinds of "able editors," *blithering* stump orators, penny-a-liners, or guinea-a-worders,

> "Sweet friends, for Jesus' sake forbear
> To dig the dust inclosèd here."

This is all of essential I had to say.' [1]

The Carlyle-Emerson correspondence as edited by Norton was published in two volumes in 1883.

Norton's part in editing the Carlyle-Emerson letters led to his selection by Mary to supervise the publication of the papers returned by Froude. He set himself promptly to the task, and brought out the 'Early Letters of Thomas Carlyle' in 1886, the 'Correspondence between Goethe and Carlyle' and the 'Reminiscences' in 1887. He published

[1] *Norton Letters*, ii. 138–139.

meanwhile in the *New Princeton Review*, July 1886, an article in which he criticised very severely Froude's editorial methods.

During the summer of 1925 I was allowed to examine the journal kept by Froude during his West Indian travels of 1887. I have permission to give the following extracts. They bring before us the intimate processes of Froude's mind, and enable us to understand still more of the conditions under which he carried out Carlyle's commission. The passages reveal that the work thus undertaken by Norton was the occasion of Froude's writing what was later published under the title of 'My Relations with Carlyle.'

'Saw in an advertisement that Eliot Norton is to bring out the "Reminiscences" immediately [run the words of the entry at Havana, Cuba, March 8, 1887]. I was foolish enough to have a bad night about it. I know that my own heart and purpose was perfectly clear in that matter. Why should I vex myself because I have infuriated a certain number of people? Carlyle ought to have known his own mind. If he trusted me at all, he ought to have trusted me altogether. Of course had I known that after I had done my best the persons into whose hands the papers were to pass were to be at liberty to vilify me and what I might do, I would have had nothing to do with it, nor would anyone in such a situation. . . . I can now only protect myself by laying open frankly my exact position, and the exact circumstances.

'March 11, 1887.—Vedado, seven miles from Havana. Sick of the hot city and the crowded and noisy hotel, I came down here to recover. I fell in love with this place when I dined here with the Montelo party. It is close to the sea, the waves breaking on the coral rocks close to the window, and a fresh sea breeze streaming in through the window. My host,

M. Petit, a Frenchman, is the best cook in Cuba. I have a suite of rooms, instead of a single garret, for the same sum, and here mean to stay and gather myself together again. . . .'

'I came down here yesterday, looked at the rooms, gathered heart, and began to be better. I have a bit of autobiography, the whole of my connection with Carlyle, which I mean to write, and, if necessary, publish by and by. It ought to be done, nor shall I have any peace till it is done. This is the place where I shall see no one, shall, I hope, get some sound sleep, and collect my courage and my senses. I cannot enjoy enough the sweetness of the air, and am in better spirits since I determined what to do.

'March 19, 1887.—In a few hours I must leave Vedado where I have enjoyed myself much for eight days. Among other things, as if in retreat, I have written a complete account of all my connection with the Carlyle business. . . .

'March 23, 1887.—Two years ago I thought I had got clear of the shadow that had been on me for so long. Now it is back again. The more distant I get from the position in which I was placed the more unfair and unjust it appears to me.'

Frederick Chamberlin, quoting from Norton's criticisms of Froude, refers to Norton as 'that typical Harvard professor with the voice so cultivated and so softly and evenly modulated that nobody ever heard it.' [1] In writing of Froude, however, it is quite evident that Norton uses little restraint, and to him 'the questionable Froude' is 'insincere,' 'a Mephistopheles,' 'a continental liar,' 'a hesitator,' 'a coward,' 'a moral contemporary of Warburton,' 'an accomplished flatterer.' Indeed, he goes farther. 'I am tempted . . . to say "Damn him!"' he wrote on March 1, 1883. One is surprised to find the judicious scholar lapsing into such extravagances, and

[1] *The Sayings of Queen Elizabeth*, p. xiv.

is inclined to believe that he has been influenced by Carlyle's own 'habit of humorous exaggeration.' The motives which actuated him are not far to seek. He appears to have conceived a strong dislike of Froude which made it impossible for him to see any good in the man. His own words may speak for him.

'I have never taken to Froude [wrote Norton in his journal, January 25, 1873]. His face exhibits the cynical insincerity of his disposition. Carlyle is fond of him, and assures me I should like him better, if I knew him better. But he is an out and out disciple of Carlyle, in thought and in literary form ; he, doubtless, has his good qualities which Carlyle sees, and Carlyle is not insensible to the flattery of being accepted as master by a man of Froude's capacity.

'The wisest of the wise
Listen to pretty lies,
  And love to hear 'em told.
Doubt not that Solomon
Listened to many a one,
Some in his youth and more when he grew old.'[1]

When Froude's edition of Carlyle's 'Reminiscences' appeared, Norton wrote on April 15, 1881, in reply to a letter from Mary. At this remote date one reads Norton's reply with a feeling of mild compassion for the weakness of human nature. Norton is clearly doing his utmost to condemn Froude for giving the 'Reminiscences' to the world, and in the same breath admitting the value of the material and asserting that hostile criticism cannot endure. At least one paragraph of the letter—the third—might have been written by Froude himself.

'It was very kind in you to write me, and your letter has touched me deeply [are Norton's words to Mary]. The incidents of your uncle's last days of which you tell me, held sacred in your memory, will

[1] *Norton Letters*, i. 461–462.

be held sacred in mine. To have known and loved him, and to have received such expressions of his regard as he gave me, are among the most substantial and permanent blessings of my life. . . .

'I have read the "Reminiscences" with deepest interest. I have the same feeling as you in respect to Mr. Froude's publication of them. More than once I spoke to your uncle, with even more freedom, perhaps, than was altogether becoming, of my mistrust of Mr. Froude. He used to assure me that if I knew him better I should think better of him. Reading as I did between the lines of the "Reminiscences," with such illustrations of their meaning as my knowledge of your uncle afforded, there were few sentences that I regretted to read,—could they have been read only by me and a few others who could rightly interpret them. It was only as they would give false impressions to the curious public, and be misinterpreted by it, that I regretted certain passages. I feel for the pain which the publication of what never should have been given to the public has brought and must continue to bring you.

'But the clamour against the book and the misinterpretation of it will in great part be short-lived. The great and noble qualities of your uncle's character are too manifest in the book for it not to become to many persons one of the most precious of their possessions. It is one of the most human of books; as sincere and serious a record of life as exists anywhere; a book to strengthen and to elevate whoever can read it aright. The very parts of it with which most fault is found are either evidences of an uncompromising sincerity, or of an exaggeration of expressions that indicate the simplicity and tenderness of the heart from which they proceeded.

'To my eyes there is not a word in the book that distorts or dims the image of your uncle in my heart,—an image formed with as strict a sincerity as one would learn from his example. I hold him but the dearer for it all.'[1]

After Norton had read the first two volumes of Froude's 'Thomas Carlyle' he wrote of his impressions and emotions to Mary, July 5, 1882:

'I felt much for you, and, I trust, with you, in reading Froude's two volumes of the "Life." I have never read a book that gave me more pain, or that seemed to me more artfully malignant. I could not have believed, even of Froude, bad as I thought him, a capacity for such falseness, for such betrayal of a most sacred trust, for such cynical treachery to the memory of one who had put faith in him. I am at a loss to discover a sufficient motive for this deed.

'No unbiased person can, I believe, read the "Life" without a conviction that the original text—the letters—does not support Mr. Froude's comment; that he has throughout glossed the letters in a false and evil spirit, that he has distorted their plain significance, and misinterpreted them with perverse ingenuity. The process is too open; he has revealed his own nature, and he has not succeeded in obscuring, for more than a brief moment, the real character of those to whom he has done wrong. His blows are vain, malicious mockery.

'This misrepresentation of his is, indeed, not so much a sin against those whom he called friends, as a crime against human nature itself. To attempt to pervert the image and to degrade the character of a man like Mr. Carlyle, is to do an injury to mankind.

'It is impossible to forgive him for the gross indelicacy of publishing the most private, sacred, and tender expressions of the love of two such lovers as those whose lovely letters he has ventured to print. But a more noble love-story is not to be read,—and these letters will be precious and sacred to many who

[1] *Norton Letters*, ii. 118–120.

will be the better for reading them, though they cannot but shrink from being the innocent accomplices in such a breach of faith. I wish that at some time you might print these letters by themselves, so that they should make their true impression, and be relieved from the ugly setting in which they are now preserved. Indeed, it seems to me that you may have to write the true story of your uncle's life, or rather to give the true account of him.

'You may perhaps remember that nine years ago Mr. Emerson confided to me your uncle's letters to him, and that your uncle approved his doing so. Since Mr. Emerson's death his letters to Mr. Carlyle have also been put into my hands. I propose to edit this most interesting correspondence, and though there will be little need of my saying much, I hope in the little I may have to say to be able to do something to redress the wrong that Froude has done. . . .' [1]

A few weeks later, after he had been working over the Carlyle-Emerson letters, Norton in a letter to John Simon, September 21, 1882, reiterated his hope that the correspondence would act as a corrective to Froude's work. 'The letters are the record of forty years of admirable friendship,' he wrote. 'They will dispel some of the false impressions concerning Carlyle which, thanks mainly to Froude, are so prevalent just now. "Froude is a villain," writes —— [2] to me, and I do not think her far wrong. But Carlyle will always suffer from the lack of the sense of humour in mankind, and from the impossibility that the insincere should understand the frankness of genuine sincerity.' [3]

Norton sent a copy of the 'Carlyle-Emerson Correspondence' to Leslie Stephen. Somewhat later, on March 1, 1883, he wrote to Stephen as if to deliver himself in regard to Froude.

[1] *Norton Letters*, ii. 135–137.
[2] The omitted name is most certainly that of Mary Carlyle.
[3] *Norton Letters*, ii. 139.

'The best part of your last letter . . . was the sentence in which you told me that your wife's sentiments about Froude coincide pretty much with mine. I should feel safe in believing about anybody as she does; and I am glad no longer to have to suspect myself of discrimination or of charity about a man of whom I have no better opinion than I have of Froude. I believe that some day he himself will compel you to give more than a half-hearted assent to your wife's opinion. Good women always recognise the true colours of Mephistopheles long before the Fausts find them out. It went against the grain with me that the closing words of Carlyle's letters to Emerson should be in praise of this false friend and the expressions of trust in him.[1]

'Carlyle's letters will, I hope, do something to set right public opinion concerning him, which the questionable Froude has had such success in misleading and perverting. (I am tempted to follow your bad example, and to say "Damn him"! I save myself by quoting the words from you.)'[2]

It was in a letter to Stephen written after Norton had finished reading the last two volumes of Froude's 'Thomas Carlyle' that he wrote the bitterest indictment of Froude.[3] The letter is dated November 29, 1884.

[1] Little wonder that Norton shrank from Carlyle's words. They run thus: 'Froude is coming to you in October. You will find him a most clear, friendly, ingenious, solid, and excellent man; and I am very glad to find you among those who are to take care of him when he comes to your new Country. Do your best and wisest towards him, for my sake, withal. He is the valuablest Friend I now have in England, nearly though not quite altogether the one man in talking with whom I can get any real profit or comfort.' See the first English edition of *The Correspondence of Thomas Carlyle and Ralph Waldo Emerson*, ii. 353.

[2] *Norton Letters*, ii. 142–143. It would be instructive to have the full text of Leslie Stephen's letter to Norton dated June 15, 1903. Most of what Stephen wrote about the controversy is omitted. See Frederic Maitland's *Life and Letters of Leslie Stephen*, p. 483.

[3] *Norton Letters*, ii. 170. Norton's attitude was recognised at the time by Edward FitzGerald, who wrote in August 1882 that he did not like to see Norton going about the work of editing the correspondence of Emerson and Carlyle 'with such an animus against his fellow-editor.' See *Letters of Edward FitzGerald to Fanny Kemble*, p. 246.

'As for Froude, the spirit of truth is not in him. These last volumes are not so openly malignant as the first, but covertly they seem to me quite as much so. Froude's praise generally rings false. I know nothing else so bad against the Sage of Chelsea, as that this man should be his chief disciple and representative. Carlyle is expiating his sins. He, the lover and believer in truth, has "a continental liar" (one of the phrases of our late political campaign) to report him to the world,—this is the penalty of extravagance of speech; and he, the steadfast and courageous man, has a hesitator—"just hint a fault," etc.,—and a coward to praise him for not having sold his birthright for a mess of pottage. Ah! dear old Thomas, why did not you know that your exaggerations and outcries were the windy food of humbugs and falsifiers? Well, the poor old Thomas is having a pretty hard Purgatorial experience, and it isn't clear that he will ever get quite into Paradise. I hope so. I fancy Mrs. Carlyle turning to him with a slightly sub-acid smile, and while he is sunk in gloomy patience, whispering to him, a little maliciously,—

'"Caina attende chi vita ci spense."'

When Ruskin wrote from Oxford, March 10, 1883, that he was much disappointed at having no word of epilogue from Norton on Emerson and Carlyle by way of finial to the 'Correspondence,' and assured him that he was not with him in thinking Froude wrong about the 'Reminiscences,'[1] Norton replied: 'The sentiment of the book was too intimate for a third person to intervene in it. Moreover, believing as I do that great and grievous wrong has been done to Carlyle since his death, and that the feeling toward him is still too excited to be set right, I thought that the best service to be rendered him was to let him show himself as he was in one of the most

[1] *Ruskin-Norton Letters*, ii. 189–191.

characteristic relations of life, and to allow the impression made by this display of his real nature to work its effect unaccompanied by any expression of a judgment that might be controverted, or charged with the partiality of affection.' Norton then took occasion to remind Ruskin that perhaps Ruskin himself did not have a proper estimate of Carlyle. 'The effect of the book in modifying the harsh and false opinion of the public, so far as I can judge of it, seems to me to indicate that I was right,' continued Norton. 'Even you, I sometimes fancy, underrate the worth of the man, and let the trivial and external traits of his unique individuality go for too much in your estimate of him.'[1]

Ruskin, however, was not to be moved from his position. He grew more and more impatient as Norton went on with his editorial work, and frequently lapsed into long silences.[2] A letter of August 28, 1886, expresses his attitude. Norton had written to commiserate him upon his recent illness. 'It is not the Lord's hand, but my own folly, that brings these illnesses on me; and as long as they go off again, you needn't be so mighty grave about them,' replied Ruskin. 'How many wiser folk than I go mad for good and all, or bad and all, like poor Turner at the last, Blake always, Scott in his pride, Irving in his faith, and Carlyle, because of the poultry next door. You had better, by the way, have gone crazy for a month yourself than written that niggling and naggling article on Froude's misprints.'[3] When Norton published Ruskin's letters to him he added

[1] *Norton Letters*, ii. 146-147.

[2] Ruskin was out of sympathy with Norton from the time Froude began to publish the volumes about the Carlyles. August 30, 1882, he wrote to Norton: 'I have not been so glad of anything for many a day as about those Emerson letters; nevertheless, one of my reasons (or causes) of silence this long time has been my differing with you (we *do* differ sometimes) in a chasmy manner about Froude's beginning of his work.' Norton hides the remainder of Ruskin's remarks behind the three dots of omission which editors have always found helpful in concealing what they do not want the public to know. See *Ruskin-Norton Letters*, ii. 175-176.

[3] *Ruskin-Norton Letters*, ii. 216.

this footnote by way of explanation of this last sentence: 'For some years past Ruskin had been on terms of cordial friendliness with Froude, and much influenced by him, especially in his view of Froude's dealings with the trust committed to him by Carlyle.' The fact is, however, that Ruskin always supported Froude in his handling of the Carlyle matter and opposed Norton. The full extent of his opposition to Norton is considered elsewhere.[1]

There is no doubt that Norton took pleasure in doing all within his power to injure Froude. After the publication of the 'Early Letters of Carlyle' he wrote to call Lowell's attention to the fact that the notice of the book in the London *Times* was hostile to Froude. '*The Times*,' he wrote, 'has hitherto supported Froude, but this is a *volte-face*. Indeed it looks as if the "Letters" had dealt Froude a heavier blow than even I expected.'[2] In a letter to Mary, dated September 18, 1887, Norton in a way summarises his attitude towards Froude:

'You reproach yourself too much [he writes to Mary] in regard to your part in confirming the relations between your uncle and Froude. Your uncle's regard for him was natural enough. Froude is an accomplished flatterer. His insincerity of nature and his talent for external agreeableness fit him for his part. Your uncle did not distrust him, did not discover his insincerity, because such genuine opinions as Froude has were in important respects derived from him, and Froude played skilfully the part of a disciple, with a show of independence. Your uncle, as I may have told you, asked me once why I did not like Froude, and when I told him it was because I thought him lacking in the sense of truth, he assured me I was wrong, and should like him better if I knew him better. But Froude's talk with your uncle and his manners confirmed my distrust of

[1] See pp. 210–212 of this volume.

[2] *Norton Letters*, ii. 177–178.

him. Still I did not think so ill of him, as he has since compelled us to think. . . .'[1]

I have given sufficient evidence, perhaps, to show the spirit in which Norton prosecuted his work. It is significant that Ruskin was not in sympathy with his attitude, and that Leslie Stephen by no means was of Norton's opinion. A clear expression of Leslie Stephen's judgment is on record. 'I have heard Froude accused . . . of a malicious misrepresentation of the man whom he chose as his prophet. I believe such a view to be entirely mistaken,' he wrote.[2] Norton even seems to have had qualms of conscience, as when he admitted to Leslie Stephen that he was glad no longer to have to suspect himself about a man of whom he had no better opinion than he had of Froude.

Norton's account of Froude's editorial work on the Carlyle manuscripts has been accepted and passed on evidently without investigation. Ordinarily the Norton edition of the 'Reminiscences' is referred to by those who are citing references to works on Carlyle. The reason is clear. In his preface to the 'Reminiscences,' Norton wrote: 'The first edition of the 'Reminiscences' was so carelessly printed as frequently to do grave wrong to the sense. The punctuation, the use of capitals and italics, in the manuscript, characteristic of Carlyle's method of expression in print, were entirely disregarded. In the first five pages of the printed text there were more than a hundred and thirty corrections to be made, of words, punctuation, capitals, quotation marks, and such like; and these pages are not exceptional.' Such positive and apparently condemning assertions have influenced the public. Few have ever tested the conclusions at first hand. Elsewhere I give the results of my own examination into these charges.[3]

[1] *Norton Letters*, ii. 183.
[2] *Studies of a Biographer*, iii. 206, American edition.
[3] See pp. 352–358 of this volume.

A careful study of Norton's part in the controversy leaves one with the impression that he was spitefully malicious towards Froude. There can be no doubt that in assuming the editorship of the Carlyle papers, in the face of Carlyle's wishes as embodied in his will, he was lacking in the courtesy which men of letters are accustomed to extend to fellow-workers. His attitude throughout seems petty. Ruskin's 'niggling and naggling' phrase is not too severe a summary of Norton's article on Froude's misprints. Norton's own editorial work is not letter-perfect, although he had the advantage of all the work which Froude had performed over the manuscripts, as well as the help of Mary and Alexander Carlyle and their confederates. One is forced to the conclusion that much of his work on the Carlyle papers was motivated by a personal dislike which one is not happy to find in a man of Norton's abilities.[1]

Norton's influence is discernible in one other incident of the controversy. In 1890 there was an exchange of correspondence between Froude and Mary Carlyle in regard to a new edition of the 'Thomas Carlyle.'[2] Froude asked for permission to compare the text of the biography with the original documents in Mary's possession. In reply she suggested an elaborate plan of having the manuscripts 'examined by two competent men of letters (with an

[1] A little volume published in 1927 by Kate Stephens, *A Curious History in Book Editing*, throws much additional light upon Norton. Miss Stephens tells how Mr. Heath and Mr. Norton removed her name from the title-page of *The Heart of Oak Books*, in the preparation of which she did most of the editorial work. Her story introduces a new question into the Froude-Carlyle controversy. Was Charles Eliot Norton's name simply placed on the title-pages of the Carlyle correspondence to give an air of authority to work edited chiefly by Mary and Alexander Carlyle? It is significant that in the preface to the *Letters of Thomas Carlyle*, Norton says: 'In the editing of this series of letters, as in the preceding volumes, I have been greatly assisted by Mrs. Alexander Carlyle. A small part of her share in the work is indicated by her initials affixed to some of the footnotes.' Here is an interesting question for someone to investigate.

[2] See the correspondence as given among the illustrative documents in this volume on pp. 332–336.

umpire if necessary), one to be named by Mr. Froude, the other by Professor Norton.' She suggested also that 'the remuneration of these nominees should be liberal, so as to ensure a thorough examination and a decision as to Mr. Froude's accuracy or otherwise which may be regarded as final.'

No man of letters of Froude's standing and character could for a moment consider such a proposal. Froude's solicitor summarised the matter admirably. 'It seems to me that your original proposal was reasonable enough,' he wrote to Froude, March 17, 1890. 'Mrs. Carlyle has rejoined by an elaborate proposal of referees and a covert suggestion that you or your representatives are not to be trusted with the papers. As you had them for so many years in your own hands, the proposition requires only to be stated to show the absurdity of it. I think Mrs. Carlyle's elaborate proposal about the payment of referees, umpires, etc., shows she is making difficulties in complying with your request.' In the end the proposal came to nothing. Mary Carlyle died in 1895. Norton, pleading advanced years, withdrew from editorial work after supervising his edition of the 'Reminiscences,' and Mary's cousin and husband, Alexander Carlyle, became chief sponsor of the controversy.

CHAPTER IX

THE CONTROVERSY IS REVIVED

AFTER Norton's edition of the 'Reminiscences' was published in 1887 there was a lull in the controversy until 1898.[1] In that year appeared David Wilson's 'Mr. Froude and Carlyle,' with the announcement that it was only the forerunner of a biography which, however, was 'not likely to be finished for many years.' In the preface Wilson stated that his book was not a complete account of Carlyle's life, but only an argument on certain aspects of it. 'There are,' he maintained, 'delusions current which must be demolished before any truthful biographer can hope for a hearing.'

Wilson, a native-born Scotsman, a graduate of the University of Glasgow, and a barrister, was in 1898 in the British Civil Service in Burma. He early came under the influence of Carlyle's writings, and arrived at the conclusion that Carlyle was a sage after the order of Confucius. His association with the enemies of Froude helped to arouse in him a dislike of Froude as strong as was his admiration for Carlyle. In 1895 Wilson visited Canada and the United States. According to his own statement, it was at the instigation of Charles Eliot Norton that he entered the lists against Froude.[2]

[1] The *Early Letters of Jane Welsh Carlyle*, edited by David G. Ritchie, were published in 1889, but the book was not directly controversial. Later, however, attempts were made to have it count against Froude.

[2] See Wilson's *East and West*, pp. 269–272, and *The Truth about Carlyle*, pp. 28–29.

Wilson's 'Mr. Froude and Carlyle' is a queer volume. Its tone throughout is hostile and disagreeable, motivated by intense feeling against Froude. The text is woven of gossip and is replete with unsupported statements. It is not a scholarly or judicial examination of the matters in hand, and to anyone conversant with the facts and possessed of an elementary knowledge of logic and the laws of evidence it cannot carry conviction. So manifestly absurd and valueless was it that Froude's children passed it by without public notice. Wilson seemingly had great confidence in the volume as a refutation of Froude's work on Carlyle. Within a few years after its publication he bought all the copies which remained in the hands of the publishers and advertised that he would be glad to give copies free to public and university libraries.

The publication of Wilson's 'Mr. Froude and Carlyle' revived memories of the old contentions which many hoped were in a fair way of being forgotten, as far as anything which had gathered such an extensive literature about itself could be forgotten; and it prepared the way for the next important phase of the controversy. This phase began in 1903 with the publication by Alexander Carlyle of the 'New Letters and Memorials of Jane Welsh Carlyle,' with an introduction of eighty-seven pages by Sir James Crichton-Browne, a Scots physician, who was at that time Lord Chancellor's Visitor in Lunacy in London. This introduction marked Sir James's first formal connection with the controversy, a connection which he has since made emphatic by a number of contributions which have embarrassed even his best friends.

Although this introduction is the most temperate of anything which Sir James has written on the controversy, it can scarcely be called mild or judicial. It manifests much of the extravagance which one has learned to associate with his discussions of the matter. One of his epigrams is worthy of a place here. 'He began with hero-worship and ended in a study of demoniacal possession,' says Sir James by way of summarising Froude's biography of Carlyle. Such rhetoric is amusing, even though it fails to impress as conclusive argument. One of the most interesting features of the introduction, however, and the one which Sir James doubtless intended to carry most weight, is the consideration of Mrs. Carlyle's life from a medical point of view. Although Mrs. Carlyle had been dead for more than thirty-six years, and despite the fact that he had never known or treated her, Sir James speaks as if with authority on the nature of her illness, and declares that Froude was utterly mistaken in saying that her life with Carlyle had anything to do with breaking her health. He represents the time spent by the Carlyles at Craigenputtock as 'halcyon days,' wherein Jane 'rode with her husband every fine morning,' read 'Don Quixote' and Tasso with him in the evenings, 'gathered flowers, galloped about the country on her own account, entertained illustrious visitors like Emerson and Lord Jeffery.'

Alexander Carlyle's contribution to the work was the preparation of such notes as he felt were necessary to supplement those which his uncle Thomas had already attached to the letters. Throughout Alexander's annotations there is an emphasis upon details calculated to destroy any belief in Froude's accuracy. The cumulative effect of these annotations is overwhelming upon the reader who does not take the time and do the work necessary to arrive at the truth. After pointing out what he alleges are guesses and delusions on the part of Froude in regard to Mrs. Carlyle's life at Craigenputtock, Alexander remarks: 'These, though they could be added to indefinitely, must suffice. One cannot, in any reasonable space, point out all his perversities. For truly, one may say, "of making many" corrections in "Froude" "there is no end." One makes two or three, or it may be two or three hundred, and then feels inclined to give up in despair ; for the number of errors still remaining seems to reach so far away into infinity that the task of overtaking them all would throw the labours of Hercules quite into the shade.' [1]

Here, indeed, was a work beside which David Wilson's 'Mr. Froude and Carlyle' was insignificant. The 'New Letters and Memorials of Jane Welsh Carlyle' was authentic material, annotated by Thomas Carlyle, and now published by his nephew, who affirmed that he was taking it upon himself to rescue his uncle's reputation and memory from the grasp of a man who, as he informed the public, had betrayed the solemn trust which Carlyle had committed to him. Was there anything to say in refutation of such evidence?

[1] *New Letters and Memorials*, i. 27.

CHAPTER X

FROUDE'S POSTHUMOUS PAMPHLET

ONE with a knowledge of the past history of the controversy is somewhat surprised that Alexander Carlyle should have deliberately renewed it. Froude had given public warning in Mary's lifetime that if his good faith and honour were attacked he might find it necessary to reveal what he preferred to withhold as being none of the world's business. He gave this warning first, I believe, when Mary was making the stir about the note prohibiting publication which Carlyle had attached to the memoir of his wife. The warning was renewed in correspondence which passed between Mary and Froude at the time Froude made over the copyright of the 'Reminiscences' to her. This correspondence is now published for the first time.

On December 23, 1885, Froude wrote to his solicitor to inform him that the 'Reminiscences' had been out of print for some time, and that, as he was not in possession of the manuscripts he was unable to correct the typographical and other errors. 'As the profit of the book is to go to Mary Carlyle, she may now have the editing,' he continued, 'provided always that the memoir of Mrs. Jane Welsh Carlyle is withdrawn. That is my own property in all senses of the word. It is not to appear any more with the "Reminiscences," but will be attached as a preface to the letters of Mrs. Carlyle. The edition for which she received payment years ago was only exhausted last summer.'

A reply from Mary's solicitor, dated April 3, 1886, stated that 'Mrs. Carlyle would be glad to have the copyright of the "Reminiscences" assigned to her as arranged,' and suggested that perhaps Froude might no longer desire to reserve the literary control. 'If Mr. Froude should still desire to make this reservation Mrs. Carlyle cannot object to his doing so,' continued the solicitor. 'Mrs. Carlyle would, however, be quite willing to prepare a new edition of the work if Mr. Froude will authorise her to revise it as suggested by you.'

To this letter Froude through his solicitor replied on April 19, 1886, as follows :

'I have no fault to find with Mr. Benson's letter. I never questioned that Mrs. A. Carlyle was to receive all the future profits. Mr. Benson does not deny that I had reserved the literary control. I wrote to you in the winter to say that I was willing to relinquish this control over two-thirds of the book. It was now out of print and needed revision. Mrs. A. Carlyle being in possession of the original manuscripts was the fittest person to do it, and I had no wish to interfere further.

'I still reserved the control over his memoir of Jane Welsh Carlyle, partly because it was specifically bequeathed to me and I had the copy which was made at Carlyle's direction in my own hands ; but chiefly for another reason which I have explained in the accompanying note to Mrs. A. Carlyle herself. If I receive from her satisfactory assurance on the point which I there mention the entire book shall at once become her own and all rights over it shall be conveyed to her in a legal form. Otherwise I can only allow the republication of this particular memoir under my own supervision. It will then perhaps be better that I should republish the entire book

26th. The chief interest of today expressed in bluemarks on my wrists!

27th. Went with Geraldine to Hampstead; preferring to be broiled on a heath to being broiled in Cheyne Row. Dined at the Spaniard; & came home to tea, — dead-weary, & a good many shillings out of pocket.

28th. Dined at Lord Goderich's with Sir Colin Campbell, whom I hadn't seen for some fifteen years. He is not much of a Hero, that; he may be a brave man, & a clever man at his trade; but beyond soldiering, he knows nothing: & is nothing I think. In fact, Heroes are very scarce.

29th (Sunday) Nobody but Geraldine this forenoon. In the evening I was surprised by the apparition of Mrs Newton,

FACSIMILE OF MARY CARLYLE'S COPY OF A PORTION OF JANE WELSH CARLYLE'S JOURNAL FOR THE PERIOD APRIL 15, 1856, TO JULY 5, 1856.

This portion of the 'true copy' of the material constituting the 'Letters and Memorials of Jane Welsh Carlyle' which was willed to Froude by Carlyle, is perhaps the only copy of the entry for June 26, 1856, now in existence. The original of this facsimile has been in the possession of the Froude family from the time that Carlyle gave it to J. A. Froude.

myself, paying the profits from the edition to Mrs. A. Carlyle.'

'The accompanying note' from Froude to Mary reads thus:

5 Onslow Gardens, S.W.
April 20, 1886.

'In the part of Mrs. Carlyle's journal which Carlyle inserted in his memoirs of her there is a passage referring to the "blue marks on her wrist." It was this passage which caused him so much pain in looking back. It was this also which determined me from the beginning in the course which ought to be pursued.

'I am perhaps the only person now living who knows the circumstances to which the entry refers. I know also that on this as on some similar occasions Mrs. Carlyle had made up her mind to destroy herself. I intend that if possible this knowledge shall die with me. To have made it public would have answered at once the accusations which have been brought against me. I preferred to bear them in silence—a silence which I earnestly hope that I shall not be compelled to break.

'If you will assure me that you will not publish this passage—as you might do inadvertently—not knowing to what it referred; if you will assure me also that you will not again raise a question of my good faith in the discharge of the duty which your uncle laid upon me, I will pass over this memoir with the rest to you and you can re-edit it in any form that you please.

'You can find any other faults that you like with me, but if accusations are raised against my honour and integrity, I owe something to myself. I did not seek the responsibility which your uncle put upon me. I accepted it only at his own entreaty, and you may compel me to tell the whole truth. The responsibility will then be yours.

'J. A. FROUDE.

'To Mrs. Alexander Carlyle.'

Five days later Mary's reply came :

3 Chalcot Gardens,
Haverstock Hill, N.W.
April 25, 1886.

'In reply to your letter : I will not print the passage in Mrs. Carlyle's journal which you refer to, and need hardly add that I should never have dreamt of doing so.

'As to the value of confidences given to you I presume by Miss Geraldine Jewsbury, and as to your keeping or not keeping them, you will no doubt judge for yourself and act exactly as you please. But I may mention that I have by me a packet of letters which I have read and which were given to me to keep because they were too private to be seen by you. They would throw some light upon the matter you refer to. I am willing to show this packet to your lawyer as it has remained since Mr. Carlyle closed it up, with his docketing upon it, and with its seal unbroken.

'I am quite willing to see to the correcting of the "Reminiscences," but although I have no intention of writing anything there or elsewhere likely to give rise to further controversy, I should refuse the right to do so as *a gag*. The copyright I claim by my lawyer's advice in accordance with the agreement.

'MARY CARLYLE.

'J. A. Froude, Esq.'

'Here is the young woman's answer,' wrote Froude to his solicitor. 'I think she may be trusted to avoid dangerous subjects. . . . I do not think that there is any occasion for your seeing the packet which Mrs. Carlyle speaks of. You can make over the copyright ; at least I have no objection. She speaks of an agreement. No agreement that I know of was ever contemplated ; none was ever sent to me for signature. I uniformly answered that I had nothing to agree to. I would do what I had meant and promised from the beginning ; namely, return the manuscripts when I had done with them, and give her the future profits of the "Reminiscences," reserving the literary control. But this was never to my knowledge put into any further form or contract, nor was I ever informed that she had taken the £1700 till I learnt it long after from Farrer. But there is no occasion to enter into this matter. All I wish is to be quit of Mary Carlyle and all connexion with her henceforth.'

Mary's letter to Froude reveals that her knowledge of the cause of the blue marks on Mrs. Carlyle's wrist was sufficient to make her wish to keep the matter quiet. Her intimation that perhaps Froude's knowledge of the matter came from Geraldine Jewsbury points to the fact that Mary had reason to believe that Geraldine knew the facts. At any rate the passage was removed from the original copy of the journal, and was never printed in Mary's lifetime.[1] Thereby hangs a story which I reserve for a later chapter.

In the light of such knowledge one would have deemed it wise for Alexander Carlyle to allow matters to rest. He may have thought, however, that because the Froudes did not notice Wilson's 'Mr. Froude and Carlyle' they were tired of controversy. Or he may have concluded that as Froude had been dead for nine years, and the journal entry destroyed, no one would be the wiser. Whatever his reasoning, he published the 'New Letters and Memorials of Jane Welsh Carlyle' and found fault with Froude as sharply as he could. In particular, he printed Mrs. Carlyle's journal for 1856 with the assurance that he gave it to the public 'without suppression of more than a proper name or two, exactly as it stands and stood when it first came into my [his] possession.'[2] He was evidently not prepared for what happened next.

[1] 'It was by her hand that it was cut out of the journal,' writes Crichton-Browne in the *Contemporary Review*, July 1903, p. 48.
[2] *New Letters and Memorials*, ii. 88.

The attack was such as the Froudes could not allow to pass unnoticed. Their father's honour and good faith were now at stake. He had, as we know from his Cuban journal, taken precautions against just this contingency. For the Froudes the question of publication was serious. They took counsel with wise friends, however, and in the end a decision to publish was reached. The narrative was published under the title of 'My Relations with Carlyle.'[1] It came as a voice from beyond the grave—a voice that spoke in no uncertain terms.

In the 'Relations' Froude reveals what he had refrained from disclosing in the biography. He explains more fully his interpretation of Carlyle's association with Lady Ashburton. He enters into the details of Carlyle's personal life. He tells how Carlyle after his wife's death went through her diaries and papers and, in the light of what was written therein, saw what his faults had been. 'The worst of those faults I have concealed hitherto,' writes Froude. 'I can conceal them no longer. He found a remembrance in her diary of the blue marks which in a fit of passion he had once inflicted on her arms. He saw that he had made her entirely miserable; that she had sacrificed her life to him; and that he had made a wretched return for her devotion. As soon as he could collect himself he put together a memoir of her, in which with deliberate courage he inserted the incriminating passages (by me omitted) of her diary, the note of the blue marks among them,

[1] 'The epitome of some of the omitted matter given as an introduction to the essay undoubtedly suggests that, in the interests of veracity, omission was advisable,' write Alexander Carlyle and Crichton-Browne in *The Nemesis of Froude*, pp. 3–4. Their surmise is mistaken. In July 1925 I examined the original draft of Froude's narrative, and found the epitome entirely accurate. It was made for the reason alleged, and for no other. 'The first few pages are of too intimate a nature to be given to the public; but they are painful evidence of how acutely Mr. Froude had suffered under the criticism to which he refused to reply,' are the words of his representatives. It would have served no important purpose to print what is only an elaboration by Froude of the following sentence from an unpublished letter of his to John Skelton in 1884: 'I have suffered nothing less than purgatory for some years past.'

and he added an injunction of his own that, however stern and tragic that record might be, it was never to be destroyed.'[1]

Froude recounts once more the story of how and when the Carlyle papers came into his possession, and then passes on to a discussion of the nature of the relationship between Carlyle and his wife, about which he says there had long been rumours in the circle of Cheyne Row. 'I had observed in Mrs. Carlyle's diary that immediately after the entry of the blue marks on her arms, she had spent a day with Geraldine at Hampstead,' continues Froude. 'I asked Miss Jewsbury if she recollected anything about it: she remembered it only too well. The marks were made by personal violence. Geraldine did not acquit her friend in all this. She admitted that she could be extremely provoking. She said to me that Carlyle was the nobler of the two. Her veneration for her teacher never flagged in spite of all. She looked on his failings as aberrations due to his physical constitution. But the facts were as she told me. She did not live long after this. In her last illness, when she knew that she was dying, and when it is entirely inconceivable that she would have uttered any light or ill-considered gossip, she repeated all this to me, with many curious details. I will mention one, as it shows that Carlyle did not know when he married what his constitution was. The morning after his wedding-day he tore to pieces the flower-garden at Comely Bank in a fit of ungovernable fury.'[2] In closing his references to this matter Froude writes: 'I have since learnt that the nature of Carlyle's constitution was known to several persons, that in fact it was an open secret.'[3]

After saying what he thought necessary to explain his position Froude closes with a few general remarks.

'If I have now told all [he writes], it is because I

[1] *Relations*, p. 11. [2] *Ibid.*, pp. 22–23. [3] *Ibid.*, p. 24.

see that nothing short of it will secure me the fair judgment to which I am entitled. I am certain that I have done the best for Carlyle's own memory. The whole facts are now made known. The worst has been said that can be said, and anything further which can now be told about him can only be to his honour. . . . Of all literary sins Carlyle himself detested most a false biography. . . . Falsehood and concealment are a great man's worst enemies.

'Such at least is the doctrine about the matter which I learnt from Carlyle himself; such is my own opinion, and on this I have acted. I cannot discover in myself any other motive for the course which I have taken. All motives of worldly prudence lay the other way. Personally I never met with anything but the warmest kindness from Carlyle. I had no secret injuries to resent. I had always admired him, and in his later days I learnt to love him. No one does what he knows to be wrong without some object. If anyone will suggest what unworthy motive I can have had, he may perhaps assist me in discovering it. I cannot discover it myself.

'It is likely enough that I have made mistakes in matters of fact as well as in the reading of manuscripts. Let all such be made known. No one will be better pleased than I shall be. I complain only of reflections on my good faith and personal honesty, which I fling off me with legitimate indignation.

'I am told that Mary Carlyle possesses documents which show parts of Carlyle's story in another light. If so, they ought to have been communicated to me. She says now that they were considered too sacred. I cannot help that. I could judge only by what Carlyle put into my hands. She offered to show them to my solicitor. If too sacred for me to see, they were too sacred to be exposed to a lawyer. If she wished me to know what they contained she ought to have sent me copies, or have told me generally their contents.

'If I have erred in other ways I may plead the worry and perplexity in which I was involved and the nature of my task, which perhaps the wisest man could not have dealt with without stumbling in places. My book, if it is still to be condemned at present, will be of use hereafter. . . . It may not be completely correct, but it will have made concealment impossible, and have ensured that the truth shall be known. The biographies of the great men of the past, the great spiritual teachers especially, with whom Carlyle must be ranked, are generally useless. They are idle and incredible panegyrics, with features drawn without shadows, false, conventional, and worthless. The only "Life" of a man which is not worse than useless is a "Life" which tells all the truth so far as the biographer knows it. He may be mistaken, but he has at least been faithful, and his mistakes may be corrected. So perhaps may some of mine, especially if particular papers have been purposely withheld from me.

'I have discharged the duty which was laid on me as faithfully as I could. I have nothing more to reveal, and, as far as I know, I have related exactly everything which bears on my relations with Carlyle and his history. This is all that I can do, and I have written this that those who care for me may have something to rely upon if my honour and good faith are assailed after I am gone.' [1]

At last the full word had been spoken. The pamphlet created a renewal of discussion throughout the English-speaking world. Everyone recognised that its note of sincerity was unmistakable. It was a last solemn word from a man of seventy who in Carlyle's own words was 'looking steadfastly into the silent continents of Death and Eternity.' Whatever might be said against the pamphlet, it could not be ignored.

[1] *Relations*, pp. 37–41.

CHAPTER XI

THE AFTERMATH

FROUDE'S pamphlet, which appeared at the end of May 1903, brought consternation to his enemies, who lost no time in replying to it savagely. In the *British Medical Journal* of June 27, 1903, Sir James Crichton-Browne discussed the matter of Carlyle's sexual competence in a paper of considerable length. The article is violent and in bad taste throughout, and was so considered at the time. As soon as copy could be prepared Alexander Carlyle, in collaboration with Sir James, published 'The Nemesis of Froude,' adapting their title from 'The Nemesis of Faith,' Froude's book of 1849. In as strong a fashion as they could command they set forth Mary's claims as against Froude's, and did their utmost to demolish the evidence given in 'My Relations with Carlyle'.

Again it must be said that the tone is violent and the argument almost incoherent with rage. One feels throughout that the authors 'do protest too much;' that where there is such violence of opposition there must be something to oppose. The authors distort facts. They publish only fragments of such letters of Froude as are in their possession, suppressing the context which would make the quoted portions fully intelligible and refusing to reveal the full text.[1] They

[1] This is especially true of the letter quoted from at the bottom of p. 103, and the one referred to on p. 154, but not quoted. Unfortunately Froude kept no copy of the letter last mentioned.

resort to personal abuse. They appeal to the authority of Margaret Oliphant. They ridicule and slander Geraldine Jewsbury. They point to Charles Eliot Norton's espousal of their cause. In short, far from establishing their case, they involve themselves in contradictions, and succeed only in amusing a careful reader. They were not, however, troubled with any further communications from the Froudes. Carlyle's biographer had uttered his last word, and his representatives regarded it as final.

Since 1903 Alexander Carlyle has gone on intermittently with his publication of the materials which Froude as editor and biographer had used or discarded. Thus far he has published five volumes. 'The New Letters of Thomas Carlyle' appeared in 1904, the 'Love Letters of Thomas Carlyle and Jane Welsh' in 1909, and the 'Letters of Thomas Carlyle to John Stuart Mill, John Sterling, and Robert Browning' in 1923. In the preface to the 'New Letters of Thomas Carlyle' Alexander remarks that 'controversial topics have been avoided,' yet in both the preface and the footnotes he continues to attack Froude. In 1909, in the preface to the 'Love Letters,' he returns to his charges against Froude of misquoting and misinterpreting, even of failing 'to comprehend the plain meaning of the writers.' Within more recent years he has not attacked Froude openly. He is planning, however, to publish more of the Carlyle correspondence. Under date of November 27, 1926, he informed me that he had just finished editing for publication what he calls the 'After-Marriage Letters' of Carlyle and his wife, 'about 950 letters, many of them new, the old ones extended, and the whole throwing quite a new light on relations of husband and wife.'

In addition to the activities of Alexander Carlyle, mention must be made of the work of others. In 1913 David Wilson came forward once more with a small volume entitled 'The Truth about Carlyle,' in which he tries finally to refute the charge that Carlyle was sexually incompetent. The preface by Sir James Crichton-Browne is in his usual manner. Wilson also published in the same year another small book entitled 'The Faith of all Sensible People,' the purpose of which was, in his own words, 'to minimise theology' and 'to show what is meant here [in his biography of Carlyle] by such an expression and where Carlyle stood in theology.' [1] The most recent addition to Carlyle correspondence is the volume of 'Jane Welsh Carlyle Letters' edited by Leonard Huxley in 1924.

The mere bulk of the matter which has been published to confute Froude is large. The reiterated charges against him, taken up and repeated at second, third, and fourth hand, impress the casual reader with their importance. Froude himself throughout his literary career paid little attention to personal attacks. He grew accustomed to them. His children, weary of the controversy over the Carlyle biography, ignored the matter as far as possible. The result is that the field has been left pretty largely to Alexander Carlyle and his adherents. The evidence is now well in hand, and the time seems ripe to formulate a reasonable verdict.

At present there is considerable divergence of opinion in regard to the controversy, largely the result, I think, of imperfect knowledge. Mary Agnes Hamilton in her 'Thomas Carlyle' (1926) adopts wholesale the assertions of Froude's enemies. 'Froude gave a picture of the man he thought he admired as dismal as it is perverse,' she writes.[2] She then maintains that Froude reared the superstructure of his biography of Carlyle on a misquotation of 'gey ill to deal wi'.' Her conclusion is that we must 'get behind Froude' in order to see Carlyle as he was.

[1] *Carlyle*, I. p. vi.

[2] *Thomas Carlyle*, pp. 10–11.

On the other hand, Elizabeth Drew in her 'Jane Welsh and Jane Carlyle' (1928), while severe in her criticism of Froude as biographer, nevertheless displays a spirited distrust of the attitude of his enemies. 'Because Froude made her [Jane Welsh Carlyle] out an Amelia Sedley, Mr. Alexander Carlyle makes Carlyle out like the hero of "The Idylls of the King"; because Froude paints Carlyle as an irritable egotist, Sir James Crichton-Browne paints Jane as a hypochondriacal neurotic; because Froude accepted Miss Geraldine Jewsbury's stories of Jane's unhappiness as evidence, Mr. D. A. Wilson accepts second or even third hand stories of her physical and moral blemishes as evidence; because Froude suppressed or garbled all the passages in the letters which disproved his theory, the modern critics underline and isolate all the passages in the letters which they think prove theirs.' [1]

It is, however, in Norwood Young's 'Carlyle: His Rise and Fall' (1927) that we find a new and confident note in regard to Froude. Mary Agnes Hamilton and Elizabeth Drew both worked upon the available published materials. Young, on the contrary, prosecuted a vigorous study of unpublished material, and reached the same conclusion as had Herbert Paul in 1905. 'If Froude's case could have been put before Carlyle, like that of Lockhart, there can be little doubt,' writes Young in conclusion, 'that he would have given an emphatic verdict in favour of the writer of one of the best and bravest biographies in the English language.' [2]

Several have expressed surprise that Young makes

[1] *Jane Welsh and Jane Carlyle*, p. 9. If Froude represents Mrs. Carlyle as an Amelia Sedley, then I am unable to read English and draw proper inferences. The Jane portrayed by Froude is a woman of strong and imperious nature, disillusioned, disappointed, and half-embittered, yet actuated by a stern sense of duty. 'His was the soft heart, and hers the stern one,' asserts Froude in *Thomas Carlyle*, 4. p. 171. Such a Jane Carlyle can scarcely be likened to Amelia Sedley.

[2] *Carlyle: His Rise and Fall*, p. 327.

no reference to the elaborate biography of Carlyle which David Wilson has in preparation, four volumes of which were available when Young's book appeared. In my opinion, the reason is obvious. I have presented enough evidence thus far, I think, to make it clear that Wilson's biography is the culmination of a controversy that has been waging since 1879 ; that it is designed to be the final blow to Froude. It was projected as propaganda, as a reference to Wilson's 'Mr. Froude and Carlyle' reveals. It accepts and perpetuates the allegations of Mary and Alexander Carlyle and Charles Eliot Norton. It heaps up evidence in the notes by reiterated remarks upon Froude's inaccuracy. It is the work of a man who, never having seen Carlyle, has yet taken it upon himself to attempt to destroy confidence in Froude's portrayal ; for to no less a task has Wilson set himself. 'I do not want to supersede Garnett, but Froude,' he writes. In such spirit has it been prosecuted. Its very bulk carries conviction in many quarters. Size and plausibility, however, cannot save a work, if its conception is fundamentally wrong. Young undoubtedly feels that Wilson's work, as passing on conclusions which are now known to be untenable, was unworthy of notice in a book which professes to throw new light upon Froude as well as upon Carlyle. I mention Wilson's 'Carlyle' here as the last phase of the aftermath of the controversy. A more detailed study of his volumes is reserved for a later chapter.

CHAPTER XII

THE METHODS OF FROUDE'S ENEMIES

WHEN Mary and Alexander Carlyle and their followers began and carried on the attack against Froude as literary executor and biographer of Carlyle they found a method and a technique formed to their purpose. The opponents of Froude as historian had been busy since 1856, and they had succeeded in formulating and perpetuating a theory to the effect that his work was inaccurate and unreliable. I have referred previously to the fact that criticism of Froude the historian is used to buttress criticism of Froude the biographer. It becomes necessary at this point, therefore, to consider briefly the nature and the far-reaching effect of the attacks upon Froude's historical work. With such information in mind, the censure of his biographical labours will be much more easily understood.

Edward Augustus Freeman by continued assaults in the *Saturday Review* and the *Contemporary Review*—attacks which on the surface are learned and plausible—'did ultimately produce an impression, never yet fully dispelled, that Froude was an habitual garbler of facts and constitutionally reckless of the truth.' The bubble of Freeman's misrepresentation has been pricked, but it has not been easy to dispel the general impression which he implanted through a long series of years in the minds of thousands of readers. A few extracts from his letters are sufficient to reveal his spirit. 'You have found me out about the sixteenth century: I fancy that, from endlessly belabouring Froude, I get credit for knowing more of those times than I do,' he wrote to James Hook, April 27, 1857. 'But one can belabour Froude on a very small amount of knowledge, and you are quite right when you say that I have "never thrown the whole force of my mind on that portion of history."' Again he wrote to Hook: 'I find I have a reputation with some people for knowing the sixteenth century, of which I am profoundly ignorant.' [1]

The most delightful and illuminating evidence against Freeman, however, is that which was gleaned from the marginal annotations of his books. These annotations reveal that he was not speaking the truth when he remarked about his criticism of Froude, 'In truth there is no kind of temper in the case, but only a strong sense of amusement in bowling down one thing after another.' Among the marginal notes in his copy of Froude's 'History of England' occur such statements as these: 'Beast,' 'May I live to embowel James Anthony Froude'; 'Can Froude understand honesty?' 'Supposing Master Froude were set to break stones, feed pigs, or do anything but write paradoxes, would he not curse his day?' 'You've found that out since you wrote a book against your own father'; 'Give him as slave to Thirlwall'; 'Froude is certainly the vilest brute that ever wrote a book.' One asks whether criticism of value could emanate from such a mind. 'I suppose it must have amused Freeman to call another historian a vile brute,' remarks Herbert Paul. 'But it is fortunate that there was no temper in the case. For

[1] See *Life and Letters of Freeman*, i. 381–382. The two extracts here quoted have been admirably employed by Herbert Paul in his *Life of Froude*, p. 151. As recently as October 6, 1928, 'Stet,' writing in the *Saturday Review*, says: 'This, of course, is the periodical in which amends should be made to Froude, for it was in the *Saturday Review* that Freeman, in a long series of criticisms, damaged beyond repair Froude's reputation for accuracy and impartiality.'

if there had, it would have been a very bad temper indeed.'[1]

Freeman's mischief lived after him, however, and the legend which he created was adopted and augmented by men who should first have taken pains to verify the facts upon which they founded their assertions. Herbert Paul's 'Life of Froude' was published in 1905. In the meantime Herbert A. L. Fisher had published 'Modern Historians and their Methods' in the *Fortnightly Review*, December 1, 1894. Fisher's article was evidently written in haste to take advantage of the moment. In consequence, one should perhaps adopt the attitude of an anonymous reviewer of a biography of Samuel Johnson which appeared nine days after the Doctor's death, and say that 'a few trifling inaccuracies will of course be expected, and pardoned by the indulgent reader.' In all seriousness, however, a man of Fisher's reputation, writing of an historian like Froude, should have taken more care about his facts. His article really does a kind of justice to Froude. One portion of it, nevertheless, is unworthy of the author. Instead of verifying his source material at this point, Fisher borrows almost word for word from Edward Wakefield's 'New Zealand and Mr. Froude' in the *Nineteenth Century* of August 1886.

'He [Froude] was, too, constitutionally inaccurate, and apparently incapable of reporting upon the facts of his own observation, without curious and even serious errors [asserts Fisher]. Writing, for instance, of Adelaide, in Australia, he says: "Seven miles away we saw below us, in a basin with a river winding through it, a city of 150,000 inhabitants, not one of whom has ever known, or will ever know, one moment's anxiety as to the recurring regularity of his three meals a day." Adelaide is on high ground, not in a valley; there is no river running through it;

[1] See his *Life of Froude*, pp. 147-198.

its population was not more than 75,000; and, at the very moment when Mr. Froude visited it, a large portion of that population was on the verge of starvation. His fascinating book on the West Indies abounds with similar mistakes. Of Port of Spain in Trinidad he writes: "The streets are broad, and are planted with trees for shade; each house, where room permits, having a garden of its own with coffee-plants. There is abundance of rain, and the gutters which run down by the footway are flushed almost every day." As a matter of fact, the streets are narrow; they are not planted with trees; very few of the houses have gardens; and I have been assured by a resident that he has never heard of a garden being planted with the coffee-plant.' [1]

In 1897 Charles Langlois and Charles Seignobos of the Sorbonne brought out their 'Introduction aux Études historiques' which was translated into English by G. G. Berry, and published with a preface by F. York Powell in 1898. In this book we have a charming example of historical inaccuracy at second hand. The authors, after speaking of 'those who aspire to be critical scholars,' assert that 'in order to succeed in critical labours it is not enough to like them. It is necessary to possess qualifications "for which zeal is no substitute."' And they make it clear that accuracy is one of the prime requisites. There is a class of people, they assert, of whom it must be said, 'He works badly, he has the genius of inaccuracy.'

'Their catalogues, their editions, their *regesta*, their monographs swarm with imperfections, and never inspire confidence; try as they may, they never attain, I do not say absolute accuracy, but any decent degree of accuracy. They are subject to "chronic inaccuracy," a disease of which the English historian Froude is a typical and celebrated case.

[1] *Fortnightly Review*, December 1, 1894, p. 815.

'Froude was a gifted writer, but destined never to advance any statement that was not disfigured by error; it has been said of him that he was constitutionally inaccurate. For example, he had visited the city of Adelaide in Australia: "We saw," he says, "below us, in a basin with a river winding through it, a city of 150,000 inhabitants, none of whom has ever known or will ever know one moment's anxiety as to the recurring regularity of his three meals a day." Thus Froude, now for the facts: Adelaide is built on an eminence; no river runs through it; when Froude visited it the population did not exceed 75,000, and it was suffering from a famine at the time. And more of the same kind.[1] Froude was perfectly aware of the utility of criticism, and he was even one of the first in England to base the study of history on that of original documents, as well unpublished as published; but his mental conformation rendered him altogether unfit for the emendation of texts; indeed, he murdered them, unintentionally, whenever he touched them. Just as Daltonism (an affection of the organs of sight which prevents a man from distinguishing correctly between red and green signals) incapacitates for employment on a railway, so chronic inaccuracy, or "Froude's Disease" (a malady not very difficult to diagnose) ought to be regarded as incompatible with the professional practice of critical scholarship.

'Froude's disease does not appear to have ever been studied by the psychologists, nor, indeed, is it to be considered as a separate pathological entity. Everyone makes mistakes "out of carelessness," "through inadvertence,' and in many other ways. What is abnormal is to make many mistakes, to be always making them, in spite of the most persevering efforts to be exact.'[2]

[1] See H. A. L. Fisher in the *Fortnightly Review*, December 1894, p. 815. This reference is cited by Langlois and Seignobos.

[2] *Introduction to the Study of History*, pp. 124–126.

It remained for James Ford Rhodes to confirm this legend in his presidential address before the American Historical Association in 1900.

'Froude is much more dangerous [than Carlyle and Macaulay, says Rhodes]. His splendid narrative style does not compensate for his inaccuracies. Langlois makes an apt quotation from Froude. "We saw," says Froude, of the city of Adelaide, in Australia, "below us in a basin, with the river winding through it, a city of 150,000 inhabitants, none of whom has ever known one moment's anxiety as to the recurring regularity of three meals a day." Now for the facts. Langlois says: "Adelaide is built on an eminence; no river runs through it; when Froude visited it the population did not exceed 75,000, and it was suffering from a famine at the time." Froude was curious in his inaccuracies. He furnished the data which convicted him of error. He quoted inaccurately the Simancas manuscripts and deposited correct copies in the British Museum. Carlyle and Macaulay are honest partisans and you know how to take them, but for constitutional inaccuracy such as Froude's, no allowance can be made.' [1]

Eleven years later, in June 1911, James Bryce, in an address at Union College, 'On the Writing and Teaching of History,' continuing the Wakefield-Fisher-Langlois-Seignobos-Rhodes legend, said: 'The case of J. A. Froude, the last of the so-called literary historians, is not quite the same. The others whom I have just named [Bancroft, Motley, and Freeman] were solid, hard-working conscientious scholars; Froude was a brilliant stylist, who had begun his career as a writer of stories, and chose thereafter to display in the field of history his gift of picturesque narration. His ecclesiastical partisanship was usually evident enough to enable a reader

[1] *Annual Report of the American Historical Association for the Year 1900*, pp. 62–63.

to discount it. A graver fault was that superb indifference to truth which sometimes led him to regard the facts he had to deal with chiefly as so much material to be handled with a view to artistic effect, putting on them such colouring as was needed to secure the particular effect desired, and caring little for accuracy in details which did not move his curiosity.' [1]

When reputable historians, who boast that they are working in a scientific spirit in a scientific age, adopt and perpetuate charges which rest upon false statements, students may well hesitate to accept one of their conclusions without first consulting the original sources.[2] The judges have come to judgment, and are confuted by their own words. If Froude is to be consigned to the hell reserved for the inaccurate, he is sure of much and distinguished company.

A word should be said in regard to Edward Wakefield's original statements. He, as an Australasian, should have known what he was talking about. His offence cannot be palliated. Mr. Fisher, of course, was without the advantage of that immediate knowledge of topography which residence affords. He cannot, however, excuse himself on such ground. He might easily have set himself right by casual reference to a good atlas or encyclopædia. Adelaide is built on level ground at the foot of mountains over 2,000 feet high. The river Torrens divides it in half. The population, including the suburbs, was at the time of Froude's visit well over 100,000.[3] The Hon.

[1] See Bryce's *University and Historical Addresses*, p. 346.

[2] If Providence permits, I plan to publish a study of Frederick Chamberlin's attacks upon Froude's historical works.

[3] According to a series of original papers issued under the authority of the Royal Commission for the Colonial and Indian Exhibition of 1886. Under date of September 21, 1928, John Lavington Bonython, Esq., Lord Mayor of Adelaide, supplied the following information: 'Adelaide is situated midway between St. Vincent Gulf and the Mount Lofty Ranges, and its height above sea-level at the General Post Office, which is practically the centre of the city, is 154 feet. Those suburbs which lie between the city and the mountains are set on rising ground stretching up to the foothills. Viewing the metropolitan

J. G. Jenkins, Agent-General for South Australia, who was a resident of Adelaide and took a pretty active interest in municipal affairs when Froude visited the city in January 1885, says there was then 'no unusual or general distress.' With regard to the Port of Spain, Mr. Fisher's quotation is inexact. Froude wrote that the streets at Port of Spain 'are planted with trees for shade, each house where room permits having a garden of its own with palms and mangoes and coffee plants and creepers'; he does not use the expression 'having a garden of its own with coffee plants.'[1] It appears upon investigation that Froude is more in the right than Fisher. Bryce and Keith Johnston's 'Cyclopædia of Geography (1880) says (page 713) that Port of Spain is 'substantially built with wide streets.' De Verteuil's 'Trinidad' says that 'the promenade between King Street and Marine Square . . . is about a hundred feet wide;' that the same promenade is 'planted with rows of large trees . . . Almond Walk is an alley planted with almond trees . . . Many houses have large lots attached which are planted with trees and flowers. These dwellings, being generally low and almost hidden amidst the foliage, the town assumes a peculiar and in some parts a rather rural aspect.'[2]

David Wilson, calling attention to the charges contained in the obituary notice of Froude in the

area from any of the numerous vantage points on the slopes of the Ranges, however, it may in a restricted sense be said that Adelaide lies in a basin, although the usual description of the country is a plain. The River Torrens runs through the city, dividing the northern residential portion from the main business portion. The Torrens is fifty miles long, and its average width near the main centre of the city is seventy-five yards. According to the Government Statist the population in 1885 was 113,000. As to the statement that the people, or any portion of them, were on the verge of starvation in 1885, Mr. A. T. Saunders, an old resident and undoubted authority on local history, asserts that the report is entirely incorrect.' This information was given in response to specific questions submitted by me.

[1] See his *English in the West Indies*, p. 64.

[2] *Trinidad*, pp. 269 and 272, by the Hon. L. A. A. De Verteuil. De Verteuil was a minister in the Government of Trinidad.

London *Times* admits that the authorities for many statements are not given by the writer; 'but' he adds, 'the anecdotes were not contradicted or even questioned, and must have been read by persons who could have contradicted them if untrue, and assuredly would have been well pleased to do so. Under the circumstances, one can scarcely hesitate to believe them.'[1] Wilson could hardly have failed to know that under date of November 5, 1894, Sir Theodore Martin through *The Times* replied in no uncertain terms to some of the charges brought against Froude by the writer of the obituary.

'If I may venture to say so [run Sir Theodore's words], the writer of your obituary notice (October 22) of Professor Froude has given too ready credence to the critics who accused my friend of failing in the painstaking and discriminating research which must go to the production of anything that deserves the name of history. To say of a historian, as your writer says of Froude, that "he was not a student," that "he had neither the desire to probe his authorities to the bottom, nor the patience to do so," is about the heaviest charge that could be levelled against him. It strikes, indeed, at the very root of his reputation as man as well as writer. To those who, like myself, know that Froude thought no labour too great to get at the essential facts of history, and who also know how dear truth and sincerity were to him, the statement is, indeed, startling. Its accuracy fails, if it may be tested by the specimens your writer gives of the "anecdotes" on which it is based. When, he says, Froude was invited to inspect the Cecil papers at Hatfield, "he went there and stayed one day." What was the fact? Froude was there quite a month studying these papers. Again it is said that although Froude visited Simancas, "it is unquestionable that he learned comparatively little about the records there

[1] *Mr. Froude and Carlyle*, pp. 9–10.

preserved." Mr. Froude was at Simancas more than once. On his first visit, in 1861, he spent three months of hard work there, and then and subsequently he spared no pains to make himself master of every document of value that bore upon the reign of Elizabeth. This I had the best reason to know from my intimate personal communication with him at the time. Not less without warrant is the statement of your writer of his having, while engaged upon his "Life of Lord Beaconsfield," merely glanced at the Beaconsfield papers "on a Saturday to Monday visit." What the "Beaconsfield papers" are your writer does not say. But I know for certain that the letters which were of chief value to Froude, and which greatly modified and moulded his opinion of Lord Beaconsfield, if they were only glanced at "on a Saturday to Monday visit," had sunk so deeply into his mind that he was able to give me orally as full a description of their contents as I could have gained had I read the letters themselves. Every detail in them was talked over between us, and I was under the impression that they were either then or lately in his hands to consider how far they might be used.

'Mr. Froude during his entire life endured silently much misrepresentation as to his works and ways. If he were guilty of occasional inaccuracy, or mistaken conclusions, who is not, especially in a great work like his "History," where the conflict of contemporary statements and opinions is so great as it is throughout all the period with which he deals? But the charge of deliberately failing to take the only means by which accuracy in history or biography is to be arrived at might surely have been left to die with Mr. Freeman.' [1]

Sir John Skelton, also, wrote in Froude's defence. 'It seems to me,' he said, 'that the charge, even when stated in far more temperate language than was used

[1] Reprinted by Skelton in *Blackwood's Magazine*, December 1894, pp. 766–767.

at the time, rests on no sufficient basis. We must remember that he was to some extent a pioneer, and that he was the first (for instance) to utilise the treasures of Simancas. He transcribed, from the Spanish, masses of papers which even a Spaniard would have read with difficulty, and I am assured that his translations (with rare exceptions) render the original with singular exactness. As regards Scottish history, I could not accept his *conclusions*, and I had more than once to examine his statements sentence by sentence; but I have seen no reason to change the opinion I expressed in the preface to "Maitland of Lethington": "Only the man or woman who has had to work upon the mass of Scottish material in the Record Office can properly appreciate Mr. Froude's inexhaustible industry and substantial accuracy. His point of view is very different from mine; but I am bound to say that his acquaintance with the intricacies of Scottish politics during the reign of Mary appears to me to be almost, if not quite, unrivalled." And with this view, I may add, John Hill Burton concurred.'[1]

Mary Carlyle's first public act was in conformity with the methods of Froude's enemies since 1856. Her letter to *The Times* of May 5, 1881, was an attempt to induce the public to believe that Froude was utterly unreliable, that he recklessly disobeyed specific written instructions, that he was, in short, a betrayer of confidence. The charge thus made has been persistently reiterated, as I have shown. Froude's detractors are not content with plain statements of their case. They attack Froude's good faith. They express surprise at Carlyle's choice of executor and biographer. On one page they question whether Froude was ever commissioned to write the biography; on another they quote one of Froude's letters to Carlyle in which plain reference is made to the task

[1] *Blackwood's Magazine*, December 1894, p. 766.

which Carlyle had imposed upon Froude. They proclaim at one time that Froude was personally honest; at another that when he turned author he was a liar. In one breath they suggest that he took advantage of Carlyle's old age, grief, and helplessness to ingratiate himself in his favour and secure possession of his papers and authorisation to write his biography; in another they affirm that Carlyle was vigorous and in full possession of his faculties as late as 1878. Considerable evidence of the many contradictions in which they have involved themselves has already been presented. A few more examples of their methods may not be amiss.

Alexander Carlyle and Crichton-Browne would have it that Carlyle's attitude towards his wife after her death was the result of senility. 'If Carlyle did hanker after a moral cremation,' they write, 'and there is not a shred of evidence beyond Froude's imaginary conversations that he ever did so, it was a senile and morbid epiphenomenon of distracting grief, which a true friend should have taken at its real value.' [1] Likewise, in refuting Frank Harris, Crichton-Browne asserts that Carlyle, during his last years, was exceedingly feeble; indeed, almost helpless. Harris maintains that he walked with Carlyle in Hyde Park in 1877. 'In the summer of that year,' writes Crichton-Browne, 'he [Carlyle] called at my house in Regent's Park with his niece . . . and was so feeble that it was thought better that he should not make the effort of getting out of the landau. . . . *He was then quite unequal to a walk in Hyde Park.*' [2] On the other hand, David Wilson quotes the diary kept by one of Carlyle's nephews to prove Carlyle's soundness mentally and physically in his eighty-third year. 'He walks about a mile before breakfast, every morning between eight and nine,' run the words of the diary. 'I offered him my arm [on August 11, 1878],

[1] *Nemesis*, p. 117.

[2] *The Truth about Carlyle*, p. 19.

which he said he did not need, but accepted, and talked with animation all the way back.' Another entry asserts : '[His] mind is quite clear and memory strikingly good still.'[1]

The manner in which the line is drawn between Froude in his private capacity and Froude as an author is worth noting. 'In private life an honourable and straightforward man, the moment he took pen in hand he became untrustworthy,' remarks Crichton-Browne.[2] Wilson adopts this notion. Indeed, it is somewhat amusing to find Wilson, who never knew Froude, proceeding to analyse and pass judgment upon his nature with serene confidence. According to Wilson, Froude's failure as biographer lies in the fact that he lacked affection for Carlyle, was ignorant of the details of his life, was incapable of sincerity, and always thought of self first, 'measuring himself against others always to the other's disadvantage.' Notwithstanding, Wilson is disturbed by a sense of his own possible error. 'To call Mr. Froude insincere in the ordinary sense of that word would be misleading. He was seldom conscious of anything but perfect sincerity. And yet the perfect sincerity which alone makes written words perennially valuable was never quite reached by him.[3] It is . . . a matter of common experience that persons of good intelligence narrate in perfect good faith stories which on investigation are found to be false. We do not, therefore, call them liars—at least we should not! We should say they are mistaken. . . . His narrative is not a criminally false one, but it is a book of blunders.[3] He honestly did think that the faults he attributed to Carlyle were trifles, and many persons think so still. He may have been wrong, indeed there is no doubt that he was wrong in this ; but even

[1] *Mr. Froude and Carlyle*, pp. 297–298.
[2] *New Letters and Memorials*, i. p. x.
[3] *Mr. Froude and Carlyle*, pp. 80, 90 respectively.

while demonstrating his general inaccuracy, it is only fair to him to make allowance for his point of view.[1] These and the other things already discussed . . . are quite compatible with a certain honesty of intention for which he must receive credit.[1] Of course Mr. Froude had some genuine feeling of affection for Carlyle—he was only *half* a hypocrite.[1] It is needful perhaps to point out that, *judged by ordinary standards*, Mr. Froude was not guilty of any serious moral fault when he thus "stood in his own light," and by thinking of himself instead of his subject failed to see or make us see Thomas Carlyle as he truly was.' [1]

Wilson attempts to give his 'Mr. Froude and Carlyle' an air of veracity and importance by insisting upon the value of trustworthy evidence. 'In a literary inquiry,' he writes, 'we are independent of legal rules, but not of logic and common sense. We must discount hearsay evidence, and believe nothing but what there is credible evidence for.' [2] In the light of such admonition, it is curious to observe the extent to which he makes use of gossip and other anonymous testimony, a habit which he carries over to his biography of Carlyle. His pages present such phrases as 'An ex-servant of the Carlyles . . . mentioned a thing'; 'one worthy gentleman resident in Dumfriesshire . . . could have told him much about Carlyle'; Carlyle 'noticed and remarked confidentially to a very intimate friend'; 'An eye-witness . . . gave me a comical description of an evening with the Carlyles'; 'there is excellent reason to believe.' [3]

Particular attention must be called to one of Wilson's charges against Froude's veracity. Froude makes the statement that his last visit to Carlyle was on February 4, 1881.[4] Wilson asserts, on the

[1] *Mr. Froude and Carlyle*, pp. 312, 312, 316, 317 respectively.
[2] *Ibid.*, p. 96. [3] *Ibid.*, pp. 160, 186, 273–274, 315, 282 respectively.
[4] *Thomas Carlyle*, 4. p. 469.

authority of an unnamed 'eye-witness' that Froude had taken leave of Carlyle and departed weeping on January 30, 1881, 'and never again saw Carlyle alive.'[1] Then, in a note, he calls attention to the chronology printed in a volume published by the Carlyle House Purchase Fund Committee, and presents the unsigned chronology as evidence against Froude, adding a remark to the effect that the 'serious conflict of dates was intentional, not a mere slip of the pen, on the part of the editor of that volume.' It is important to know the identity of both the eye-witness and the author of the chronology. If perchance the report originated with Mary and Alexander Carlyle, the matter immediately becomes a question of their word against the word of Froude. Whatever the facts may be, we have a right to ask whether the public should be required to accept anonymous evidence.[2]

Charles Eliot Norton follows similar methods. The main strength of his attack is founded on a repetition of the charge that Froude disobeyed Carlyle's injunctions against publication.[3] He further charges in substance that when Froude did publish he failed to make proper omissions, departed from the original manuscripts to such an extent as to change and even destroy the sense, in addition to making 'many mis-statements of fact and misrepresentations

[1] *Mr. Froude and Carlyle*, p. 185.

[2] Just as I complete my manuscript Reginald Blunt informs me that he and G. A. Lumsden prepared the chronology in question. Mr. Blunt kindly writes as follows: 'I do not know where the late Mr. Lumsden got his authority for dating Froude's final interview with Carlyle on January 30th. He doubtless refers to the last time they had speech together, when Carlyle's bed had been moved into the drawing-room; on February 4th Carlyle was beyond speech or understanding.' That is exactly what Froude says in *Thomas Carlyle*, 4. p. 469: 'When I saw him next his speech was gone. His eyes were as if they did not see, or were fixed on something far away. I cannot say whether he heard me when I spoke to him, but I said, "Ours has been a long friendship; I will try to do what you wish." This was on the 4th of February 1881. The morning following he died.' Until competent proof of the contrary is brought forward, Froude's statement must therefore stand.

[3] *New Princeton Review*, July 1886, pp. 11–19.

of character and action.' When he edited the 'Early Letters of Thomas Carlyle' he made further allegations. 'The letters that passed between Carlyle and Miss Welsh from their first acquaintance in 1821 till their marriage in 1826 afford a view of their characters and their relations to each other, different both in particulars and in general effect from that given by Mr. Froude. His narrative is a story "founded on fact," elaborated with the art of a practised romancer, in which assertion and inference, unsupported by evidence or contradictory to it, often take the place of correct statement. Even if the form of truth be preserved, a colour not its own is given to it by the imagination of the writer.' [1] He adds that to give a complete demonstration of Froude's divergence from the truth it would be necessary to rewrite the whole story. He then proceeds to give a few examples in support of his statements. 'Such,' he writes in conclusion, 'is the treatment that the most sacred parts of the lives of Carlyle and his wife receive at the hands of his trusted biographer! There is no need, I believe, to speak of it in the terms it deserves.' [2]

Enough, perhaps, has been said of the spirit in which Norton attacked Froude. The results of an examination of his charges are given in a later chapter of this book. It is well to point out here one further pronouncement of Norton. 'Your uncle did not distrust him, did not discover his insincerity, because such genuine opinions as Froude has were in important respects derived from him, and Froude played skilfully the part of a disciple, with show of independence,' are his words to Mary.[3] It should be borne in mind, however, that Carlyle had thirty-two years in which to arrive at an estimate of Froude; and Carlyle, we are assured, was a keen discerner of character and a smiter of shams. Norton, on the

[1] *Early Letters of Carlyle*, ii. 367. [2] *Ibid.*, 381.
[3] *Norton Letters*, ii. 183.

other hand, upon a few months of acquaintance and with a deep-seated dislike of Froude, feels much better qualified than Carlyle to discern Froude's true character.

Indeed it is rather amusing to learn how many were surprised that Carlyle did not see matters as they saw them. 'The wonder is,' writes Crichton-Browne, 'that Carlyle, with his quick discernment and passion for truth, should have made Froude his principal literary executor. When he did so he was old, and had but few friends, though many worshippers. He was touched by Froude's personal devotion . . . and so, forgetting his instability, entrusted him with a weighty and precious burden, under which he staggered and fell.' [1] Carlyle, it seems, was the one man who did not know what he was about. It appears further that after Carlyle had selected Froude to act as his literary executor and biographer, Froude failed to consult those who could have saved him from errors of taste and fact. 'I have often mourned,' writes Moncure Conway, 'that William Allingham and I, who had so long and intimately worked with him on "Fraser," did not together offer our assistance in assorting the enormous mass of letters and papers by which Froude was overwhelmed.' [2]

In studying the methods of Froude's enemies one is impressed first of all with the intense partisanship and heat which they display. They are not content with plain statements of fact. They depart from the question in hand to attack Froude's personal character

[1] *New Letters and Memorials*, i. p. xi.

[2] *Autobiography*, ii. 213. Now and then Conway dropped hints which reveal that he knew Froude had good authority for writing as he did. On p. 402 of *The Nation*, November 29, 1894, Conway says: 'It is to be hoped that Froude's papers will fall into careful hands. Not only are there, to my knowledge, invaluable memoranda among them that have never seen the light, but facts will be discovered which will much soften the asperities with which his own failures, as I deem them, in dealing with Carlyle's papers have been judged.'

and motives. Even grave and sober students of history are lured into the most extravagant utterances. In writing of Froude's 'Life and Letters of Erasmus,' Professor Ephraim Emerton remarks that it 'illustrates the author's familiar qualities—his remarkable distinctness of view and his complete indifference to accuracy of detail.'[1] It is admitted even by Froude's enemies that he did take pains to be accurate, but could not be so. Certainly Professor Emerton does not mean 'complete indifference'; only a fool or a knave could be guilty of such. One can only conclude that Mr. Emerton has been betrayed into an unscholarly lapse similar to that of Langlois and Seignobos when they wrote that 'Froude was . . . destined never to advance any statement that was not disfigured by error.' There is no need, perhaps, to say more of the methods of Froude's enemies. Enough has been said to reveal the necessity and the importance of careful investigation.

[1] In his *Desiderius Erasmus*, p. xxv.

CHAPTER XIII

SOMETHING ABOUT FROUDACITY

One of the methods employed to destroy confidence in Froude is that of emphasising and exaggerating his errors of fact. His enemies avow that these are so many and so serious as to vitiate the whole of his work. To convey briefly and forcibly, if not maliciously, an idea of the type of error peculiar to his writings they have coined two words. A Froudacity or a Froudulency, we are to understand, is an error possible only to Froude or to those few whose minds are likewise constitutionally incapable of formulating reliable statements.

Such criticism started at the point of merely technical error. Norton, as we have seen, began the attack with an assertion that the first five pages of Froude's edition of the 'Reminiscences' contain more than a hundred and thirty errors. David Wilson has zealously promulgated and augmented these charges. After pointing to certain mistakes in one page of the biography, he asks the public to 'multiply these errors by 1860, and then consider seriously what such a book is worth.' [1] He also asserts that Norton once told him that he would undertake to find far more than an average of one error to the page of Froude's 'Carlyle'; that in some parts the average is about one error to each sentence.[2] In the light of such statements, repeated

[1] *Mr. Froude and Carlyle*, p. 103.

[2] *Ibid.*, p. 307.

year after year, it is not strange that the public has come to regard Froude's work with grave suspicion.

Omitting for the present the matter of punctuation and other strictly technical details, let us pass to a consideration of the so-called 'misprints by which the sense is changed and even destroyed.' I have collated the text of the Jane Welsh Carlyle memoir as printed in Froude's edition of the 'Reminiscences' with that printed in Norton's edition, and find seventeen differences which somewhat affect the sense. Of these only two can fairly be called serious deviations from the original text. One of these has been stressed by David Wilson. The following sentence relative to the effect upon Mrs. Carlyle of her father's death appears in Norton's edition: 'It broke her health, permanently, within the next two or three years; and, in a sense, almost broke her heart.'[1] In Froude's edition the sentence appears in this form: 'It broke her health for the next two or three years, and in a sense almost broke her heart.'[2] Says Wilson: 'The significance of this mistake is worth examination. It was the principal one of several mistakes which led Mr. Froude to enrich modern fiction with the pathetic figure of a new Griselda.'[3] Wilson does not tell us, however, that in 1882 in the first volume of the biography Froude gave the following version of the passage: 'It broke her health permanently, and in a sense almost broke her heart.'[4] There, it should be observed, is the word 'permanently,' which Wilson would have us believe Froude passed over and concealed, intentionally or otherwise! It is certain that Froude was not endeavouring to conceal anything, or to wrest the passage from its original meaning. If he had wished to employ the sentence to buttress a theory, he would surely have taken more pains to harmonise the passages. Moreover, he knew that

[1] *Reminiscences*, i. 72.
[2] *Ibid.*, ii. 94.
[3] *Mr. Froude and Carlyle*, p. 158.
[4] *Thomas Carlyle*, I. p. 124.

the manuscripts were to be given ultimately to Mary Carlyle.

The other passage Norton[1] prints in this form: 'She *read* the first two volumes of 'Friedrich,' much of it in printer's sheets (while on visit to the aged Misses Donaldson at Haddington); her applause (should not I collect her fine Notekins and reposit them here?) was beautiful and as sunlight to me,—for I knew it was sincere withal, and unerringly straight upon the blot, however exaggerated by her great love of me.' Froude[2] gives this version: 'She read the first two volumes of "Friedrich," much of it in printer's sheets (while on visit to the aged Misses Donaldson at Haddington); her blame was unerringly straight upon the blot, her applause (should not I collect her fine notekins and reposit them here?) was beautiful and as sunlight to me, for I knew it was sincere withal, however exaggerated by her great love of me.' The reader may make what he will of the differences. To me, the version given by Froude seems to make better sense. I can understand how blame may be 'unerringly straight upon the blot'; I cannot easily understand how applause may be so. At any rate, the sense is affected but little; it certainly is not destroyed. Only by collation of manuscripts and texts can the exact form be determined.

The foregoing are the two most serious differences between the texts of the Jane Welsh Carlyle memoir as given by Norton and by Froude. One can better understand how such differences arose when one considers that several copies of the memoir were made. There is Carlyle's original manuscript. Of this Mary Carlyle made two copies, a perfect and an imperfect copy. The perfect copy, which Carlyle willed to Froude, was corrected in blue pencil by Carlyle himself, and a number of the corrections, noted by Miss Margaret Froude, are in

[1] *Reminiscences*, i. 203.

[2] *Ibid.*, ii. 243.

my possession. They help to explain some of the differences between Norton's text and Froude's. It is beyond reason to charge all departures from Carlyle's original manuscript upon Froude. He printed the first edition of the memoir from the 'perfect' copy made by Mary and corrected by Carlyle himself. No adequate and just understanding of this matter can ever be reached unless the history of the texts is kept in mind.

I have made a similar collation of the sketch of James Carlyle, and find twenty-two differences which affect the sense. One of these differences—the most serious—certainly does give a wrong impression. In Froude's edition [1] we read: 'I knew Robert Burns, and I knew my father.' Norton [2] prints correctly: 'I know Robert Burns, and I knew my father.' As Burns died in 1796, one year after Carlyle's birth, it is evident that Carlyle never made his acquaintance. An impartial judge would say that the 'knew' of Froude's edition is a misprint. It is not difficult to account for every error in the first edition of the 'Reminiscences.' It is impossible to point to one which affords any ground for asserting that Froude altered or suppressed material with a view to establishing any preconceived notion about the Carlyles. One is not surprised to find that Ruskin took Norton to task for his 'niggling and naggling article on Froude's misprints.' [3]

The most trivial details are emphasised by Froude's enemies, often to their own confusion. All who are familiar with Froude's books know that he employs the spelling 'Comely' in referring to the first home of the Carlyles in Edinburgh. David Wilson, in a note on p. 194 of his 'Mr. Froude and Carlyle,' remarks: 'Correctly, *Comley*, misspelt by Mr. Froude.' Alexander Carlyle himself may correct Wilson.

[1] *Reminiscences*, i. 18. [2] *Ibid.*, 13.
[3] *Ruskin-Norton Letters*, ii. 216.

'Comley Bank (now spelt Comely, though Carlyle uniformly, and Edward Irving generally, spelt it Comley) is a terrace of small houses in the northern suburbs of Edinburgh. Carlyle remained tenant of No. 21 till the 26th of May 1828.' [1]

In like manner Alexander Carlyle seizes upon a similarly trivial detail as a means of taxing Froude with misrepresentation. 'Francis Jeffrey, whom Mr. Froude repeatedly but erroneously calls Mrs. Carlyle's cousin,' writes Alexander. 'There was no trace of consanguinity between them beyond being, of course, son and daughter of Adam and Eve!' [2] Let us turn to one of Froude's own statements. 'He [Jeffrey] wrote to her as cousin: what the exact relationship was I know not; but it was near enough, as he thought, to give him a right to watch over her welfare.' [3] Froude was thinking, in fact, of one of Carlyle's own statements. 'They discovered mutual old cousinships by the maternal side,' are Carlyle's own words in his account of Jeffrey.[4] It occurs to the reader that if there was no trace of consanguinity between them Carlyle should be taken to task for assigning the relationship to the maternal side. Those who know anything about relationships in Scotland know that they are traced to remote sources, but always, if the tracers are honest, to actual sources.

David Wilson seems to have discovered the facts about this cousinship, which he attempts to gloss over in his latest work. He explains that, although Mrs. Jeffrey and Mrs. Carlyle avoided friction, they never quite harmonised.[5] The result was, he affirms, that the one thing possible to Jeffrey was to be very

[1] *New Letters and Memorials*, i. 17, *note*. See also *Early Letters of Jane Welsh Carlyle*, 121, *note*, where David G. Ritchie says: 'The place is, now [1889] at least, always spelt "Comely Bank."' And David Wilson at last concedes the point. 'Now spelled Comely,' he writes in his *Carlyle*, 1. p. 431, *note*.

[2] *New Letters and Memorials*, i. 45, *note* 2.

[3] *Thomas Carlyle*, 2. p. 126.

[4] I quote from Norton's edition of the *Reminiscences*, ii. 239.

[5] *Carlyle*, 2. p. 53. See also p. 32 of the same volume, *note* 1.

affectionate and gallant towards Mrs. Carlyle, a thing which circumstances made it easy to do. 'She was young enough to have been his daughter,' writes Wilson, 'and he always called her "My dear child," and as soon as they discovered some distant connection called cousinship in Scotland but never heeded in England, it was "My dear child and cousin."' Thus, according to Wilson, were the Carlyles conciliated; 'and that,' he assures us, 'is the key to the courtesies of Jeffrey towards the younger woman.' In the face of Wilson's open letter [1] to Frank Harris, wherein he avouches disbelief in 'keys' and 'secrets' it is amusing to find him offering this and other keys in his biography of Carlyle.

One sentence in Froude's posthumous pamphlet, 'My Relations with Carlyle,' was the occasion of much ado. 'The morning after his wedding-day he tore to pieces the flower-garden at Comely Bank in a fit of ungovernable fury,' wrote Froude on the authority of Geraldine Jewsbury.[2] 'But, unfortunately for Miss Jewsbury,' Sir James Crichton-Browne informed the public, 'there was no flower garden at Comely Bank, but only a bit of a border, in which there were not likely to be many flowers in Scotland on October 18th.' [3] It is illuminating to read the following sentence from one of Jane's letters, dated June 28, 1826: 'For there is a real flower garden in front, over-shadowed by a fair-spreading tree; while the windows look out on the greenest fields with never a street to be seen.' [4] And on February 3, 1827, Carlyle wrote to his brother Alexander to this effect: 'I assure you many a time on a soft mild night, I smoke my pipe in our little flower-garden.' [5] Alexander Carlyle himself contradicts Sir James's assertion. 'It is well known that

[1] It is printed in *The Truth about Carlyle*, pp. 71–87.
[2] *Relations*, p. 23.
[3] *British Medical Journal*, June 27, 1903.
[4] *Love Letters*, ii. 301.
[5] *Letters of Carlyle*, i. 28.

Miss Welsh was exceedingly fond of flowers, especially roses,' he writes. 'The house at Haddington had (and still has) a beautiful flower-garden; so also at Comley Bank, on a small scale; and even at Craigenputtock, "the loneliest and dreariest spot in all the British Dominions," one of her first cares was to have rose-bushes planted.'[1] As to Sir James's statement that there were not likely to be many flowers in Scotland on October 18, my own diary for 1914 records that on November 10 of that year, chrysanthemums and other flowers were blooming freely in the parks of Glasgow.

When I called Alexander Carlyle's attention to the discrepancies of statement in regard to the flower garden, he replied that the Comely Bank garden could be called such only in 'the language of flattery,' as Mrs. Carlyle wrote of her Cheyne Row garden. 'It was,' he asserts, 'simply a plot in front of the house, with a flagged path and a border leading up to the front door of their little "pepperbox" of a house. In sober truth it lay on the border-line between a garden "on a small scale" and no garden at all. And if two writers at widely different times, each with different aims in view, did not call it by the same name the disagreement hardly deserves to be called remarkable.' As to the merits of the whole matter, the impartial reader may draw his own conclusions.

I think it is worth while at this point to present several 'niggling and naggling' assertions of errors which have been exalted to the rank of Froudacities. Extended comment will not, in my opinion, be necessary; the facts speak for themselves. Referring to Froude's account of the life of the Carlyles at Craigenputtock, Alexander Carlyle writes: 'Mr. Froude reluctantly confesses that there were *two* horses in the stable; and that Carlyle and his wife occasionally rode or

[1] *Love Letters*, ii. 378–379, *note*.

walked together.'[1] There is, however, no 'reluctance' discoverable in Froude's account. He makes a plain statement of fact. 'There were two horses in the stable—Larry, the Irish horse of "genius," and Harry, Mrs. Carlyle's pony.'[2] The 'reluctance' appears to be pure fabrication on the part of Alexander Carlyle.

The matter of dating one of Carlyle's bits of verse has given Alexander another occasion to reflect unfavourably upon Froude's statements. 'The poem by Carlyle, called "My Own Four Walls," was not written at Hoddam Hill, however, but at Craigenputtock; probably in 1829. The handwriting and paper of the original, and the expressions "whinstone house," "moorland house," and the mention of a wife are alone sufficient to prove this. Carlyle's biographer seems to have doubted that anything so cheerful . . . *could* have been composed at Craigenputtock.'[3] In reply it may be said that Froude does not 'seem to doubt' at all. He quotes[4] from Carlyle's letter of April 2, 1826, written from Hoddam Hill, and then says: 'This expression ["my own four walls"] repeated twice, suggests the possible date of a poem—the only poem, perhaps, that Carlyle ever wrote which is really characteristic of him. It was written either at Hoddam or at Craigenputtock. In some respects—in the mention of a wife, especially—it suits Craigenputtock best. But perhaps his imagination was looking forward.'

In regard to the death of one of Carlyle's horses at Craigenputtock Alexander makes the following comment: 'Mr. Froude says with his usual inaccuracy, "Old Larry, doing double duty on the road and in the cart, had laid himself down and died—died from overwork."'[5] It appears that Froude founded his

[1] *New Letters and Memorials*, i. 26.
[2] *Thomas Carlyle*, 2. p. 45.
[3] *Love Letters*, ii. 263, *note.*
[4] *Thomas Carlyle*, 1. pp. 323–324.
[5] *New Letters and Memorials*, i. 33, *note.* For Froude's account see his *Thomas Carlyle*, 2. p. 152.

narrative on a passage in one of Carlyle's own letters which Norton had printed seventeen years before the publication of the 'New Letters and Memorials of Jane Welsh Carlyle.' The passage reads: 'We are all thrown into real sadness to-day by poor Larry. The poor old toilworn stout-hearted Nag is dead! . . . I imagine it is mere hard work that has killed Larry: such riding to and fro about that *Mill*, then quite incessant harrowing for extra hours, etc., etc.; till about a week ago the beast grew sick with swelled throat and so on; then seemed to grow better, but on Friday relapsed worse than ever . . . and now *is* not.' [1]

With regard to the foregoing Alexander Carlyle made the following comment in a letter to me: 'Carlyle "imagined" Larry died from "mere hard work"; Froude states unconditionally he died from "overwork"; Carlyle after he had learned that Larry died from a horse epidemic gave the real cause of death. Froude had before him both accounts, the imagined and the true: yet he gave the former (in an altered and vitiated form) and suppressed the latter entirely! I might have used with propriety a much stronger word than "inaccuracy" in describing this duplicity of Froude.'

The evidence which Alexander charges Froude with having suppressed is a letter of Jane's with annotations by Carlyle, which was published in 1903.[2] There is nothing whatever in either the letter or the annotations to contradict Froude. It cannot be proved that Carlyle was ignorant of the prevalence of the epidemic when he wrote the account of Larry's death to John. Carlyle's letter suggests that the overwork of Larry had so reduced his strength as to make him susceptible to illness. How excessive the work

[1] *Letters of Carlyle*, i. 284. The letter, dated May 8, 1831, is addressed to John Carlyle.

[2] *New Letters and Memorials*, i. 33–34.

was the account emphasises. With the evidence now in hand readers may endeavour to discover what in this instance constitutes the duplicity of Froude, and judge for themselves the nature and extent of it.

Enough, however, of these trivial matters. Let us pass to something of greater importance. Shortly before her marriage Jane Welsh wrote to her aunt, Mrs. George Welsh, a letter about Carlyle. With reference to this Alexander Carlyle says : 'It is one of the letters which Carlyle himself selected and annotated for insertion in "The Letters and Memorials of Jane Welsh Carlyle," and which Mr. Froude omitted.' [1] Such a statement sounds damning. What is the truth ? According to the terms of Carlyle's will all materials were left to Froude to edit as he saw fit. It must always be borne in mind that final editing was left to Froude. Moreover, and this is the important fact in connection with this particular charge, the letter in question appears in Froude's 'Thomas Carlyle,' on pages 356–358 of the first volume, and hence was omitted from the 'Letters and Memorials' to avoid repetition. Readers must always keep in mind the fact that Froude was projecting and carrying forward a series of books about the Carlyles—nine volumes in all—and was endeavouring not to repeat more than was absolutely necessary.[2]

Alexander also objects strongly to those portions of Mrs. Carlyle's correspondence from October 1863 to the end of December 1864 which Froude chose to

[1] *Love Letters*, ii. 328.

[2] Froude took pains to give cross-references. Such sentences as the following occur : 'For this, too, the reader is mainly referred to the "Reminiscences," which need no correction from contemporary letters ; and to which those letters, though written when the scenes were fresh, can still add little, save a further evidence of the extreme accuracy of his memory.' The sentence is from the *Thomas Carlyle*, I. p. 240. A note at the bottom of *Thomas Carlyle*, I. p. 247, reveals that Froude, contrary to the representations of Alexander Carlyle, studied the documents with great care. All the evidence points to the fact that Froude was eager to have readers become familiar with all the available printed material. He tried, however, to avoid repetition.

publish in the 'Letters and Memorials.' He maintains that on the whole her letters during this period are much less gloomy and despairing than the extracts given by Froude would lead one to infer. Froude's selection, he avers, was motivated by a desire to represent Mrs. Carlyle's condition in the worst light. 'For some reason or other,' remarks Alexander, 'Mr. Froude has clearly done his best (or worst) to paint her condition, especially at Holm Hill, in the darkest colours possible, by picking from different letters the most gloomy and despondent sentences and placing them together as an extract from one letter—many of these citations being of necessity under wrong dates.' [1] On the face of it, that sentence seems to me to say that Froude has placed together extracts from a number of Mrs. Carlyle's letters of this period—especially those of the period when she was at Holm Hill with Dr. and Mrs. Russell—in such a way as to cause readers to think that they constituted one letter and only one. The fact is, however, that Froude has taken care to inform his readers that he is giving selections. He plainly heads those of this period 'EXTRACTS FROM LETTERS,' and in a note adds this remark: 'A series of short extracts from the letters to her husband will convey a sufficient picture of her condition in body and mind.' [2]

I informed Alexander Carlyle that, in my opinion, his remarks about this particular portion of the correspondence are misleading. 'What I say s strictly and absolutely true,' he replied; 'not a single word of it requires emendation.' He asserts that Froude prints extracts from letters of different dates, as an extract from one letter. He has not, however, reprinted the letters from this period of which Froude gives extracts, nor has he granted me permission to

[1] *New Letters and Memorials,* ii. 293.
[2] *Letters and Memorials,* iii. 204.

examine them. What he has printed in the 'New Letters and Memorials' are those of the period in question which Froude discarded as being merely repetitions of substance as given in the letters which he had selected for publication. A careful examination of this discarded material reveals that it neither adds to the value of what Froude gave nor detracts from it.

As a matter of fact, Sir James Crichton-Browne has revealed the nature of this discarded material. 'The letters,' he writes, 'are residual in character for they are those which Mr. James Anthony Froude mutilated or put aside, and he of course selected from Mrs. Carlyle's writings whatever was of most literary merit or popular interest; but they are still intrinsically worthy of publication, for even her 'notekins,' as her husband called them, contain pungent particles and happy turns of expression, while adscititiously they deserve attention, because they clear up some obscure points in a complicated controversy and help towards a just judgment of two prominent figures in our English Pantheon. Like the letters published in 1883, they are open to the objection that they are overloaded with domestic details about spring-cleanings and other housewiferies, trivial incidents of travel, intricate itinerary arrangements and complaints of postal irregularities; but as Froude who had a free hand with Mrs. Carlyle's correspondence introduced such superfluities while he omitted much that was essential to the understanding of her story, it is undesirable that there should be any avoidable elisions in the letters that are intended to refute his errors. Had Mrs. Carlyle's correspondence as a whole to be edited *de novo* a very different method of dealing with it from that adopted would have been followed, but Froude's indiscretions have made complete candour necessary.'[1] These admissions are important. The statement that the

[1] *New Letters and Memorials*, i. v.–vi.

letters are 'residual in character' proves that Froude did exercise a considerable editorial supervision over the matter which went into the 'Letters and Memorials'; he discarded enough to fill the 612 pages of two large volumes. Sir James's further remarks about the nature of the discarded material justify Froude's omissions. The two volumes of 'New Letters and Memorials' add almost nothing to a vital knowledge of the Carlyles. They are concerned mostly with details of little importance, constituting repetitions very largely of material already printed by Froude. They abound in omissions which, in the light of what is now known about some of the omitted passages, arouse grave suspicion. Indeed, that remark about 'complete candour' is unfortunate, as the facts prove.

Norton's strictures on the biography likewise do not abide close scrutiny. As an example we may take his discussion of the nineteenth chapter of Froude's first volume, wherein the biographer narrates events preliminary to the marriage of Carlyle and Miss Welsh. At one point Froude observes: 'However deeply she honoured her chosen husband, she could not hide from herself that he was selfish—extremely selfish.' [1] Norton avers that Froude is wrong.[2] 'This charge,' he asserts, 'Miss Welsh may be allowed to deny for herself.' To sustain his affirmation he quotes from two of Jane's letters to Carlyle—the first dated March 4, 1826; the second, June 28, 1826. 'At the bottom of my heart,' run the words of the first, 'far from censuring, I approve of your whole conduct.' The second reads: 'It is now five years since we first met—five blessed years! During that

[1] The sentence is from Froude's *Thomas Carlyle*, I. p. 337. To arrive at a correct understanding of Froude's treatment of the relations between Carlyle and Jane Welsh one should read consecutively in his *Thomas Carlyle*, I. pp. 181–367.

[2] *Early Letters of Carlyle*, ii. 376–377. Note the variations between the passages as given by Norton and by Alexander Carlyle, and then consider Norton's note on p. 376.

period my opinion of you has never *wavered*, but gone on deliberately rising to a higher and higher degree of *regard*.'

The matter is not so simple, however, as would appear by thus tearing two sentences from their context. I quote a more considerable portion of the letter of March 4, the text being that printed by Alexander Carlyle. 'I am not surprised,' writes Jane, 'that you feel hurt by my raillery on the subject of your plans, since you view it as an indication of an unfair theory of your character. But, in truth, it is nothing of the sort. I think you neither whimsical nor inconstant; think you nothing but what is noble and wise. I know full well you have more serious distresses than idleness and a diseased imagination; and, at the bottom of my heart, far from censuring, I approve of your whole procedures.'[1] Observe that Norton, who brings such serious charges of inaccuracy against Froude, has altered the word 'procedures' to 'conduct,' with what degree of change in meaning readers may determine for themselves. Bear in mind that this letter of March 4 is an apology on Jane's part for her letter of February 21, in which she refers to Carlyle as 'the most tantalising man in the world' in a manner which he took to be an accusation of 'fluctuations and change of purpose' on his part in regard to where they should live after marriage. Jane avowed that she had written the letter of February 21 in a 'fit of jesting,' although she had used the word 'seriously' in introducing the objectionable reference to Carlyle. The important fact, however, is that the letter of March 4 does not refer to selfishness in Carlyle at all, but to his seeming 'fluctuations and change of purpose,' and cannot therefore be used in support of the charge which Norton brings. Those who will read Jane's letter of

[1] *Love Letters*, ii. 246. I urge all who are interested to read the complete text of the letters immediately connected with this portion of the controversy.

June 28 will understand that she could say all that she does say therein and still recognise Carlyle's limitations—his selfishness among them.

I must call attention to one other attempt to convict Froude of misrepresenting Carlyle. 'Froude would have us believe,' writes Alexander Carlyle, 'that in relation to his wife Carlyle was an iconoclast and a faith wrecker, an atheist of the most blatant type.' He then gives statements to prove the essentially religious foundation of Carlyle's life, and points to Pope's 'Universal Prayer' as indicative of the best expression of Carlyle's spiritual needs.[1] The whole criticism is directed against a portion of a paragraph in Froude's posthumous pamphlet.[2] The criticism, however, distorts the substance of Froude's remarks. Froude does say, on the authority of Mrs. Carlyle, that Carlyle had taken from her the creed in which she had been bred, and that he had been unable to put anything in the place of it. But he also says that Carlyle himself had a confidence which sustained him in his uncertainties that 'the Maker of all things would do right'; that he believed, in short, or thought he believed, in a special Providence.

At no time did Froude ever represent Carlyle as 'an atheist of the most blatant type.' Such a thought never entered his mind. On the contrary, Froude prints the passage from Carlyle's journal in which Pope's 'Universal Prayer' occurs with extended comments upon it by Carlyle himself.[3] Moreover, throughout the biography Froude has written in no uncertain terms of Carlyle's essentially religious nature. Two examples are enough. 'His mind had been formed in his father's house upon the Old Testament and the Presbyterian creed, and, far as he had wandered and deeply as he had read, the original lesson had remained indelible. . . . To this

[1] *Nemesis*, pp. 31–32.
[2] *Relations*, pp. 7–8.
[3] *Thomas Carlyle*, 4. p. 371.

simple creed Carlyle adhered as the central principle of all his thoughts. The outward shell of it had broken. He had ceased to believe in miracles and supernatural interpositions. But to him the natural was the supernatural, and the tales of signs and wonders had risen out of the efforts of men to realise the deepest of truths to themselves.'[1] And again: 'Carlyle's faith . . . was that without a spiritual belief—a belief in a Divine Being, in the knowledge of whom and obedience to whom mortal welfare alone consisted—the human race must degenerate into brutes.'[2]

I could give hundreds of other examples of the manner in which Froude's meaning has been perverted or misrepresented, but these must suffice. No one of the citations which I have given is in itself of supreme importance. It is the amassing of such trivial details, the emphasising and re-emphasising of them that has gone far to destroy confidence in Froude. With these examples before them readers may evaluate for themselves the importance of such criticism, and may take care not to heed the cry of Froudacity without investigating the matter at first hand.

[1] *Thomas Carlyle*, 3. pp. 12–13.

[2] *Ibid.*, p. 424.

CHAPTER XIV

EDWARD IRVING AND JANE WELSH

AMONG the welter of more important charges brought against Froude as biographer four emerge as of major importance. We are told that he misunderstood and misrepresented the relations between Edward Irving and Jane Welsh ; that his portrayal of the life of the Carlyles at Craigenputtock is not true to fact ; that his narrative of the episode between Carlyle and Harriet Lady Ashburton is ' gratuitous and inexcusable, not only untrue, but the opposite of the truth ' ; and that he built the superstructure of the biography on a misquotation of a remark that Carlyle's mother once made to the effect that Carlyle was ' gey ill to deal wi'.' Let us examine each of these charges in turn.

An adequate discussion of the relations between Edward Irving and Jane Welsh would fill a volume. It is not possible in this chapter to do more than give in summary the narrative as related by Froude, the arguments used against him, and a few remarks upon the issues involved. Froude, after describing the circumstances under which Irving and Miss Welsh became acquainted, relates the story of the love which sprang up between them, of the discovery on Jane's part that Irving was already engaged to Miss Isabella Martin, and of her consequent turning from Irving when Miss Martin refused to release him from the engagement. ' Mrs. Carlyle's character was profoundly affected by this early disappointment, and cannot be understood without a knowledge of it,' writes Froude. 'Carlyle himself, though acquainted generally with the circumstances, never realised completely the intensity of the feeling which had been crushed.'[1]

These statements Alexander Carlyle emphatically denies. 'The romantic story of Irving and Miss Welsh being disappointed, broken-hearted, thwarted lovers, is not reconcilable with fact, and can be believed only by those who are unacquainted with the true story of the affair,' he writes.[2] Upon reading Alexander's own account of the episode, however, one gathers an impression that the true story cannot be ascertained, and is therefore inclined not to place too much confidence in the statements of Froude's critics. Alexander appeals to the authority of Margaret Oliphant's biography of Edward Irving, forgetting that Carlyle himself refers to it as 'a loyal and clear, but feeble kind of book.'[3] He questions the value of Jane's own confession that she had '*once* loved Irving passionately,' and remarks that Froude's account of the love-affair 'is the reverse of creditable to either Irving or Miss Welsh,' as if the latter statement could in any way affect the truth of the matter.[4] 'The only basis the story has,' affirms Alexander, 'is to be found in Irving's florid, exuberant, and extravagant letters to Miss Welsh, and her confession to Carlyle that she had once loved Irving passionately,' as if any further basis were needed! And then follows an attempt to prove that Irving wrote to most people in the same strain that he wrote to Jane.[5]

Charles Eliot Norton's comment of 1886 upon Froude's account shows that Norton's knowledge of

[1] *Thomas Carlyle*, I. p. 156.
[2] *Love Letters*, ii. 409.
[3] *Reminiscences*, Norton edition, i. 73.
[4] See *Love Letters*, ii. 409.
[5] *Love Letters*, ii. 410.

Jane's girlhood and young womanhood was quite inadequate. 'It was an affair discreditable to Irving, and for a time it brought much suffering to Miss Welsh,' are Norton's words.[1] He then asserts that Froude's excuse for telling the story is contradicted by the evidence, and gives the public to understand that Froude had no adequate knowledge of the matter. 'Her letters show that her feelings for Irving, first controlled by principle and honour, soon underwent a very natural change. Her love for him was the passion of an ardent and inexperienced girl, twenty or twenty-one years old, whose character was undeveloped, and who had but an imperfect understanding of the capacities and demands of her own nature.' Norton's conclusion is that the contrast between Irving's nature and Carlyle's was the thing which did 'affect her profoundly,' and that 'her temporary passion for Irving was succeeded by a far deeper and healthier love'—that for Carlyle.[2] Norton's comments were written, as I have said, in 1886. Ritchie's volume of Jane's youthful correspondence revealed that she was far from being an undeveloped and inexperienced young girl, and Froude's critics began to revise Norton's statements. In 1898 David Wilson still felt that Norton's remark about 'character undeveloped' was doubtless true, but he was constrained to add that if Ritchie's book had been available to Norton in 1886, the adjective 'inexperienced' would probably have been modified![3]

Wilson's own comment upon Froude's account is to the effect that he 'mixes up a grain of fact with a bushel of fiction in perhaps the most audacious manner ever attempted in any narrative not expressly fictitious,' and adds that 'Mr. Froude passes over in silent contempt Carlyle's account of his wife's early lovers.'[4] Again let us appeal to facts. Froude had

[1] *Early Letters of Carlyle*, ii. 368.
[2] *Early Letters of Carlyle*, ii. 369.
[3] *Mr. Froude and Carlyle*, p. 110.
[4] *Ibid.*, p. 105.

already published Carlyle's account of his wife's early lovers. It is a portion of the memoir of Jane Welsh Carlyle which appeared in the 'Reminiscences' in 1881, more than a year before the publication of the first two volumes of the biography. Moreover, Froude himself called special attention to the previously published material, giving as his reason the fact that 'what is already there does not need repeating.'[1] Wilson's expression 'silent contempt' attracts attention. By what power of divination, one asks, does Wilson know so much of the secret processes of Froude's mind?

We turn next to Margaret Oliphant's opinion of the love affair. 'My first interview with Mrs. Carlyle,' she writes, 'was on the subject of Irving, her first tutor, her early lover, and always her devoted admirer and friend. . . . There were some points about which she was naturally and gracefully reticent —about her own love, and the preference which gradually swept Irving out of her girlish fancy if he had ever been fully established there, a point on which she left her hearer in doubt. But there was another sentiment gradually developed in the tale which gave the said hearer a gleam of amusement unintended by the narrator, one of those sidelights of self-revelation which even the keenest and clearest intelligence lets slip—which was her perfectly genuine feminine dislike of the woman who replaced her in Irving's life, his wife, to whom he had been engaged before he met for the second time with the beautiful girl grown up to womanhood, who had been his baby pupil and adoration, and to whom—with escapades of wild passion for Jane, and wild proposals to fly with her to Greece, if that could be, or anywhere—he yet was willingly or unwillingly faithful. This dislike looked to me nothing more than the very natural and almost universal feminine objection to the woman who has

[1] *Thomas Carlyle*, I. p. 299.

consoled even a rejected lover. The only wonder was that she did not herself, so keen and clear as her sight was, so penetrating and impartial, see the humour of it, as one does so often even while fully indulging a sentiment so natural, yet so whimsically absurd.'[1]

In my opinion Margaret Oliphant has revealed quite enough. She discloses the facts of Irving's love for Jane. She speaks of Jane's rival as 'the woman who replaced her in Irving's life.' She does not, however, recognise the genuineness of Jane's dislike for Isabella Martin. If a stupid man dared to disagree with a woman in a matter concerned with human love he would be inclined to say that for once Margaret Oliphant was obtuse. Charles Eliot Norton, it seems to me, unwittingly came much nearer the truth. 'It was an affair,' he wrote, 'discreditable to Irving, and for a time it brought much suffering to Miss Welsh.' Such testimony is all the more valuable as coming from one of Froude's chief critics.

We must now examine the testimony of Jane herself to the effect that she had '*once* loved Irving passionately.'[2] The confession came about in this way. Upon Irving's marriage to Miss Martin, October 13, 1823, after an engagement of eleven years, he returned to his pastorate in London. He had made the acquaintance of Mrs. Basil Montagu, to whom he confided the story of his love for Jane Welsh. Carlyle, also, had become acquainted with Mrs. Montagu. At Carlyle's suggestion, she began corresponding with Miss Welsh and advising her upon her love affairs. Assuming that Carlyle was cognisant of the relations which had existed between Irving and Miss Welsh, Mrs. Montagu wrote to

[1] Article 'Thomas Carlyle,' *Macmillan's Magazine*, April 1881.

[2] See *Love Letters*, ii. 147. The 'once' is italicised on the authority of Alexander Carlyle. Froude does not italicise it. The original letter I have not seen.

Carlyle about them under date of May 30, 1825.[1] The information was rather mystifying to Carlyle, who wrote to Miss Welsh, June 24, 1825, in this strain: 'I am glad that you have answered Mrs. Montagu, and liked her. She labours under some delusion, I believe, about your secret history, but she has skill to manage anything. I have had a letter from her, full of eloquence, in which she tells me that "your heart is in England your heart is not here." This is the "romance of real life."'[2]

At the end of a letter to Carlyle, dated July 19, 1825, Jane added these remarks: 'I had *two* sheets from Mrs. Montagu, the other day, trying to prove that I knew nothing at all of my own heart! Mercy! how romantic she is!'[3] So far as I know, the text of the two sheets here mentioned has never been published. It seems to me probable that they provided Froude with the information which he gives in his account of Mrs. Montagu's correspondence with Carlyle and Miss Welsh, for which he has been so severely criticised.[4] Jane must have replied to Mrs. Montagu's two sheets promptly, for on July 20, 1825, Mrs. Montagu responded in a letter which Alexander Carlyle has published.[5] Mrs. Montagu's reply Jane forwarded to Carlyle under cover of her own letter of July 24, 1825, which is now known as the letter of confession. In Jane's letter occur these passages:

'I thought to write to you from this place with joy; I write with shame and tears . . . I cannot come to you, cannot be at peace with myself, till I

[1] Alexander Carlyle prints part of the letter in *Love Letters*, ii. 134, *note*. What he prints verifies the summary given by Froude in *Thomas Carlyle*, I. p 304.

[2] *Love Letters*, ii. 134.

[3] *Ibid.*, 146.

[4] See his *Thomas Carlyle*, I. pp. 303–308.

[5] *Love Letters*, ii. 148–150. Alexander makes a peculiar reference to the text of this letter. 'The version,' he says, 'gives Mrs. Montagu's meaning as accurately as possible.' See *Love Letters*, ii. 146, *note*. If he has printed the letter as it was written, it can scarcely fail to give the meaning accurately.

have made the confession which Mrs. Montagu so impressively shows me the need of.

'Let me tell it then at once. I have deceived you,—*I* whose truth and frankness you have so often praised, have deceived my bosom friend! I told you that I did not care for Edward Irving; took pains to make you believe this. It was false: I loved him—must I say it—*once* passionately loved him. Would to Heaven that this were all! it might not perhaps lower me much in your opinion; for he is no unworthy man. And if I showed weakness in loving one whom I knew to be engaged to another, I made amends in persuading him to marry that other and preserve his honour from reproach. But I have concealed and disguised the truth; and for this I have no excuse; none, at least, that would bear a moment's scrutiny. Woe to me then, if your reason be my judge and not your love! I cannot even plead the merit of a *voluntary* disclosure as a claim to your forgiveness. I make it because I *must*, because this extraordinary woman has moved me to honesty whether I would or no. Read her letter, and judge if it was possible for me to resist it.' [1]

Carlyle's reply is dated July 29, 1825. Alexander has printed the letter, but with some omissions which are indicated and some which are not. I am printing the complete text of the letter from a copy, now in my possession, made by Froude when he was preparing the biography.[2] When he came upon this phase of the matter Froude hesitated. I am able to present for the first time a portion of the original draft of the biography which reveals his attitude at the moment.

'The responsibility of Carlyle's biographer never weighed more heavily on him than when he was

[1] *Love Letters*, ii. 146–147. The whole of the letter should be read.

[2] See the illustrative documents on pp. 336–340 of this book. I offer this letter, copied by Froude, as an example of his accuracy in following the originals. Compare this version with that printed by Alexander Carlyle in *Love Letters*, ii. 150–155.

called to decide whether to print or to omit this most touching letter [wrote Froude in regard to Jane's confession of love for Irving]. To lay bare unnecessarily to vulgar curiosity the nearest secrets of such a heart as Mrs. Carlyle's would be more than a literary offence, it would be a moral crime, and had Carlyle himself wished that his wife's history should remain unknown, this story with all belonging to it would have been consigned through the flames to the safe keeping of everlasting silence. Desiring, however, that his last work should be (as was said in the preface) a monument to the companion who had fought the battle of life at his side, Mr. Carlyle himself prepared his wife's correspondence for publication. Although these earlier letters were not in his hand when his collection was made, and were believed to be lost, they came eventually under his eye. On the back of this one he had endorsed that it was not to be copied, but the injunction was struck through, was left to his biographer's discretion.

'Had I considered that Carlyle was but a literary meteor to blaze but for his own generation and to be forgotten the next, my reluctance might still have been invincible. Believing, however, as I do, that Carlyle's influence will be felt and that his name will be held in honour in centuries yet far distant, that he has been one of those who have seen truly into the essential nature of things, and that he has become a fixed star to shine while English literature remains with a piercing and growing radiance, I have concluded not to leave untold a story in which he and all others concerned in it carried themselves with a true nobility. The lives of great men belong to mankind. Happy those among them, happy though, alas! rare, who teach by their example as well as by their intellect, and in the record of whose lives the accusing angel himself can find nothing to reproach. Fate had thrown into connection with each other three persons of extraordinary power and character. From the collision the mind of one of them was overthrown. With the others the effects of what had been were never wholly obliterated. Yet those who suffered most had suffered because with stern integrity they had sacrificed their wishes to their duty. Generosity never assumed a nobler form than in the tender affection with which Carlyle treasured the memory of Edward Irving, though on Irving had been centred the only passionate love his own wife had ever to bestow. To Carlyle she was the truest of companions, but her heart had been partially paralysed.

'Miss Welsh's self-reproaches only awoke in Carlyle a sense of his own unworthiness. Most touching is the conflict of generosity between these two singular spirits; most striking the sudden window that it opens into the spiritual depths of Carlyle's still struggling soul. It seemed almost as if in a moment of self-recognition he felt that he never could be to her what Irving might have been, and tried to repel him from her by his self-depreciation. He had his confessions to make and he did not spare himself.'

Originally, Froude intended to print the full text of Carlyle's reply immediately following the paragraphs which I have just given. Instead, after commenting upon Carlyle's state of mind, he gave a summary of the reply in his own words.[1] Froude's summary is confirmed by the actual text of the letter. Alexander Carlyle, however, condemns it in strong terms. 'Carlyle's biographer, seeming to cite from this letter, says: "His infirmities, mental and bodily, might make him an unfit companion for her or indeed for any woman." The words "or indeed for any woman" are a pure—or rather an impure—invention of the biographer. There is nothing the least like

[1] *Thomas Carlyle,* I. pp. 307–308. Froude's summary begins with the sentence, 'He knew, he said, that he could never make her happy.'

them in this or in any other of Carlyle's letters. . . . Carlyle's only " bodily infirmity " was dyspepsia ; he was never afflicted with any " mental infirmity." '[1] We must remember that Froude had before him the full text of Carlyle's letter. Let us bear in mind the portions which Alexander Carlyle has omitted : ' the affection you rejoice in is worse than worthless. It is hurtful. It may be your ruin. I can no longer love. You do not know me ; believe me, you would be wretched with me in a week.' May we not conclude that Froude was justified in summarising the document as he did ? In any event, the portions of the letter which Alexander Carlyle omits are such as to suggest that their omission is due to the fact that they support Froude too strongly.

Whatever interpretation may be placed upon Jane's letter of confession, there can be no doubt that the substance of it was serious to her and to Carlyle. There is plenty of evidence, too, that the love existing between Edward Irving and Jane Welsh was what Froude represents it to be both in itself before her marriage to Carlyle, and later in its effects upon Irving and Mrs. Carlyle. It is not difficult to show that for a long time Carlyle was ignorant of the facts in the case, and that Alexander Carlyle's assertion that Irving and Carlyle ' had no secrets from one another ' is not strictly true.

Carlyle himself has placed on record a short passage which reveals much in regard to Irving.

' It was in one of those visits by Irving himself [to Edinburgh, where Carlyle was then staying], without any company, that he took me out to Haddington . . . to what has since been so momentous through all my subsequent life ! . . . I think there had been, before this, on Irving's own part some movements of negotiation over to Kirkcaldy for *release* there, and of hinted hope towards Haddington,

[1] *Love Letters*, ii. 153, *note*.

which was so infinitely preferable! And something (as I used to gather long afterwards) might have come of it, had not Kirkcaldy been so peremptory, and stood by its bond (as spoken or as written), "Bond or utter Ruin, Sir!"—upon which Irving had honourably submitted and resigned himself. He seemed to be quite composed upon the matter by this time: I remember in our inn at Haddington that first night, a little passage: we had just seen, in the Minister's house (whom Irving was to *preach* for), a certain shining Miss Augusta,—tall, shapely, airy, giggly, but a consummate fool, whom I have heard called "Miss *Dis*gusta" by the satirical;—we were now in our double-bedded room, George Inn, Haddington, stripping, or perhaps each already in his bed, when Irving jocosely said to me, "What would you take to marry Miss Augusta, now?" "Not for an entire and perfect chrysolite the size of this terraqueous Globe!" answered I at once, with hearty laughter from Irving.—"And what would you take to marry Miss Jeannie, think you?" "Hah, I should not be so hard to deal with there I should imagine!" upon which another bit of laugh from Irving; and we composedly went to sleep.' [1]

Who that understands the nature of a young man in love can fail to see in Irving's casual questioning of Carlyle the fear that at last Jane Welsh was face to face with one who might claim her permanently? Of Irving's jealous fears and hopeless love Carlyle, the one from whom Irving 'had no secrets,' knew nothing at the time. That one significant clause—'as I used to gather long afterwards'—and the scant references on the part of Carlyle to the whole matter help us to understand how serious the affair was for Irving and Miss Welsh.[2] When Carlyle dismisses

[1] *Reminiscences,* Norton edition, ii. 85–87.

[2] See Jane's reference to Irving in a letter to Carlyle of November 10, 1824, in the *Nineteenth Century,* January 1914, pp. 101–102.

a subject briefly, it is not because of its lack of significance to him ; it is often because he does not wish to admit the degree of its significance.

It is impossible to dismiss Froude's account of the affair with a gesture. After careful study of all the available evidence I am convinced that his version is substantially correct. At any rate, Alexander Carlyle's account fails to impress me as a refutation of Froude's.

CHAPTER XV

JANE'S MISALLIANCE

FROUDE, in narrating the circumstances of the courtship of Carlyle and Jane Welsh, stresses the differences in their social status. He points out that Jane, as the daughter of a successful physician, was born and grew up in comparative ease and comfort, and moved in a town and city social circle well above the ranks of the lower middle class. Carlyle, he affirms, came of good and respectable, but peasant stock. He says that Jane came to a recognition of the sterling worth of Carlyle's peasant family, and 'was willing to share their method of existence, sharply contrasted as it was with the elegance and relative luxury of her home at Haddington.' [1] He makes it clear, however, that Jane's mother did not agree. 'It was natural, it was inevitable independent of selfish considerations, that she could not look without a shudder on the purposed marriage with the son of a poor Dumfriesshire farmer, who had no visible prospects and no profession, and whose abilities, however great they might be, seemed only to unfit him for any usual or profitable pursuit.' [2] In a word, Froude interprets the whole affair in a contemporary light; as it looked to those who were concerned at the time. With his gift of imagination he was able to reconstruct the past, and to shut out all thought of Carlyle's future success as effectually as if it had never been. To one unable to do this, to

[1] *Thomas Carlyle*, I. p. 313. [2] *Ibid.*, p. 314.

one who keeps thinking of Jane's choice in the light only of what Carlyle became, Froude's presentation will doubtless remain difficult.

Alexander Carlyle and his followers have strongly resented Froude's version of the matter. 'Froude misunderstands the whole situation as regards Carlyle's marriage,' asserts Crichton-Browne.[1] 'Miss Welsh knew well what she did when she married Carlyle and there is no pretext for Froude's contention—on which he harps again and again—that she lowered her station in doing so; or for his allegations that her mother was violently opposed to the marriage on account of Carlyle's inferior worldly situation; and that Carlyle himself felt remorse for having entangled in an engagement one so much above him.'[2] In 1898 David Wilson asserted that 'it is the historical fact that the *mésalliance* was unheard of in Edinburgh society, and so was Miss Welsh, until after she married Carlyle.'[3] He repeated this statement with additional explanations in 1923. 'The word "misalliance" was never heard. On the contrary the Haddington gossips . . . explained that she never had much and that her richer suitors shied at her plainness and departed on discovering how little of an heiress she was.'[4] The issue could scarcely be more sharply defined.

If we are to understand the matter aright, however, it would seem advisable to forget all that happened after 1826, and look at the situation from 1821 to 1826 through the eyes of Thomas and Jane themselves. Their correspondence has much to say

[1] *New Letters and Memorials*, i. p. xxxvi. [2] *Ibid.*, p. xxxviii.

[3] *Mr. Froude and Carlyle*, pp. 141–142. Wilson is referring to a remark in Froude's *Thomas Carlyle*, 4. p. 297: 'When Miss Welsh, of Haddington, announced that she was to be married to him, the unheard of *mésalliance* had been the scoff of Edinburgh society and of her father's and mother's connections there.' By 'Edinburgh society' it would be manifestly unfair to say that Froude meant other than such portion of that society as knew of the Welshes and of Carlyle.

[4] Wilson's *Carlyle*, 1. p 427. Observe that the evidence offered by Wilson is anonymous gossip.

about the disparity of their relative positions in life. On February 13, 1822, Carlyle wrote to Jane as follows: 'Besides, do I not know how we stand related towards each other? I understand what is your rank and what your prospects: I understand too what are my own; and perhaps there are feelings of integrity and honest pride within me, which I am as chary of as some who make more noise about them. Do not *you* look upon me as a slave, however others may look upon me.'[1] Again, on January 9, 1825, he wrote: 'At times, I confess, when I hear you speak of your gay cousins, and contrast with their brilliant equipments my own simple exterior, and scanty prospects, and humble but to me most dear and honourable-minded kinsmen, whom I were the veriest dog if I ever ceased to love and venerate and cherish for their true affection, and the rugged sterling [worth] of their characters; when I think of all this, I could almost counsel you to cast me utterly away, and connect yourself with one whose friends and station were more analogous to your own.'[2]

In reply to the foregoing Jane wrote on January 13, 1825, a letter which should be read in full, such is its importance. 'I do not wish for fortune,' she told Carlyle, 'more than is sufficient for my wants; my natural wants, and the artificial ones which habit has rendered nearly as importunate as the other; but I will not marry on less, because in that case every inconvenience I was subjected to would remind me of what I had quitted; and the idea of a sacrifice should have no place in a voluntary union. Neither have I any wish for grandeur. The glittering baits of titles and honours are only for children and fools. But I conceive it a duty which every one owes to society, not to throw up that station in it which Providence has assigned him; and having this conviction I could not marry into a station inferior to my

[1] *Love Letters*, i. 29. [2] *Ibid.*, ii. 67.

own with the approval of my judgment, *which* alone could enable me to brave the censures of my acquaintance.' [1] That certainly is explicit. With such evidence before him is it any wonder that Froude wrote as he did? 'All her friends, the social circle of which she had been the centre, regarded the marriage with Carlyle as an extraordinary *mésalliance.* To them he was known only as an eccentric farmer's son without profession or prospects.' [2]

Froude's critics, however, would have it that the 'inferior station' and 'the censures' of acquaintances were figments of Jane's imagination, or ruses on her part to impress Carlyle with the sacrifice she was making.[3] It would be pleasant to believe so, if one were not compelled to do violence to one's common sense. The critics would have it, also, that Carlyle, throughout the remainder of his life, laboured under the delusion that Jane had married out of her station. Froude is charged with ignorance of conditions in Scotland, such ignorance as prevented him from understanding properly the relative social position of the two lovers. Do they not realise that in maintaining delusion on the part of Carlyle they imply a similar ignorance in his case? It appears, however, that Froude knew very well what conditions among the Carlyles were. A striking bit of evidence is tucked away in one of the pages of David Wilson's biography of Carlyle. 'They were working women,' writes Wilson of Carlyle's mother and sisters, 'not encumbrances. The mother herself worked both in the house and in the fields, and set a good example by being cheery. Once she had been out hoeing turnips all day, and in the evening the other workers gave her a start, and there was a merry race home to the farm-house.' [4] Those words corroborate Froude. He meant just what those statements reveal; that

[1] *Love Letters*, ii. 70.
[2] *Thomas Carlyle*, 1. p. 349.
[3] See Wilson's *Carlyle*, 2. p. 49.
[4] Wilson's *Carlyle*, 2. p. 289.

Carlyle was brought up among women who worked long and hard at labour such as the women of the Welsh family knew nothing of at first hand ; and having been brought up so, he unconsciously looked upon most women, particularly those among whom he lived, as equal to such tasks. To say this, is not to decry honest labour or worthy farm people like the Carlyles ; it is but to emphasise a difference in station.[1]

All of this Carlyle knew well. On January 17, 1826, he wrote in this fashion to Jane : 'Can *you* suffer poverty ? Do you know what it means ? It is a word of three syllables, easily written, and looks romantic when spoken by the side of household love. Alas ! alas ! the bearing of it is a different matter. For myself I am happy, and *rich* in the midst of it ; but you, my poor Jane, would die before you learned this wisdom as I have had to learn it. There are many miracles in this world : but for a woman to descend from superfluity to live with a sick ill-natured man in poverty, and not in wretchedness, would be the greatest miracle of all.'[2] Alexander Carlyle, however, will have none of this. In a note upon this letter he attempts to explain away the meaning of 'superfluity' by saying that after the death of Jane's father, her mother had to be economical in household management.

The facts about the circumstances of the Welshes are these. Jane's father paid £10,500 for Craigenputtock and his home in Haddington, saving the entire amount from his medical practice in twenty years. To do that necessitated an annual average saving of £525. The income from Craigenputtock was at least £180 a year, in addition to which there

[1] In 1903 Andrew Lang wrote in *Longman's Magazine*, xliii. 24, as follows : 'They were not equal by birth. We have only to look at the portraits of Carlyle's mother, on one hand—an old peasant woman—and of Mrs. Carlyle's father and mother, who have the air and dress of gentlefolk.'

[2] *Love Letters*, ii. 216–217.

was the sale price of the Haddington home after Dr. Welsh's death. After the final settlement of his estate there was, in addition to Craigenputtock and the Haddington home, a cash balance of £145 12*s*. 3*d*.[1] One fancies that Mrs. Welsh and her daughter must have managed fairly well in the first half of the nineteenth century on an income of at least £200 a year.

It is certain that Carlyle, when first introduced into the Welsh home, was impressed by its air of opulence in a manner which clearly reveals his unfamiliarity with the surroundings of the well-to-do. 'The drawing-room,' he wrote, 'seemed to me the finest apartment I had ever sat or stood in. . . . I felt as one walking transiently in upper spheres, where I had little right even to make transit.'[2] He says too, that when Edward Irving used to talk to him of Dr. Welsh and Jane, both seemed 'far away . . . objects of distant reverence and unattainable longing.'[3] Nor did he ever cease to feel that she had left comparative ease. 'My chief pity is for Jane,' he wrote to his brother John in 1837. 'She hoped much of me; had great faith in me; and has endured much beside me, not murmuring at it. I feel as if I had to swim both for her deliverance and my own.'[4] One of two things is true; Carlyle was either entirely mistaken throughout his life, or he was speaking facts. Froude, who knew both of the people concerned, and knew them intimately for many years, believed that Carlyle was speaking the truth.

Five months before the marriage Jane wrote to Carlyle in this way, on May 9, 1826: 'One thing I

[1] See *New Letters and Memorials*, i. 1–2, 226 *note*, and *Love Letters*, ii. 269.
[2] *Reminiscences*, Norton edition, i. 147.
[3] *Ibid.*, 74.
[4] Wilson's *Carlyle*, 3. p. 3. In describing Carlyle's state of mind during a dinner at David Masson's home after the Rectorial address at the University of Edinburgh, John Tyndall says: 'In the background slumbered the consciousness of success. In the same region lay thoughts of his wife, whose pride in his triumph would reverberate its glow upon him. Clinging to her image were memories of a time when her union with him was deemed a *mésalliance*.' See Tyndall's 'Personal Recollections of Carlyle' in the *Fortnightly Review*, liii. 17. This article is reprinted in Tyndall's *New Fragments*.

must entreat of you : if the thought of maintaining a wife begins to press more hard on you than you at first supposed it would, hesitate not to tell me that we must live apart till a more auspicious season ; but if not, if you are still determined to make me your own at all haps and hazards, for heaven's sake, dearest, speak not another word to me about your *poverty*. Every such word comes home to me with the force of a *reproach*. And truly this poverty is a circumstance of which I need not to be any more warned ; for I have long since looked it full in the face, and left it out in none of my calculations. Even when I proposed our taking up house in Edinburgh, it had by no means escaped my recollection that we should be very poor.'[1]

In the face of all this discussion on the part of the lovers themselves, who knew, if anyone did, their respective positions in life, Alexander Carlyle and those who support him maintain that Jane did not marry out of her station. To show that the social status of the Carlyles was equal to that of the Welshes, if not superior to it, Alexander offers the pitiful rag of a Carlyle pedigree to gild over the inequality of birth. It is as though Jack Durbeyfield should have offered to a well-born and comfortably endowed lover of Tess the genealogical history of the Durbeyfield family. As Norwood Young has pointed out with reference to Carlyle's supposed descent from Scottish royalty, 'The blood of Duncan must by this time have spread all over Great Britain. We are all descended from every person living in Scotland in the time of Duncan, whether royal or plebeian.'[2] Carlyle himself saw the humour of it all. 'What laughing my darling and I had when that document arrived,' he wrote in regard to the work of a local antiquarian.[3]

[1] *Love Letters*, ii. 281–282.

[2] *Carlyle : His Rise and Fall*, p. 12.

[3] *Love Letters*, ii. 329, *note*. 'When Carlyle became famous, a Dumfries antiquary traced his ancestry with apparent success through ten generations to the first Lord Torthorwald. There was much laughter about it in the house in Cheyne Row, but Carlyle was inclined to think on the whole that the descent was real,' says Froude in *Thomas Carlyle*, 1. pp. 2–3, *note*.

Besides the evidence which has already been given, it is not necessary to do more than quote from the letter which Jane wrote to her aunt, Mrs. George Welsh, of Boreland, Southwick, Dumfries, October 1, 1826, by way of announcing the prospective marriage.

'It were no news [run the words of the letter] to tell you what a momentous matter I have been busied with ; " not to know *that* would argue yourself unknown." For a marriage is a topic suited to the capacities of all living ; and, in this, as in every known instance, has been made the most of. But, for as much breath as has been wasted on " my *Situation*," I have my own doubts whether they have given you any *right* idea of it. They would tell you, I should suppose, first and foremost, that my Intended is *poor*, (for *that* it requires no great depth of sagacity to discover), and, in the next place, most likely, indulge in some criticisms scarce flattering on his birth (the more likely, if their own birth happened to be mean or doubtful) ; and, if they happened to be vulgar-fine people with disputed pretensions to good looks, they would, to a certainty, set him down as unpolished and ill-looking. But a hundred chances to one, they would not tell you he is among the cleverest men of his day ; and not the cleverest only but the most enlightened ! that he possesses all the qualities I deem essential in *my* Husband, a warm true heart to love me, a towering intellect to command me, and a spirit of fire to be the guiding star of my life. Excellence of this sort always requires some degree of superiority in those who duly appreciate it : in the eyes of the *canaille*—poor soulless wretches ! —it is mere foolishness, and it is only the *canaille* who babble about other people's affairs.

'Such then is this future Husband of mine ; not a *great* man according to the most common sense of the word, but truly great in its natural, proper sense ; a scholar, a poet, a philosopher, a wise and noble man, one who holds his patent of nobility from Almighty God, and whose high stature of manhood is not to be measured by the inch-rule of Lilliputs !—Will you like him ? No matter whether you do or not—since I like him in the deepest part of my soul. I would invite you to my wedding, if I meant to invite any one ; but to *my* taste, such ceremonies cannot be *too* private : besides by making distinctions among my relatives on the occasion, I should be sure to give offence ; and, by God's blessing, I will have no one there who does not feel kindly both towards *him* and *me*.[1] '

Froude printed this letter in the biography.[2] He knew that it summarised the whole matter. It touches upon the question of poverty, of station, of outward culture, as well as upon the actually intrinsic quality and worth of Carlyle. It makes clear, too, the open criticism of Carlyle among the circle of Jane's relatives and acquaintances. To say, in the face of this letter, that ' no breath had been wasted ' in Scotland on Jane's ' situation ' is to make an assertion which I for one cannot believe.

[1] *Love Letters*, ii. 328–330. [2] *Thomas Carlyle*, I. pp. 356–358.

CHAPTER XVI

CRAIGENPUTTOCK

ALEXANDER CARLYLE, seconded by Crichton-Browne and David Wilson, maintains that Froude's version of the life of the Carlyles at Craigenputtock is untrue to the facts, that it is, in brief, a series of 'guesses' founded upon 'hallucinations and delusions.' In summary they charge him with having 'depicted Mrs. Carlyle's life at Craigenputtock as one of the loneliest and dreariest possible.'[1] According to his detractors Froude is wrong at every turn; he exaggerates the natural surroundings of Craigenputtock; he misrepresents the kind of life Mrs. Carlyle experienced there; he is wrong in saying that her health suffered there; his version of the Craigenputtock days does not harmonise with that of either Carlyle or his wife. In the face of such sweeping assertions it is wise to ascertain just what is Froude's version of the life at Craigenputtock.[2]

It should be remembered that Froude presents a full canvas of the Craigenputtock scene, the details of which are supplied mostly in the words of the two people chiefly concerned. The biographer gives lights as well as shadows. He alternates descriptions of pleasant aspects with those of unpleasant aspects. He gives contemporary accounts along with recollections written many years later. He directs

[1] *New Letters and Memorials*, i. 24.
[2] For the substance of Froude's account see his *Thomas Carlyle*, 2. pp. 23–424.

readers to Carlyle's own version of the life as given in the 'Reminiscences.' It is no one-sided account that Froude gives. He allows the facts to tell their own story, and the cumulative effect is difficult to ignore. It is only just to add that Alexander Carlyle and his friends maintain that Froude has so arranged his materials as to produce a cumulative effect which is entirely misleading.

In closing his long narrative of the Craigenputtock days Froude gives the following summary :

'Thus the six years' imprisonment on the Dumfriesshire moors came to an end. To Carlyle himself they had been years of inestimable value. . . . The solitude had compelled him to digest his thoughts. . . . His religious faith had gained solidity. . . . He had been tried in the furnace. Poverty, mortification, and disappointment had done their work upon him, and he had risen above them elevated, purified, and strengthened. . . .

'He had lain in, too, on the moors a stock of robust health. Lamentations over indigestion and want of sleep are almost totally absent from the letters written from Craigenputtock. . . . On the moors, as at Mainhill, at Edinburgh, or in London afterwards, he was always impatient, moody, irritable, violent. These humours were in his nature, and could no more be separated from them than his body could leap off its shadow. But, intolerable as he had found Craigenputtock in the later years of his residence there, he looked back to it afterwards as the happiest and wholesomest home that he had ever known. He could do fully twice as much work there, he said, as he could ever do afterwards in London ; and many a time, when sick of fame and clatter and interruption, he longed to return to it.

'To Mrs. Carlyle Craigenputtock had been a less salutary home. She might have borne the climate, and even benefited by it, if the other conditions had been less ungenial. But her life there, to begin with, had been a life of menial drudgery, unsolaced (for she could have endured and even enjoyed mere hardship) by more than an occasional word of encouragement or sympathy or compassion from her husband. To him it seemed perfectly natural that what his mother did at Scotsbrig his wife should do for him. Every household duty fell upon her, either directly, or in supplying the shortcomings of a Scotch maid-of-all-work. She had to cook, to sew, to scour, to clean ; to gallop down alone to Dumfries if anything was wanted ; to keep the house, and even on occasions to milk the cows. Miss Jewsbury has preserved many anecdotes of the Craigenputtock life, showing how hard a time her friend had of it there. Carlyle, though disposed at first to dismiss these memories as legends, yet admitted on reflection that for all there was a certain foundation. The errors, if any, can be no more than the slight alterations of form which stories naturally receive in repetition. A lady brought up in luxury has been educated into physical unfitness for so sharp a discipline. Mrs. Carlyle's bodily health never recovered from the strain of those six years. The trial to her mind and to her nervous system was still more severe. . . . The loneliness of Craigenputtock was dreadful to her . . . Her hard work, perhaps, had so far something of a blessing in it, that it was a relief from the intolerable pressure. For months together, especially after Alick Carlyle had gone, they never saw the face of guest or passing stranger. So still the moors were, that she could hear the sheep nibbling the grass a quarter of a mile off. For the many weeks when the snow was on the ground she could not stir beyond the garden, or even beyond her door. . . .

'Carlyle himself recognised occasionally that she was not happy. Intentionally unkind it was not in his nature to be. After his mother, he loved his wife better than anyone in the world. He was only occupied, unperceiving, negligent ; and when he *did* see that anything was wrong with her he was at once the tenderest of husbands.' [1]

As over against the narrative of which the foregoing passages are a summary, Crichton-Browne maintains that Froude does not make a statement about Craigenputtock and Mrs. Carlyle's avocations there that is not open to correction. [2] He asserts that Mrs. Carlyle 'went there with cheerful acquiescence' ; that her health did not suffer there but 'benefited immensely' ; that the account of her 'alleged drudgery' is 'as mythical as the injury to her health.' Let us see what the evidence reveals.

From the first Jane was opposed to going to Craigenputtock. Months before their marriage she ridiculed the notion of Carlyle's even considering residence at the Craig, adjuring him to 'think of some more promising plan than farming the most barren spot in the county of Dumfriesshire.' She made no effort to conceal her aversion to the project. 'What a thing that would be to be sure !' she exclaimed. 'You and I keeping house at Craigenputtock ! I would just as soon think of building myself a nest on the Bass Rock. Nothing but your ignorance of the place saves you from the imputation of insanity for admitting such a thought. Depend upon it you could not *exist* there a twelvemonth. For my part, I would not spend a month at it with an angel.' [3] And later she continued : 'Will you be done with this wild scheme of yours ? I tell you it will *not* answer ; and you must positively play Cincinnatus somewhere else. With all your tolerance of places, you would not find at Craigenputtock the requisites you require. The light of heaven, to be sure, is not denied it ; but

[1] *Thomas Carlyle*, 2. pp. 416–421.

[2] *New Letters and Memorials*, i. p. xl–xli.

[3] *Love Letters*, ii. 70–71.

for green grass? Besides a few cattle-fields, there is nothing except a waste prospect of heather and black peat-moss.'[1]

It is clear that to her the prospect was never pleasing. How, then, did it come about that she consented to go? The answer is that, having married Carlyle, the move to Craigenputtock became almost inevitable. Carlyle was in the habit of being obeyed; he believed that a man should be *Herr im Hause*; indeed, he had taken pains before marriage to make his position clear upon all such matters. His attitude towards women was the logical result of the Puritan doctrine in which he had been reared. Even in these modern and very liberal days the influence of that doctrine is still powerful. Very early in her married life, Jane came to understand that she must resign herself to the inevitable. In such a marriage the will of one was sure to dominate; the desires of one were sure to be subordinated. It is hardly necessary to say that in the Carlyle household the will of the husband was supreme. That she accommodated herself to him, Carlyle admits; her acquiescence he takes for granted. Writing to his brother, March 29, 1827, of the Craigenputtock plan, Carlyle says: 'As for Jane, I think there is little fear that her tolerance would be less than mine: in good sooth, she is a *true* wife, and would murmur at no scene or fortune which she shared along with me.'[2] That letter is in keeping with what he wrote many years later. 'She liked London constantly; and stood in defence of it against me and my atrabilious censures of it; never had for herself the least wish to quit it again, though I was often talking of that, and her *practice* would have been loyal compliance for my behoof.'[3]

As to the settlement at Craigenputtock, Froude

[1] *Love Letters*, ii. 86.
[2] *Letters of Carlyle*, i. 40.
[3] *Reminiscences*, Norton edition, i. 171.

says : 'To Mrs. Carlyle herself the adventure might well seem desperate. She concealed the extent of her anxiety from her husband, though not entirely from others. Jeffrey especially felt serious alarm.' [1] It appears, however, that she was not entirely successful in concealing her anxiety from her husband. On March 7, 1828, from Comely Bank, Carlyle wrote thus to his brother John : 'How matters stand at Craigenputtock I can only guess, but am going down to see. I am in no small uncertainty. This Edinburgh is getting more agreeable to me, more and more a sort of home ; and I *can* live in it, if I like to live perpetually unhealthy, and strive forever against becoming a *hack*, for that I cannot be. On the other hand, I should have liberty and solitude for aught I like the best among the moors—only Jane, though like a good wife she says nothing, seems evidently getting more and more afraid of the whole enterprise. She is not at all stout in health. But I must go and look at things with my own eyes, and now as ever there is need of mature resolve, and steadfast when mature.' [2]

The foregoing letter is not in harmony with what Carlyle has recorded elsewhere. Looking back to the removal from Edinburgh he wrote :

'Her modest days, which never demanded much to make them happy, were beginning to have many little joys and amusements of their own in that bright scene [at 21 Comely Bank, Edinburgh], and she would have to change it for one of the loneliest, mooriest, and dullest in nature. To her it was a great sacrifice, if to me it was the reverse ; but at no moment, even by a look, did she ever say so. Indeed I think she never felt so at all. She would have gone to Nova Zembla with me, and found *it* the right place had benefit to me or set purpose of mine lain there.' [3]

[1] *Thomas Carlyle,* 2. p. 24. [2] *Ibid.*, 1. p. 426.
[3] *Ibid.*, 1. pp. 386–387.

In this passage Carlyle has voiced several things correctly. The removal to Craigenputtock was of benefit chiefly to him. He recognises what a sacrifice it was to a woman like Jane. He brings into clear light the self-denial of the wife who had determined at any cost to forward his interests. He is mistaken only in forgetting that she did hesitate. Alexander Carlyle is always emphasising the value of contemporary letters as a means of understanding the Craigenputtock days. It is true that contemporary letters do reveal the facts. Alexander's assertion that the Craigenputtock scheme, rejected in 1825, was gladly adopted by her in 1828, is not supported by the facts.

One of Jane's letters to Carlyle, who was then (September 11, 1831) in London—a letter which remained unpublished until 1914—summarises the whole situation at Craigenputtock admirably. As usual, Jane goes right to the heart of the matter. She recognises the good work which Carlyle did there without in any way concealing her eagerness to get away. Froude is justified in writing as he did of the Carlyles at the Craig, if only on the authority of this letter:

'At Craigenputtock we have always had a secret suspicion that we were quite wrong; removed out of the sphere of human activity fully as much through cowardice as superior wisdom (am I not right in regard to you as well as myself?), and thus all our doings are without heart and our suffering without dignity. With a goal before me I feel I could leap six-bar gates; but how dispiriting, tethered on a barren heath, running round and round. Yet let it not be forgotten that at Craigenputtock you have written 'Teufelsdreck'! Yes, the candle sometimes burns its way *through* the bushel; but what a waste of light! Nevertheless, I am taking all possible pains to preserve the poor Putta in habitable order;

for no more than you would I *renounce* it. It is a safe haven (though but a desert island) in stress of weather.[1]

It is not surprising that when the opportunity came to leave the 'desert island' Jane should urge, 'Let us burn our ships, and get on march.'[2] Nor that Carlyle should write to Jane, September 14, 1831: 'Poor Puttock! Castle of many chagrins; peatbog Castle, where the Devil never slumbers nor sleeps! . . . I shall always look upon it with a mixture of love, horror, and amazement; a quite supernatural abode, more like Hades than the Earth.'[3]

Froude describes Craigenputtock as 'a high moorland farm' which lies in solitude sixteen miles from Dumfries. 'The manor house, solid and gaunt, and built to stand for centuries, lies on a slope protected by a plantation of pines, and surrounded by a few acres of reclaimed grass land—a green island in the midst of heathery hills, sheep-walks, and undrained peat-bogs. A sterner spot is hardly to be found in Scotland.'[4] Elsewhere, thinking of the place as it was before the Carlyles took possession and did something to reclaim it, recalling its distance from the nearest town and doctor, its isolation in the winter and its unbroken silence in the summer, he refers to it as 'the dreariest spot in all the British dominions.' If dreariness arises from solitude, if it afflicts the spirits of those who are compelled to withdraw into themselves for amusement and renewal of strength, if it is augmented by a stern and sombre landscape, then Froude is right.[5] Let those who think otherwise go into residence at Craigenputtock for a twelvemonth.

Carlyle's contemporary letters abound in evidence

[1] 'New Letters of Jane Welsh Carlyle,' *Nineteenth Century*, August 1914.

[2] *Reminiscences*, Norton edition, ii. 211.

[3] *Letters of Carlyle*, i. 339.

[4] *Thomas Carlyle*, I. p. 108.

[5] Carlyle in a letter to Goethe dated September 25, 1828 remarks: 'for this is one of the most solitary spots in Britain, being six miles from *any* individual of the formally visiting class.' See *Correspondence between Goethe and Carlyle*, pp. 124–126.

corroborative of Froude. They are full of references to the wildness, the sternness, the bareness, the loneliness, and the dullness of the moorland waste. During a visit to London he wrote as follows on January 14, 1832, to his brother Alexander, who had given up the struggle as tenant-farmer at the Craig: 'Often does the picture of that lone mansion in the Dunscore wold come before me here; it has a strange, almost unearthly character, as it comes before me standing in the lone Night in the wintry moor, with the tumult of London raging around me . . . we shall wander no more along the Glaisters Hill: it is the ugliest of hills, and none of us saw cheerfulness on the face of it, or anything but toil and vexation; nevertheless now when it is all past, how can we be other than sad?'[1] And a few months later, August 12, 1832, once more on the moors after his visit in London, in another letter to Alexander, he said: 'I have now and then enough ado to keep myself stiffly at work: as you know well, however, there is no other course for one in this lone Desert; where if a man did not work, he might so easily run mad. When vapours of solitude, and longings after the cheerful face of my fellow-man are gathering round me, I dash them off, and the first lusty swing of Industry scatters them away, as cock-crowing does spectres of the Night.'[2] And in 1835 he told Alexander that 'one's very dispiritment in these peopled spaces of London' was 'nothing to the gloom of Puttock.'[3]

After settling in London Carlyle, notwithstanding occasional longings to flee into the wilderness and rest—longings which come to every hard-pressed son of Adam—seems never to have changed his mind about Craigenputtock. To his mother, if to anyone, he revealed his inmost heart. I give two passages from his letters to her in 1835. The first is from a letter of February 17: 'I go out to walk daily,

[1] *Letters of Carlyle*, ii. 1–2. [2] *Ibid.*, 47–48. [3] *Ibid.*, 263–264.

and . . . the tumult of these, my brethren, sons of Adam, amuses me. How different from the lone musing stroll along the Glaisters Hill-side! I never think of that now without a kind of shudder at it; of thankfulness that I am away from it.'[1] Again, on March 25, in regard to his life in London, he wrote: 'It is very different from Puttock; which indeed I never think of without feeling that we did well to leave it.'[2] Indeed, while on the moors, Carlyle always had the feeling of one who was lost to the world. One strong figure of speech was firmly fixed in his mind. 'We are quite buried alive here, and must try to rise of ourselves,' he informed his sister, Mrs. James Aitken, February 25, 1834.[3] And when telling his brother John of the proposed removal to London, he wrote, March 27, 1834: 'To go thither seems inevitable, palpably necessary; yet, contrasted with these six years of rockbound seclusion, seems almost like a rising from the grave.'[4] Such were Carlyle's feelings at the time. More than thirty years after he had left it, he called the Craigenputtock settlement 'a kind of humble russet-coated epic.' He did not forget, however, that 'poverty and mean obstruction had given origin to it, and continued to preside over it,' and knew well enough that in retrospect it looked far different from the actual experience. Only from the vantage-point of many years could he say that the Craigenputtock experience was 'not without an intrinsic dignity greater and more important than then appeared.'[5] Many men since Æneas have in some happier hour found that even the most unpleasant experiences may be transmuted into beautiful memories.

Alexander Carlyle indulges in one strange bit of criticism. In the biography of Carlyle, Froude prints

[1] *Letters of Carlyle*, ii. 271–272.
[2] *Ibid.*, 306.
[3] *Ibid.*, 132.
[4] *Ibid.*, 138–139.
[5] *Reminiscences*, Norton edition, ii. 244.

a letter to Miss Eliza Miles in which Jane gives a rather attractive account of her life on the moors. 'This is pretty, and shows Craigenputtock on its fairest side,' remarks the biographer. 'But there was a reverse of the picture.'[1] Alexander asserts that Froude should not have used the letter at all, as 'it was neither written by Carlyle nor to Carlyle,' and suggests that it should have been printed only in a collection of Mrs. Carlyle's letters.[2] Whether or not certain material should be used in a book depends upon the author's purpose, and it is clear that this letter serves the exact purpose which Froude had in mind. He was intent upon presenting all aspects of the life at Craigenputtock. Had he wished to conceal the pleasant side, he would most certainly have taken care to withhold this letter. Alexander himself admits that 'Mrs. Carlyle's picture of life at her ancestral home is slightly coloured for a purpose.' Of course it is. That, Froude knew quite well. No critic is dealing fairly with the biographer when he condemns him for putting the proper tones into the picture.

There remains the question of Jane's work at Craigenputtock, upon which Froude and his critics are so sharply at variance. Again, fortunately, it is possible to appeal to contemporary evidence. Under date of July 2, 1832, Carlyle wrote to his brother John these words : 'As to Craigenputtock, it is, as formerly, the scene of scribble-scribbling. Jane is in a weakly state still, but I think clearly gathering strength. Her life beside me constantly writing here is but a dull one ; however, she seems to desire no other ; has, in many things, pronounced the word *Entsagen*, and looks with a brave if with no joyful heart into the present and the future. She manages all things—poultry, flowers, bread-loaves ; keeps a house still like a bandbox, then reads, or works (as at

[1] *Thomas Carlyle*, 2. p. 290.
[2] *New Letters and Memorials*, i. 40–41, *note*.

present) upon some translation from Goethe.'[1] Again, on October 17, 1832, he wrote to John: 'Jane is sitting in the dining-room; reads, sews, rules her household, where cow, hens, human menials, garden crop, all things animate and inanimate, need looking to.'[2] Much is made of the fact by Froude's opponents that the Carlyles had servants at the Craig. As to that Carlyle may speak. '*Good* servants . . . were hardly procurable; difficult anywhere, still more so at Craigenputtock where the choice was so limited.'[3] Alongside these statements, Froude's narrative appears eminently satisfactory.

It is definitely on record that at Craigenputtock Jane, among other things, sewed, baked, cooked, salted butter, helped doctor sick horses in the middle of the night, galloped sixteen miles and return to Dumfries on errands, and superintended the packing of household goods for shipment to London. That she had at some time done 'all the housemaid work' herself appears in a letter which she wrote to Carlyle, August 9, 1865.[4] A curious confirmation of the fact that Jane herself worked at household tasks appears in a statement used by David Wilson to prove that 'she never really needed to do hard work.' Wilson gives the testimony of the sister-in-law, who lived in the farmhouse at Craigenputtock, to this effect: 'Mrs. Carlyle used often to do nothing at all except read and write for many days. Then she would wake to the fact that the household work was in arrears, and have it all done in a spurt in a few days, overfatiguing herself of course. Then she would rest several days, doing nothing but write letters.'[5] Why should not the household work have gone forward even though the mistress of the house were reading and writing? The answer seems evident. Mrs. Carlyle herself, just

[1] Quoted in Froude's *Thomas Carlyle*, 2. p. 296. [2] *Ibid.*, p. 312.
[3] *Reminiscences*, Norton edition, i. 96.
[4] *New Letters and Memorials*, ii. 334.
[5] *Mr. Froude and Carlyle*, p. 204.

as she and her husband steadily affirm, did a large part of it with her own hands. Carlyle was not blind to the fact that she had a hard life of it on the moors. Writing once to his wife, who was taking a vacation at Moffat, he said, September 7, 1833 : 'Take a little amusement, dear Goody, if thou canst get it. God knows little comes to thee with me, and thou art right patient under it.' [1]

'He was doing his duty with his utmost energy,' writes Froude. 'His wife considered it to be part of hers to conceal from him how hard her own share of the burden had become. Her high principles enabled her to go through with it. . . . Her courage never gave way ; but she had a bad time of it.' [2] Froude clearly understood the motives of the man whose life he portrayed. 'Carlyle was a knight errant, on the noblest quest which can animate a man. He was on the right road, though it was a hard one ; but the lot of the poor lady who was dragged along at his bridle-rein to be the humble minister of his necessities was scarcely less tragic.' [3] In Froude's opinion Carlyle had to work in his own way, and is not to be judged by ordinary standards. 'Selfish he was, if it be selfishness to be ready to sacrifice every person dependent on him, as completely as he sacrificed himself to the aims to which he had resolved to devote his life and talents.' [4] Nor does Froude fail to present the other side of the picture. 'When Carlyle was in good spirits,' he writes, 'his wife had a pleasant time with him. "Ill to live wi'," impatient, irritable over little things, that he always was ; but he was charming, too ; no conversation in my experience ever equalled his ; and unless the evil spirit had possession of him, even his invectives when they burst out piled themselves into metaphors so extravagant that they ended in convulsions of laughter with his whole body

[1] *Thomas Carlyle*, 2. p. 367.
[2] *Ibid.*, p. 266.
[3] *Ibid.*, p. 293.
[4] *Ibid.*, 1. p. 279.

and mind, and then all was well again. Their Spanish studies together were delightful to both.' [1] What Froude has actually done is to represent Carlyle just as he was, 'not one man but many,' a strange combination of inconsistencies, a personality not easily catalogued or understood.

On the evening of December 4, 1831, Carlyle, then in London for a few months, wrote to his brother at Craigenputtock. After giving a brief account of Jane's health, he said, 'any other woman might have gone mad beside me.' [2] They had then been married a little more than five years, three of which had been spent on the Dumfriesshire moors. His remark is entirely in keeping with one of Jane's own statements of twenty-five years later. In a letter to Miss Mary Smith, after telling of the comfort which she derived from likening her first loaf of bread to Benvenuto Cellini's statue of Perseus, Jane added: 'I cannot express what consolation this germ of an idea spread over my uncongenial life during the years we lived at that savage place, where my two immediate predecessors had gone *mad*, and the third had taken to *drink*.' [3]

David Wilson, who, like Alexander Carlyle, never knew Jane, denies the value of the letter to Miss Smith as competent evidence. Its purport, however, is confirmed by reliable personal testimony. Henry Larkin, an intimate and trusted friend of both the Carlyles, knew the truth. He published a valuable account of his experiences through ten years at Cheyne Row in the *British Quarterly Review* of July 1881. It is fitting to close this chapter with his words. 'I have heard her, many times, speak of their life at Craigenputtock with absolute shuddering.'

[1] *Thomas Carlyle*, 2. pp. 49–50.
[2] *Letters of Carlyle*, i. 375.
[3] Froude's *Thomas Carlyle*, 2. pp. 29–31, *note*.

CHAPTER XVII

HARRIET LADY ASHBURTON

FROUDE's account of Carlyle's relations with Harriet Lady Ashburton has been seriously distorted and upon the basis of the distortion unjustly criticised, as anyone can see who will take the time to read his version at first hand. Indeed, Froude's enemies make his account of this affair one of their chief points of attack. 'The most serious injury done to Carlyle by Froude was not, however, by the cumulative effect of venial oversights and selfish indulgences,' writes Crichton-Browne, 'but by the immediate coup administered by the gross wickedness which was openly laid at his door in connection with the "Ashburton episode," as it is called.' [1] Alexander Carlyle, although obviously cautious, writes in a similar vein. 'Mr. Froude,' he says, 'has made a mountain of a molehill in writing of the Lady Harriet episode. Nothing could exceed his exaggeration, inaccuracy, and, I fear I must add misrepresentation, in treating of this affair.' [2]

In attempting to give an adequate account of the affair Froude was confronted with a peculiarly difficult problem. In one form or another the matter was known to the public. It was not possible to omit mention of it in a truthful biography of Carlyle. Froude himself, at the beginning of his task, did not know the full particulars. When he consulted John

[1] *New Letters and Memorials,* i. xlv.

[2] *Ibid.*, 186, *note.*

Forster he was told 'that Lady Ashburton had fallen deeply in love with Carlyle, that Carlyle had behaved nobly, and that Lord Ashburton had been greatly obliged to him.' [1] Carlyle did not explain. 'I tried once,' says Froude, 'to approach the subject with Carlyle himself, but he shrank from it with such signs of distress that I could not speak to him about it again. He had put in my hands the letters and journals which told Mrs. Carlyle's views of it. He left them to speak for themselves.' [2]

On the foundation of the documents Froude gave what seemed to him the truth of the matter. His version is no wild or exaggerated account.

'She recognised the immense superiority of Carlyle to everyone else who came about her [writes Froude of Lady Ashburton]. She admired his intellect, she delighted in his humour. He at first enjoyed the society of a person who never bored him, who had a straight eye, a keen tongue, a disdain of nonsense, a majestic arrogance. As they became more intimate, the great lady affected his imagination. He was gratified at finding himself appreciated by a brilliant woman, who ruled supreme over half of London society. She became Gloriana, Queen of Fairyland, and he, with a true vein of chivalry in him, became her rustic Red Cross Knight, who, if he could, would have gladly led his own *Una* into the same enchanting service. The "Una," unfortunately, had no inclination for such a distinguished bondage.' [3]

From his account of the first meeting of Jane Carlyle and Lady Ashburton to his summary of the entire matter, Froude is eminently restrained and fair. Let us read his words :

'Mrs. Carlyle and Lady Harriet did not suit each other. Mrs. Carlyle did not shut her eyes to the noble lady's distinguished qualities : but even these qualities themselves might be an obstacle to cordial intimacy.

[1] *Relations*, p. 15. [2] *Ibid.*, p. 20. [3] *Thomas Carlyle*, 3. pp. 342–343.

People do not usually take to those who excel in the points where they have themselves been accustomed to reign supreme. Mrs. Carlyle knew that she was far cleverer than the general run of lady adorers who worshipped her husband. She knew also that he was aware of her superiority ; that, by her talent as well as her character, she had a hold upon him entirely her own, and that he only laughed good-naturedly at the homage they paid him. But she could not feel as easy about Lady Harriet. She saw that Carlyle admired her brilliancy, and was gratified by her queenly esteem. To speak of jealousy in the ordinary sense would be extravagantly absurd ; but there are many forms of jealousy, and the position of a wife, when her husband is an intimate friend of another woman, is a difficult and delicate one . . . To a proud, fiery woman like Mrs. Carlyle the sense that Lady Harriet could come in any way between her husband and herself was intolerable.[1]

'The condition into which she had wrought herself through her husband's Gloriana worship would have been ridiculous if it had not been so tragic—tragic even in its absurdity, and tragic in its consequences. Fault there was little on any side. Want of judgment, perhaps, and want of perception ; that was all. Carlyle had formed an acquaintance which he valued and she disliked, because she fancied that a shadow had risen between herself and him, which was taking from her part of what belonged to her.' [2]

I must quote Froude's account of one incident in the relations between the Carlyles and the Ashburtons, as it has been singled out by Alexander Carlyle for especially severe criticism.

'A small incident in the summer of 1856, though a mere trifle in itself, may serve as an illustration of what she had to undergo [writes Froude]. The Carlyles were going for a holiday to Scotland. Lady

[1] *Thomas Carlyle*, 3. pp. 371–373.

[2] *Ibid.*, pp. 385–386.

Ashburton was going also. She had engaged a palatial carriage, which had been made for the Queen and her suite; and she proposed to take the Carlyles down with her. The carriage consisted of a spacious saloon, to which, communicating with it, an ordinary compartment with the usual six seats in it was attached. Lady Ashburton occupied the saloon alone. Mrs. Carlyle, though in bad health and needing rest as much as Lady A., was placed in the compartment with her husband, the family doctor, and Lady A.'s maid, a position perfectly proper for her if she was a dependent, but in which no lady could have been placed whom Lady Ashburton regarded as her own equal in rank. It may be that Mrs. Carlyle chose to have it so herself. But Lady A. ought not to have allowed it, and Carlyle ought not to have allowed it, for it was a thing wrong in itself. One is not surprised to find that when Lady A. offered to take her home in the same way she refused to go. "If there were any companionship in the matter," she said bitterly, when Carlyle communicated Lady A.'s proposal, "it would be different; or if you go back with the Ashburtons it will be different, as then I should be going as part of your luggage without self-responsibility." Carlyle regarded the Ashburtons as "great people," to whom he was under obligations: who had been very good to him: and of whose *train* he in a sense formed a part. Mrs. Carlyle, with her proud, independent, Scotch republican spirit, imperfectly recognised these social distinctions. This it may be said was a trifle, and ought not to have been made much of. But there is no sign that Mrs. Carlyle did make much of what was but a small instance of her general lot. It happens to stand out by being mentioned incidentally.' [1]

Alexander Carlyle refers to the foregoing as 'a

[1] *Thomas Carlyle*, 4. pp. 181–182. Mrs. Carlyle's remark about going as part of the luggage may be found in *Letters and Memorials*, ii. 301.

most doleful and harrowing story of Mrs. Carlyle's hardships and ill-usage on this journey to Scotland.' He asserts that Froude derived his information in regard to the matter solely from Carlyle's 'Reminiscences,' but suppressed 'the all-important statement that Lady Ashburton was, at the time, in very poor health.'[1] The fact is, however, that Froude in a note refers to the very passage in the 'Reminiscences' to which Alexander calls attention. In order to show how closely Froude conforms to his sources, I quote the passage in question :

'In July 1856, as marked in her sad record, may have been about middle of month, we went to Edinburgh ; a blazing day full of dust and tumult,—which I still very well remember. Lady Ashburton had got for herself a grand "Queen's saloon" or *ne-plus-ultra* of railway carriages (made for the Queen some time before) costing no end of money ; Lady sat, or lay, in the "saloon" ; a common six-seat carriage, immediately contiguous, was accessible from it ; in this the Lady had insisted *we* should ride, with her doctor and her maid ; a mere partition, with a door, dividing us from her. The Lady was very good, cheerful though much unwell ; bore all her difficulties and disappointments with an admirable equanimity and magnanimity : but it was physically almost the uncomfortablest journey I ever made.'[2] In the light of those words of Carlyle, Froude's account seems moderate in tone and strictly in harmony with the evidence.

That Froude was right in representing the affair as one which attracted the attention of the public to such an extent as to be a topic of conversation which brought pain to Mrs. Carlyle is now made clear by a letter of hers recently published. In 1849 Jane wrote to her niece in this fashion :

[1] *New Letters and Memorials*, ii. 116, *note*.
[2] *Reminiscences*, Norton edition, i. 204–205.

'I have been to several parties—a dinner at Dickens's last Saturday where I never went before. . . . Before dinner, old Rogers, who ought to have been buried long ago, so old and ill-natured he is grown, said to me pointing to a chair beside him, " sit down my Dear—I want to ask you ; is your husband as much infatuated as ever with Lady Ashburton ? "— " Oh of course," I said *laughing*, " why shouldn't he ? "—" Now—do *you* like her—tell me honestly is she kind to you—as kind as she is to your husband ? " " Why you know it is impossible for *me* to know *how* kind she is to my husband ; but I *can* say she is extremely kind to *me* and I should be stupid and ungrateful if I did *not* like her." " Humph ! (disappointedly) Well ! it is very good of you to like her when she takes away all your husband's company from you—he is always there isn't he ? " " Oh good gracious no ! (still laughing *admirably*) he writes and reads a great deal in his own study." " But he spends all his evenings with her I am told ? " " No—not all—for example you see he is *here* this evening." " Yes," he said in a tone of vexation, " I *see* he is here *this* evening—and *hear* him too—for he has done nothing but talk across the room since he came in." Very devilish old man ! but he got no satisfaction to his devilishness out of *me*—

" On Earth the living
Have much to bear ! " '[1]

Notwithstanding the evidence of such a letter as the foregoing, Leonard Huxley says in the introduction to his volume of Jane's correspondence that these letters ' display no trace of the morbid intensity of feeling which appears in Mrs. Carlyle's journal for 1855–6.' He takes occasion, also, to refer to what he calls Froude's ' strangely perverse account of the domestic incompatibilities between the Carlyles.'

[1] *Jane Welsh Carlyle Letters*, edited by Leonard Huxley, pp. 326–327.

His own version of the affair is much like Froude's. 'We may well surmise the origin of the trouble to have been the almost inevitable rivalry for intellectual leadership between two brilliant women, each accustomed to queen it in her own sphere. Mrs. Carlyle was the superior intellectually; but the scales were weighted for Lady Harriet in her own house by her position as hostess, her social prestige, her unquestioned throne among her friends, the still youthful charm and beauty of the spoilt child of Fortune. Hers was the first word as well as the last.' [1]

Crichton-Browne explains the entire attitude of Mrs. Carlyle as the result of her physical condition, as dementia attendant upon her change of life and upon the fact that she used various drugs and was always in the habit of dosing herself with medicine. 'The true key to Mrs. Carlyle's frame of mind at the time of the Ashburton episode is to be found in her state of health,' he asserts. 'It seems clear that she then passed through a mild, but protracted attack of mental disturbance, which would be technically called on its psychical side climacteric melancholia, and on its physical side neurasthenia.' [2] As Mrs. Carlyle was born July 14, 1801, the physical disturbances consequent upon her change of life certainly must have been protracted. Crichton-Browne overlooks also an important bit of evidence. 'The plaintive and tortured expressions cited [by Froude from her journal] were written in 1855 and 1856; but in 1857 she had largely recovered her equanimity and adopted a very different strain,' writes Sir James, quoting as evidence a letter of Jane's of July 1857. He seems to have lost sight of the fact that Lady Ashburton died May 4, 1857. That Mrs. Carlyle's physical and mental condition should improve within

[1] *Jane Welsh Carlyle Letters*, p. xii.
[2] *New Letters and Memorials*, i. p. liii.

a few weeks after that event surely argues that her unhappiness was closely connected with Lady Harriet.

Sir James, ignoring contemporary correspondence, maintains that no trustworthy record exists of the relations between Carlyle and his wife during the life of Lady Harriet. He rejects Froude's account and in the end dismisses the whole matter as being on Jane's part 'a mere figment of a perverted imagination, the offspring of an excited brain.' [1] Yet there remains the indisputable evidence that the stress and strain was for the Carlyles a hard, stubborn fact. It matters not what physical condition may have caused Mrs. Carlyle to exaggerate the circumstances; the exciting cause was a fact, and all the explanations in the world cannot away with it. Reginald Blunt emphasises this truth in words all the more convincing because he is generally critical of Froude. Although believing with Crichton-Browne that Mrs. Carlyle's condition can 'be traced back to, and based upon, her highly neurotic nature,' Mr. Blunt likewise recognises that to offer such an explanation is not 'in any sense to say that these things were not, *for her*, overwhelmingly real and terrible, or that she would have felt in any way the better for being informed that her physical troubles were the outcome of "cerebral neurasthenia," and her spiritual *malaise* was a "climacteric melancholia!"' [2] In addition to the fact that a medical diagnosis thirty-seven years after the death of a patient should not be accepted too confidently, it is just as reasonable to assert that the fact of Carlyle's association with Lady Ashburton may have aggravated Mrs. Carlyle's mental and physical condition as to maintain that her mental and physical condition coloured her interpretations of the association.

Through the few glimpses into the matter which

[1] *New Letters and Memorials*, i. p. lxv.

[2] *The Wonderful Village*, p. 192.

Carlyle affords us it is evident that he himself knew well enough that to his wife the affair was disagreeable and exasperating. One of his accounts in particular is worthy of mention here. 'In 1844, late Autumn, I was first at the Grange for a few days . . . ; she with me next year, I think ; and there, or at Addiscombe, Alverstoke, Bath House, saw on frequent enough occasions, for twelve years coming, or indeed for nineteen (till the second Lord Ashburton's death), the choicest specimens of English Aristocracy ; and had no difficulty in living with them on free and altogether human terms, and learning from them by degrees whatever *they* had to teach us. *Something* actually, though perhaps not very much, and surely *not* the best. To me, I should say, more than to her, came what lessons there were. . . . *Ay de mi* : it is a mingled yarn, all that of our "Aristocratic" History ; and I need not enter on it here.' [1] Those who recognise the echo of a Shakespearean passage in the last sentence will understand how much and what kind of meaning Carlyle has compressed within brief compass.

In closing I must emphasise the manner in which Alexander Carlyle himself supports Froude's account of this episode. 'That Mrs. Carlyle was sometimes displeased with Lady Harriet cannot be denied,' he writes, 'but that there was anything between them deserving the name of "jealousy," in the ordinary sense of that word, there is no reason to believe. Mrs. Carlyle's ruling passion throughout life was to be

[1] *Reminiscences*, Norton edition, i. 128–129. On p. 235 of the same volume Carlyle, speaking of his wife's restoration to reasonable health in 1864, says : 'This was the *end*, I might say, of by far the most *tragic* part of our Tragedy. Act Fifth, though there lay Death in it, was nothing like so unhappy.' By 'the most *tragic* part of our Tragedy,' the Act Four, Carlyle evidently means the period from 1845 to 1857, which includes the association with the Ashburtons and much of the research preliminary to the writing of 'Frederick.' All students of the Carlyles know that the last twenty months of Mrs. Carlyle's life were perhaps the happiest of their companionship. The fierce fires had burned out, the chief occasions of difference were gone or had become as nothing, her health was improved. It was a brief Indian summer of life.

thought clever ; and it is tolerably plain from her letters and journal that her chief grievance against Lady Harriet arose from chagrin at unexpectedly finding herself much inferior to her in witty and brilliant conversation. . . . She found she was no match at all for this highly gifted Lady ; and she was pained at, and perhaps in a sense, jealous of, the admiration Lady Harriet was wont to receive,'[1] Alexander's words read like a summary of the statements of Froude quoted at the beginning of this chapter. Why say more to vindicate Froude's version, when even his bitterest opponent corroborates it in this fashion? And it should never be forgotten, in any consideration of this affair, that Froude was compelled to found his interpretation upon the documents which were placed in his hands. By holding closely to the burden of these, he was able to steer a safe course through the dangers of contemporary report, and arrive at a conclusion which time has substantiated.

[1] *New Letters and Memorials*, i. 187–188.

CHAPTER XVIII

THE MEANING OF A PHRASE

One of the amusing features in connection with the controversy is the manner in which Froude's enemies have attempted to explain the phrase 'gey ill to deal wi',' and thus minimise its importance. Carlyle's own single reference to it is a note upon one of his wife's letters of December 23, 1835, where he refers to the phrase as 'mother's allocution to me once, in some unreasonable moment of mine.' [1] This explanation would seem, indeed, to imply that the expression was one of little importance; that it was used once by Carlyle's mother, and then ceased to have currency or value. In 1898 David Wilson seized upon the phrase as a means of attacking Froude, whom he charges with harping upon the expression, 'using it as a sort of refrain,' and 'always with the significant change of the word "deal" to "live"—"gey ill to live wi'." At least six times in the course of his narrative does he repeat it in this form.' He then defines the phrase, 'gey ill to deal wi'' as applicable to one who is 'difficult to make a bargain with,' or to 'a man whose decision could not be anticipated.' With Froude's interpretation he has of course no sympathy. '"Gey ill to live wi'," on the other hand, is applicable to a man who is selfish and unreasonable at home, "difficult to live with," and, strange as the fact may seem to those whom Mr. Froude has misled, it does

[1] *Letters and Memorials*, i. 49, *note*.

not appear that anybody ever found Carlyle such a man.' [1]

Passing over for the present Wilson's sweeping statement that nobody ever found Carlyle difficult to live with, I must call attention to the manner in which he misleads those who do not read the 'Thomas Carlyle' for themselves. He asserts that Froude always uses the phrase in the form 'gey ill to live wi'.' In the first place, we must remember that Froude, as editor of the 'Letters and Memorials of Jane Welsh Carlyle,' printed Carlyle's explanatory note in 1883. Furthermore, anyone who turns to page 91 of the fourth volume of the original edition of the biography will find there printed the following quotation from one of Jane's letters to Carlyle's mother: 'I am surprised that so good and sensible a woman as yourself should have brought up her son so badly that he should not know what patience and self-denial mean—merely observing "Thou'st gey ill to deal wi'." Gey ill indeed, and always the longer the worse.' Froude, then, we may conclude, by printing the original version of the phrase, as well as Carlyle's note upon it, seems not to have been intent upon deception.

In Wilson's opinion the manner in which Froude interprets the phrase 'completely alters' its meaning. Nor that only. 'How often it has been written and said, "Carlyle must have been ill to live with, for he confesses it and *his mother said it*,"' writes Wilson, as he proceeds to affirm that the simple truth of the matter is that 'though Mr. Froude says she said it,' she 'never used any language that could bear such a construction.' [2] There can be no doubt whatever that in Froude's opinion the phrase used by Carlyle's mother could bear such a construction. He was so firmly convinced of it that after printing the phrase twice in its original form, together with Carlyle's explanation of its origin, he felt no hesitancy in using it to mean

[1] *Mr. Froude and Carlyle*, p. 254.

[2] *Ibid.*, pp. 254–255.

'difficult to live with.' I find among others the following adaptations of the phrase in the biography :

Carlyle had a strange temper, and from a child was 'gey ill to live with.'[1]

But he knew that he was 'gey ill to live wi'.'[1]

Yet it is perfectly true that Carlyle would have been an unbearable inmate of any house, except his father's, where his will was not absolute. 'Gey ill to live wi',' as his mother said.[1]

Carlyle knew too well 'that he was a perverse mortal to deal with.'[1]

'Ill to live wi',' impatient, irritable over little things, that he always was ; but he was charming too.[1]

Inasmuch as Froude evidently thought 'ill to live with' equivalent in meaning to 'ill to deal with,' it is important to ascertain whether he had any good ground for doing so. He had the documents before him ; he had known Carlyle intimately for years. What did documents and acquaintance reveal ? As early as April 2, 1826, Carlyle was writing to Jane from Hoddam Hill in this fashion : 'They [the members of his family] simply admit that I am *Herr im Hause*, and act on this conviction. Here is no grumbling about my habitudes and whims : if I choose to dine on fire and brimstone, they will cook it for me to their best skill ; thinking only that I am an unintelligible mortal ; perhaps in their secret souls, a kind of humourist, *fascheous* to deal with, but no bad soul after all, and *not* to be dealt with in *any* other way.' Alexander Carlyle himself explains that *fascheous* means 'troublesome.'[2] Again, August 12, 1826, Carlyle writes to Jane in this manner : 'I swear it will break my heart if I make thee unhappy.

[1] *Thomas Carlyle*, 1. pp. 183, 345, 347, 358, and 2. p. 49 respectively. In the edition of 1890 Froude revised all of these passages to conform to the phrase used by Carlyle in *Letters and Memorials*.

[2] *Love Letters*, ii. 263–264.

And yet I am a perverse mortal to deal with, and the best resolutions make shipwreck in the sea of practice.' [1] When in a letter of March 25, 1835, Carlyle informed his mother of the loss of the manuscript of 'The French Revolution,' he wrote: 'If anyone had asked me to throw the writing into the fire, and said, What would I take? I could have given him no definite answer—except that I would be *ill, ill indeed* to deal with.' [2]

It may be well, also, to look at the matter from Jane's point of view. In writing to Carlyle's mother, December 23, 1835, Jane remarked: 'I count this fatness [of a grandchild] a good omen for the whole family; it betokens good nature, which is a quality too rare among us. Those "long, sprawling, ill-put-together" children give early promise of being "gey ill to deal wi'."' [3] Once more, November 28, 1838, she wrote to his mother: 'Carlyle keeps saying he is very bilious, etc., but he looks very passably, is not so desperately "*ill to deal wi'*" as you and I have known him, and has always a good "harl o' health at meal-time."' [4]

Do not such passages as the foregoing reveal that the 'allocution' which Carlyle says his mother 'once' used with reference to 'some unreasonable moment' of his was a permanently established and frequently employed phrase; that it was, in fact, a proverb in the family circle? And that the phrase did not mean among the Carlyles simply what David Wilson would have it mean—'difficult to make a bargain with' or 'difficult to anticipate'—is clear. Even Sir James Crichton-Browne admits that Carlyle was difficult. 'Undoubtedly he was,' writes Sir James, 'but when we come to think of it so are most men except the nincompoops.' [5]

[1] *Love Letters*, ii. 309.
[2] *Letters of Carlyle*, ii. 303.
[3] *Letters and Memorials*, i. 49.
[4] *New Letters and Memorials*, i. 72.
[5] *New Letters and Memorials*, i. p. xxxv. In *Thomas Carlyle*, 4. p. 242, Froude says: 'He never understood that a delicate lady was not like his own robuster kindred, and might be shivered into fiddle-strings while they would only have

In his recent biography of Carlyle David Wilson gives the following version of the origin of the phrase :

'His mother did not speculate about the cause of his sickness [in 1820]. The sight of it was enough to make her see little else. The only flesh he could digest was that of chickens, and she often provided it, 'almost daily,' this summer, as his young sisters remarked. They were in charge of the poultry, and observant of this elder brother, an interesting and petted invalid. The custom thereabouts was for the children to chase and catch and kill whatever bird the farmer's wife had indicated for execution ; and they thought nothing of the screeching that invaded every room and disturbed their brother at his books indoors. It seemed queer to the young barbarians that he objected to the *suffering* of the birds which he was about to *eat* ! So they never heeded his remonstrances, and made the fowls screech more than ever, and mother never bothered, till one day he said :

' "If you cannot stop the screeching, mother, I can stop the eating. I won't eat another chicken if it's killed in that way."

' "Eh !" cried his mother amazed, "What'll thou eat then ?" And presently she added in mockery : "Thou's gey ill to deal wi'," to the huge delight of the listening youngsters who thought she petted him too much, and never let it be forgotten. It became a family joke, misleading to a simple stranger.' [1]

One has to admit that Wilson has there given a pretty little explanation. He informs us that he got it from Carlyle's sister, Janet Hanning, whom he

laughed.' What the Carlyles were like is well expressed by Thomas in a letter of December 2, 1832, to his brother John : 'Alick . . . has lost none of his . . . biting satire, which however his wife is happily too thick-skinned to feel.' See Froude's *Thomas Carlyle*, 2. p. 318. There is no doubt that when Jane Welsh married Carlyle she, too, found it necessary to develop a thick skin.

[1] Wilson's *Carlyle*, i. 198.

visited in Canada. In the biography he does not give the date, but Alexander Carlyle obligingly assures us that it was told to Wilson at the time of Wilson's visit to Canada in 1895.[1] The origin of the phrase is so interesting that one wonders at Wilson's omitting it from his 'Mr. Froude and Carlyle' in 1898. It would have illuminated his chapter on 'Gey Ill to Live Wi',' and saved him from guessing at the meaning of the phrase as he does in that volume. I believe it will be admitted that the origin of the phrase does not determine its meaning, or the extent to which it was employed. The examples which I have given are sufficient, I think, to show exactly what meaning it conveyed to the Carlyles, and how frequently it was used.

It is well known that Carlyle was difficult both to deal with and to live with. No man has expressed the gist of the matter more sharply and more clearly than he himself. On March 4, 1831, he wrote to his brother John to this effect: 'Thou knowest me and my ways. I have decided on living on mine own bottom (*Grund und Boden*) for I can be a guest, beyond two days or so, with no mortal known to me, without mutual grief.'[2] The truth is written all over the story of his life from his dealings with his home people, with Jeffrey, with his wife, down to his last year at Cheyne Row. Those only got along with Carlyle who allowed him to have his own way, who were not in very frequent or intimate contact with him. It

[1] *New Letters of Carlyle*, ii. 162, *note*.

[2] *Letters of Carlyle*, i. 268. In the *Reminiscences*, Norton edition, i. 101, Carlyle utters the rhetorical question, 'Could I be easy to live with?' Margaret Froude, who was in her thirty-first year when Carlyle died, assures me, on the basis of her intimate knowledge of her father's association with Carlyle and his work upon Carlyle's biography, that the phrase 'gey ill to live with' was as commonly used in the Carlyle family circle and the Cheyne Row circle as the phrase 'gey ill to deal with.' Much truth was spoken in both circles before Alexander and Mary Carlyle were as yet born or thought of. John Tyndall, who always represents Carlyle in as favourable a light as possible, gives a clear account of how tenderly he had to be dealt with in his 'Personal Recollections of Carlyle,' *Fortnightly Review*, January 1, 1890.

appears that Froude was singularly fortunate in getting on with Carlyle. Perhaps that fact helps to explain why Carlyle valued his friendship so highly.

Mary Agnes Hamilton's assertion that Froude founded his four-volume biography of Carlyle upon the misquotation of this phrase is only another example of the inanity to which a following of second-hand authority may lead.[1] She takes her information from David Wilson and Alexander Carlyle, apparently without investigation of the matter on her own responsibility. That Froude, a man who had been intimately acquainted with both of the Carlyles for many years, who had been taken into Carlyle's confidence to such an extent that he was chosen to be his literary representative and biographer, and who was in possession of all the documents, should have founded a great work on so slender a foundation is nothing less than ridiculous. Froude based the biography on vaster first-hand knowledge than was possessed by anyone before him or could be by anyone since ; his knowledge rested upon acquaintance extending over more than thirty years, upon private conversations, upon vast collections of documents. He occupied a unique position. Alexander Carlyle knew his uncle for about eighteen months, at the very close of the sage's life. Mary knew him well enough to wish to keep much information about him concealed from the public. David Wilson knew him not at all ; and for one who knew not Joseph to assume the office of censoring the work of Froude will appear sufficiently rash to those who think.

So far as this phrase is concerned, Froude's knowledge was adequate and exact. He knew that upon occasions Carlyle was difficult to deal with, and that the difficulty of dealing with him made him difficult to live with. The expressions ' difficult to deal with ' and ' difficult to live with ' are, as Froude implies,

[1] See her *Thomas Carlyle*, pp. 10–11.

interchangeable. A man who is difficult to deal with is always difficult to live with. Such difficulty was one of the outstanding phases of Carlyle's character, and in their unguarded moments Alexander Carlyle, Charles Eliot Norton, David Wilson, and all others who know anything at all about Carlyle, admit the fact.

CHAPTER XIX

A JOURNAL ENTRY

ONE of the most persistent charges against Froude is that he manipulated documents to suit his own purposes, made omissions without indicating them, did everything, in short, to buttress his own mistaken theories of Carlyle's life. It has been affirmed with emphasis by Alexander Carlyle and Charles Eliot Norton that their own editorial work is to be relied upon, 'trusted implicitly' is the expression used by Alexander Carlyle in a letter to me. David Wilson, strangely enough, adopts one of Froude's practices, and frankly informs his readers that for their 'comfort' he prints without 'the dots of omission in quotations,' leaving them to infer, I suppose, that he also is to be trusted implicitly.[1]

It is already possible to form a preliminary estimate of the value of Alexander Carlyle's editorial work, although a complete evaluation cannot be arrived at without consulting the original manuscripts and such copies of them as remain. We have a right, in examining the work of those who have brought serious charges of inaccuracy against Froude, to demand freedom from the kind of errors which they denounce. The fact is, however, that Norton's editorial work, as well as that of Alexander Carlyle and David Wilson, is marred by numerous errors of the very kind which they charge upon Froude—

[1] See his *Carlyle*, I. p. vi.

misprints, misreadings of manuscripts, mistaken dates. Such errors, of course, any reasonable person who has had experience in editorial work should be ready to excuse. On the other hand, there are methods of editing which must of necessity arouse immediate suspicion. One such method Alexander Carlyle has employed in printing from one of Jane Carlyle's journals.

It appears that Mrs. Carlyle's journal was written in two small notebooks which, for convenience, were labelled No. 1 and No. 2. The record of the first extends from October 21, 1855 to April 14, 1856; that of the second from April 15 to July 5, 1856. Carlyle inserted the leaves of No. 2 at the proper point into his manuscript notebook of his sketch of Jane Welsh Carlyle.

'When Mr. Froude published the "Reminiscences" [writes Alexander] he omitted Mrs. Carlyle's journal, without making any reference to it at all; and reserved it for use apparently at a later date in the "Letters and Memorials." At some date subsequent to the writing of the "Reminiscences," notebook No. 1 (the earlier part of Mrs. Carlyle's journal) was found; but there is no evidence to show that Carlyle intended that it should ever be published . . . he has not annotated it or prepared it in any way for publication; and the natural inference is that he did not wish it to be published. Mr. Froude, however, has taken nearly all his extracts from Mrs. Carlyle's journal out of this notebook No. 1 . . . whilst he cites less than half a page from the part of the journal selected by Carlyle and prepared by him for possible publication.

'Under these circumstances, I have thought it the better plan not to choose extracts from both notebooks, which would necessarily be inconclusive and more or less unsatisfactory, as all "extracts" are, however fairly chosen, but to give one of the notebooks in full—since I have not space to spare for both, were there no other objection. For this purpose I, of course, choose the notebook selected by Carlyle. It follows here, without suppression of more than a proper name or two, exactly as it stands and stood when it first came into my possession.' [1]

Those explanations are straightforward and clear. The last sentence, in particular, is emphatic ; one feels that it is a trifle too insistently specific. When Alexander Carlyle printed the explanations and the journal to which they have reference he could scarcely have foreseen what the publication would lead to. Within a short time after the appearance of the 'New Letters and Memorials' Froude's children published the pamphlet, 'My Relations with Carlyle,' in which it was revealed that there was an entry in the journal which had been suppressed. Alexander Carlyle and Sir James Crichton-Browne made an attempt to supply the words of the missing entry, but succeeded only in giving a version far from accurate. In the same breath they endeavoured to fasten suspicion upon Froude. 'It is in itself suspicious that Froude does not quote the exact words of the incriminating passage in the diary. We are able to supply this omission. This was the entry. "26th June. Nothing to record to-day but two blue marks on the wrist." That is all.' [2]

Alexander's statement that he printed the journal without suppression of more than a proper name or two, exactly as it came into his possession, is just the kind of statement which carries conviction to an innocent reader. It contains much truth. Tennyson has called attention to the danger latent in an utterance which is half a truth. The statement was intended, of course, to react upon Froude. It must not be permitted to count longer against Carlyle's biographer. On the contrary it brings Froude's enemies into condemnation. At this point Alexander

[1] *New Letters and Memorials*, ii. 87–88.

[2] *Nemesis*, p. 69.

Carlyle's good faith towards Froude must stand or fall. Moreover, his treatment of this journal entry forces one to question his integrity as an editor. The imposing array of volumes of Carlyle correspondence which he has edited, however valuable in many ways, cannot be accepted as authoritative until they are collated with the originals by disinterested scholars. Even in the event of collation, it would still be necessary to know in what ways the manuscripts have been altered since leaving Froude's hands. Unfortunately, such knowledge, except in a few instances, cannot now be obtained.

Happily the circumstances in regard to this journal entry are not in doubt. The correspondence between Froude and Mary about the journal I have given in a previous chapter.[1] I am also able to present an extract from an hitherto unpublished letter of Froude to John Skelton in explanation of the entry. On May 4, 1883, in reply to an inquiry, Froude wrote Skelton to this effect : 'The mystery of the diary is that Carlyle was once (I believe only once) tempted into physical violence with the poor lady. He had transcribed the record of it which she had made, and it came to me written out without a word of the Lady Harriet entries to explain. Something was wanted to make intelligible the estrangement which followed. I omitted the story, and substituted for it what is now in the text [of the 'Letters and Memorials of Jane Welsh Carlyle, ii. 273–275]. In Carlyle's will the manuscript is described as *not yet fit for publication* and as *put into my hands to complete.* He leaves me all other documents elucidatory of the letters to be used as I please, and desires that my judgment shall be taken as his own. I mean to rest entirely on these words. I will give no explanation, for I cannot give any without showing that something is concealed.'

[1] See pp. 93–94.

Alexander Carlyle knew of the correspondence between his wife and Froude. He knew that the passage in question had been removed from the journal. He did not hint such knowledge, however, until he was driven into the open by an article in the *Contemporary Review* [1] by Ronald McNeill, now Lord Cushendun, and by the publication of 'My Relations with Carlyle.' Unless he had been so constrained the facts would, in all probability, never have been known. To say the least, it was disingenuous to assure the public that the journal was printed just as it was when it came into his possession. In reply to my criticism of his action, he wrote under date of November 27, 1926, as follows: 'What I say about my copy of Mrs. Carlyle's journal in "New Letters and Memorials," ii. 88, is accurately true: in fact, it is the truth, the whole truth, and nothing but the truth. I did not put omission marks, because I made no omissions, there being nothing to omit. I copied from the original, from which the record of the blue marks had been removed a good many years before. Froude had made it a condition that that record should not be published, and the only sure way of running no risk of its being published by some one some day or other, was to destroy it.' [2]

[1] 'The New Carlyle Letters: A Vindication of Froude,' by Ronald McNeill, *Contemporary Review*, June 1903. The following extract is pertinent: 'Do these words ["exactly as it stands and stood when it came into my possession"] imply a consciousness on the part of Mr. Alexander Carlyle that the document was mutilated before it came into his hands? If so, whom does he suspect of having tampered with it? . . . It is not easy to understand how this significant entry can have been erased from the original journal without Mr. Alexander Carlyle's knowledge; and considering the amount of righteous indignation which he and his fellow-detractors of Froude have expended over the latter's supposed "garblings," "suppression," and other similar iniquities, the circumstance is one that seems to require some explanation.'

[2] This is only a repetition of what was said in 1903. In the *Contemporary Review* of July 1903, under the heading 'Carlyle and Froude,' Crichton-Browne replied to Ronald McNeill's statements about the journal entry as 'a pitiable perversion of the facts.' Sir James maintains that it was Froude who suppressed the entry, 'and that he did so out of respect not for the reputation of Carlyle, for which he cared little, but for that of Mrs. Carlyle, who had bewitched him. He required from Mrs. Alexander Carlyle, on handing over to

When the entries were published in the 'New Letters and Memorials,' the facts should have been stated. At any rate, the public should not have been duped into believing that the exact record was given, nor should the use of the journal material by Froude have been made to appear unfair and contrary to Carlyle's wishes. The fact is that Froude protected Carlyle at this point. Quite apart from the omission of the entry in regard to the blue marks, Alexander's statement about the journal's being printed without the omission of more than a proper name or two is not correct. Here is one portion as he prints it :

'27th June.—Went with Geraldine to Hampstead, preferring to be broiled on a Heath to being broiled in Cheyne Row. Dinner at The Spaniards, and came home to tea, dead weary and a good many shillings out of pocket.

'28th June.—Dined at Lord Goderich's with Sir Colin Campbell, whom I hadn't seen for some fifteen years. He is not much of a hero that. In fact heroes are very scarce.' [1]

The actual text of the perfect copy made by Mary Carlyle for Froude reads thus :

'26th. The chief interest of today expressed in blue marks on my wrists !

'27th. Went with Geraldine to Hampstead ; preferring to be broiled on a heath to being broiled in

her the literary control of the "Reminiscences," an undertaking that she would not publish this passage, and it was by her hand, in fulfilment of her promise to Froude, that it was cut out of the journal, which has therefore been published exactly as it stands and stood when it came into her husband's possession on her death.' The publication of Froude's letter to Mary enables the public to judge between McNeill and Crichton-Browne. Alexander Carlyle's specious statement that he published the journal exactly as it was when it came into his possession needs no further comment. Mary Carlyle's ungracious half-promise to Froude was kept only in so far as it related to the suppression of the offending entry. In passing over the 'Reminiscences' and the correspondence of Carlyle to Charles Eliot Norton for editing she was deliberately attacking the good faith of Froude and furnishing occasion for further controversy. Froude silently endured the criticism which followed in the wake of Norton's publications.

[1] *New Letters and Memorials*, ii. 107.

Cheyne Row. Dined at *The Spaniard* ; and came home to tea,—dead-weary, and a good many shillings out of pocket.

'28th. Dined at Lord Goderich's with Sir Colin Campbell, whom I hadn't seen for some fifteen years. He is not much of a *Hero*, that ; he may be a brave man, and a clever man *at his trade* ; but beyond soldiering, he knows nothing : and is nothing I think. In fact, Heroes are very scarce.'

A facsimile of the manuscript is given opposite page 93. Comparison of the versions will be seen by those who are familiar with the Carlyles to be 'significant of much.'[1] A reference also to the facsimile of a portion of Mrs. Carlyle's journal given opposite page 106 of the 'New Letters and Memorials' will convince anyone that the editorial work of Alexander Carlyle does not have the literal accuracy which he demands of Froude.

The manner in which this journal has been printed convinces me that it is unsafe for a scholar to employ as authoritative the versions of any documents printed by Charles Eliot Norton or Alexander Carlyle in cases where the versions differ from the texts given by Froude. A knowledge of the matter behind the numerous marks of omission in the texts of Norton and Alexander Carlyle would help to decide many issues in question between Froude and his enemies.[2] I applied to Alexander Carlyle for permission to collate the Carlyle documents. Such permission he refused to grant, but he did offer to collate for me such passages as I would to submit to him. I frankly

[1] Jane, of course, heard enough from Carlyle about 'heroes and hero-worship.' She excelled in such remarks as those recorded on June 28. In a letter to his wife Carlyle once wrote : 'And don't mind Mrs. Henry, or take any "wits" from her that you don't return with interest. I should think you might be trusted for the rate of interest, you creosote incarnate, or spiritual "essence of soot."'

[2] For example, the matter omitted from letter 165, *New Letters and Memorials*, ii. 135, and the passage omitted from Norton's edition of the *Reminiscences*, i. 210, would undoubtedly be valuable to students of Carlyle.

told him that such collation would be of no use to me, or to any other scholar. The truth is that until the entire body of Carlyle manuscripts is edited by disinterested editors it is futile for the enemies of Froude to denounce him upon the authority of the texts edited by Charles Eliot Norton and Alexander Carlyle.

CHAPTER XX

AN INJUNCTION TO BURN

Of the same nature as his statements about the journal entry are those which Alexander Carlyle makes in regard to one of Carlyle's injunctions to burn the love-letters of Jane Welsh. 'Amongst the papers which Miss Mary Aitken too confidingly lent to Froude,' writes Alexander, 'were the love-letters which passed between Carlyle and Miss Welsh before their marriage, and which would assuredly never have been seen by his or any other eye, had she noticed what Carlyle had written respecting them. "*My strict command now is, Burn them, if ever found. Let no third party read them; let no printing of them or any part of them be ever thought of by those who love me.*" And yet in defiance of this heart-felt and, we may say, death-bed conjuration, Froude opened the packet, read all the letters, and published a selection of them in the "Early Life." He never ventured to assert that there had been any verbal withdrawal of this most earnest command, and his conduct in ignoring it may be left to the judgment of right-minded men.' [1]

Evidence which I am able to present for the first time does not support this emphatic statement. I have in my possession a copy of this injunction in Mary Carlyle's handwriting, which proves beyond all doubt that she knew what Carlyle had written about

[1] *Nemesis*, p. 109. The italics are Alexander's. The only word in this portion underlined by Carlyle is 'printing.'

[illegible]

but not often. — I wonder now what has become of all those Haddington Letters to and from. Not a letter of hers did I ever destroy; and yet not one, of all those years, can I now find. 'Letter III,' a scrap in pencil soon to be given, is proof of my having tried to keep them; and yet they are all gone, — till 1841 not a word of hers to me discoverable. I suppose she herself destroyed them, in her sortings about the House; she had a constant contempt for her own Letters, a great aversion to see them lying access=ible to the chance of foreign eyes; and would at once burn them. Mine to her I certainly once saw, about 1850, all folded out by her, and stitched into a kind of book (dear loving soul! — ah me, ah me!) — but these also, now when I might have searched them for dates at least, could I have borne to read them, are undiscoverable.+ My strict command now is, "Burn them if ever found. Let no third party read them; let no printing of them, or any part of them, be ever thought of by those who love me!" — [since [illegible]d here, — Decr 1869]

[illegible]

FACSIMILE OF MARY CARLYLE'S COPY OF CARLYLE'S NOTATIONS IN REGARD TO THE LOVE LETTERS.

The original of this facsimile has been in the possession of the Froude family from the time that Carlyle gave it to J. A. Froude

the love-letters. Nor is that all. There appears upon the manuscript a notation, also in her handwriting, to the effect that the letters in question were found December 1869. The portion of manuscript, a facsimile of which is given opposite this page, reads as follows :

'I wonder now what has become of all those Haddington Letters to and from. Not a letter of hers did I ever destroy ; and yet not one, of all those years, can I now find. "Letter III," a scrap in pencil soon to be given, is proof of *my* having tried to keep them ; and yet they are all gone,—till 1841 not a word of hers to me discoverable. I suppose she herself destroyed them, in her sortings about the House ; she had a constant contempt for her own Letters, a great aversion to see them lying accessible to the chance of foreign eyes ; and would at once burn them. Mine *to her* I certainly once saw, about 1850, all folded out by Her, and stitched into a kind of *book* (dear loving soul !—ah me, ah me !)—but these also, now when I might have searched them for *dates* at least, could I have borne to read them, are undiscoverable. My strict command now is, "Burn them if ever found. Let no third party read them ; let no *printing* of them, or any part of them, be ever thought of by those who love me !"—[since found here,—Decr. 1869].'

This document throws clear light upon Carlyle's methods. He was ever hesitating in this manner ; ever making rash vows which he seldom performed. However much he may have meant to burn the letters at the time of writing the injunction, the fact remains that he did not do so when they finally came to hand. Instead, he added a note in recognition of their discovery. He himself proceeded to examine the letters, made notations upon some of them, and later handed them over to Froude. What further proof is needed that after all he did not wish the destruction of the correspondence, but was eager and willing to have such use made of it as Froude deemed proper?

Carlyle's injunction to burn was written either in 1866, before he went to Mentone, or in 1868, when he was again occupied with his wife's letters.[1] Miss Margaret Froude tells me that the bundle of which the letters of 1825 formed a part were sent to her father either with the rest of Mrs. Carlyle's letters in 1871, or with Mrs. Carlyle's correspondence in 1873. On the back of the letter of confession Carlyle had written 'Don't copy.' This injunction he later marked through, and left the whole matter of decision to his biographer. Froude did not insert the letter. He gave a summary with brief quotations in the 'Thomas Carlyle,' 1. p. 306. We must not fail to keep in mind that after Carlyle's death Froude was left to work largely upon his own responsibility. We shall perhaps never know exactly to what extent, or in what ways, Mary and Alexander Carlyle hindered him, and actually concealed from him information which he should have had.

Mention has been made previously of material which Carlyle is alleged to have kept from Froude.

[1] Froude in *Thomas Carlyle*, 4. p. 382, gives the following entry from Carlyle's journal, September 28, 1869: 'The *task* in a sort done, Mary finishing my notes of 1866 this very day; I shrinking for weeks past from any revisal or interference there as a thing evidently hurtful, evidently antisomnial even, in my present state of nerves. Essentially, however, her "Letters and Memorials" are saved, thank God! and I hope to settle the details calmly, too.' One is forced to believe that Carlyle meant to have the *Letters and Memorials* of his wife published 'with whatever other fartherences and elucidations' were possible. Otherwise what purpose would have been served in thanking God that the papers were saved only that they might be destroyed? The injunction to burn once attached by Carlyle to the sketch of his wife which Froude printed in *Reminiscences* appears to be of the same nature as all of his other remarks about destroying material. The fact is that Carlyle was diligently preparing all of the documents for eventual publication. In his trenchant review of *The Nemesis of Froude* in *Longman's Magazine*, November 1903, Andrew Lang points out that Carlyle's assertions must be taken with the proper grain of salt. Says Mr. Lang: 'On February 6, 1873 Carlyle declares in his will that he is "for the last four years imperatively forbidden to write farther on it, or even to look farther into it." When did he break this imperative prohibition?' Lang's remarks are directed towards the assertion of Alexander Carlyle that the manuscripts of Mrs. Carlyle's letters and the sketch of her life 'contain notes by Carlyle dated 1873.' See *Nemesis*, p. 82.

On April 25, 1886, Mary wrote a letter to Froude, one sentence of which reads thus: 'But I may mention that I have by me a packet of letters which I have read and which were given to me to keep because they were too private to be seen by you.'[1] If, as Mary asserts, Carlyle withheld the letters from Froude, it leaves him under the cloud of not having been straightforward and above board with his biographer. Would not such action have convicted him of the very kind of concealment and duplicity of which Alexander Carlyle, Charles Eliot Norton, and David Wilson claim he was incapable? Mary's assertion, if true, would go far towards branding Carlyle as a hypocrite, now commissioning Froude to write his biography, again personally delivering to him so much material and, according to Mary, sending so much by her, always urging Froude to tell the truth, and through it all deliberately concealing letters of vital importance. Such a suggestion, it must be said to his credit, Froude repelled with scorn. He always maintained that toward him Carlyle was incapable of treachery. It would be better for the honour of Carlyle if the story of the reserved letters were of a piece with the account of the injunction to burn.

[1] 'These,' says David Wilson, 'were Mrs. Carlyle's letters about Lady Ashburton.' See his *Mr. Froude and Carlyle*, p. 279. Alexander Carlyle does not mention this fact in *The Nemesis of Froude*. He does speak there about Carlyle's letters to Lady Harriet, but, as he was not cognisant of the exact facts about them, his account is inaccurate. See pp. 49–50 of the *Nemesis*. To the best of my knowledge Mrs. Carlyle's letters about Lady Ashburton have never been published. It is to be regretted that Alexander Carlyle has not favoured the public with them.

CHAPTER XXI

THE SEXUAL QUESTION

Any treatment of the Froude-Carlyle controversy which omitted reference to the sex relations of the Carlyles would be incomplete. Inasmuch as the topic has gathered about itself a considerable literature—a literature not of my making—and as it is now a matter of history upon which scholars desire a verdict, I shall present a brief summary of the best available evidence. It is easier to do this now than it would have been a half-century ago. The state of mind has changed since Froude wrote his biography of Carlyle. Matters of sex are no longer taboo. In many ways this change of attitude is wholesome. Sex is a very old and a very important matter, and humanity has suffered many ills through ignorance of it. Over-emphasis, however, is as bad as under-emphasis. With reference to the Carlyles, therefore, I shall discuss the subject no farther than is necessary to clear away the penumbra of gossip and contention which has helped to obscure it.

Froude's enemies endeavour to suppress discussion of the subject by calling any reference to it filthy and obscene. Indeed, their vehemence points to some strong desire to keep the matter quiet. One finds it difficult, however, to sympathise with the exaggerated zeal of the opposition. Ruskin's case elicits no such virulence. Ruskin is known to have been sexually incompetent—his marriage to Euphemia Chalmers

Gray was annulled for this reason—but no charges of obscenity have ever been made against those who refer to the facts, nor has Ruskin's reputation as a writer ever suffered in consequence. Any harm that has come to Ruskin has come through whisperings incident upon half-knowledge. It is a painful commentary upon English biography—'bless its mealy mouth!'—that no life of Ruskin contains a brief statement of the truth. A single sentence to the effect that Ruskin was sexually incompetent would have illuminated a wide area of his life, and placed it forever beyond the whisper of gossip and surmise.

For a good many years after the publication of Froude's 'Carlyle' there was no public discussion of the sexual relations of the Carlyles. In 1898 David Wilson avoided the subject in his 'Mr. Froude and Carlyle.' 'It passed over the sexual question in silence,' he observes, 'not because I supposed there was any truth in that part of Mr. Froude's story, but because it seemed best to say nothing about such things. "Froude dealt with it indirectly—let us do likewise," was Prof. Norton's exhortation to me in 1895. Mr. Alexander Carlyle was resolute to the same effect, and till 1903 it seemed likely that this method would succeed, and the filthy libel lapse into oblivion without having ever been explicitly mentioned.' [1]

The publication of Froude's 'My Relations with Carlyle' brought the matter squarely into the open. The lamentations of Alexander Carlyle, Sir James Crichton-Browne, and David Wilson over the publication of this pamphlet are natural and sincere, and perhaps the more heart-felt because Froude's enemies now realise that they themselves are responsible. The pamphlet would never have been printed had not the attack upon Froude been pressed so persistently and so bitterly. The fact is that Froude, like Norton,

[1] *The Truth about Carlyle*, p. 29.

felt that the matter should be dealt with indirectly. And that is exactly the way Froude did deal with it when he wrote the biography. He wrote so that those who were cognisant of the truth would understand, and those who were ignorant would not. Froude had clearly in mind Carlyle's own injunction. 'The biographer has this problem set before him: to delineate a likeness of the earthly pilgrimage of a man. He will compute well what profit is in it, and what disprofit; under which latter head this of offending any of his fellow-creatures will surely not be forgotten. Nay, this may so swell the disprofit side of his account, that many an enterprise of biography otherwise promising shall require to be renounced. But once taken up, the rule before all rule is to do *it*, not to do the ghost of it. In speaking of the man and men he has to do with, he will of course keep all his charities about him, but all his eyes open. Far be it from him to set down aught *untrue;* nay, not to abstain from, and leave in oblivion, much that is true.' It would almost seem that Carlyle was thinking of his own biography when he wrote those words, and it is certain that Froude had them before him when he was writing about Carlyle. It was the sexual question which Froude selected as the matter to be abstained from and left in oblivion.

In the biography, therefore, Froude passed lightly over the entire matter. He was quite aware that London had been for years full of rumours that the marriage of the Carlyles was unsatisfactory from the sexual point of view.[1] If human testimony is to be

[1] In 1903 William H. Mallock wrote: 'There are "eminent men" and "highly gifted women" still living, and still prominent in London, to whom the facts now revealed [in Froude's *Relations*] to the general public were matters from the first, of private and intimate notoriety, and that Mr. Froude's assailants should have known nothing about them shows how ill-equipped they were for dealing with the matter in question.' See 'The Secret of Carlyle's Life,' *Fortnightly Review*, lxxx. 191. The pages of David Wilson, Sir James Crichton-Browne, and others bear witness to the prevalence of the knowledge about the unsatisfactory sexual life of the Carlyles. When I was discussing the matter

relied upon at all, there can be no doubt that Mrs. Carlyle spoke freely of her troubles to several of her intimate female friends. Knowing this, Froude made such casual references as would enable the Carlyle circle to understand that he too was cognisant of the reports. In 'My Relations with Carlyle' he speaks openly and yet with reserve. He offers no physiological explanations. He merely states, on the authority of Geraldine Jewsbury, that 'Carlyle was one of those persons who ought never to have married.' In brief, he makes it clear that the sexual relations between the Carlyles were not satisfactory, and that this fact was at the bottom of all the quarrels and all the unhappiness. Mrs. Carlyle had longed for children, he asserts, and children were denied to her.[1] That is the end of the matter so far as Froude is concerned.

When Froude's pamphlet was published in 1903 Sir James Crichton-Browne attempted to stem the rising tide of opinion in favour of Carlyle's biographer. His article in the *British Medical Journal* of June 27, 1903, is one of the curiosities of medical literature. In it, Sir James denies all of Froude's statements, and brings forward a variety of evidence as to the intimate relations of the Carlyles such as had never before been assembled in print. He affirms that Froude, on the authority of Geraldine Jewsbury alone, brands Carlyle as a Narses. 'Bold, filthy, scurrilous assertions like Froude's respecting Carlyle's impotence may mislead the unwary and the ignorant,' he remarks in closing, 'but they will scarcely deceive the

with the historian and biographer Sir George Forrest (1846–1926) at his home in Iffley, Oxfordshire, in August 1925, he said : 'Those who were at all intimate with the Carlyles knew that Froude was telling the truth about Carlyle's sexual incompetency. Jane Octavia Brookfield had the story from Mrs. Carlyle herself, as did Geraldine Jewsbury. The facts are as well authenticated as any such facts can be.' Those who were acquainted with Sir George know what a fund of information he had about the Victorian celebrities.

[1] *Relations*, p. 21.

elect who have been admitted into the communion of medical science.' [1]

Sir James himself is bold enough to assure the public that the medical profession has given judgment in his favour. 'My article,' he writes, 'must have reached the hands at any rate of more than twenty thousand medical men, and I am entitled to say that judgment was given in my favour. I received many letters from professional brethren expressing complete agreement with the conclusion at which I arrived, and not one dissenting from it. The article, though it appeared in a strictly medical journal and was addressed to medical men, was quoted by the lay press and made the subject of comment there, and there too it was generally acknowledged that I had made out my case.' [2] One can only say that Sir James is delightfully confident. One feels a desire to know how he arrived at his knowledge of the opinion of twenty thousand medical men. What his correspondents may have said to him I do not know. I believe he has not yet published their letters. I do know, however, what the medical press said about him and his article.

The *British Medical Journal* does not by any means reveal the unanimity of opinion which he claims. Editorially, the *Medical Times and Hospital Gazette* of July 4, 1903, protests against the 'wantonly indecent controversy concerning the sexual capabilities of Thomas Carlyle and his wife,' and asserts that 'the flame of controversy has unhappily been fanned by

[1] In 1903 William H. Mallock wrote in the *Fortnightly Review*, lxxx. 192, as follows: 'In the imputation referred to there [in Froude's *Relations*] there is nothing base whatever. It is the imputation of no moral fault, but of a purely natural defect. It is an imputation of precisely the same kind as that which Sir James makes against the state of Mrs. Carlyle's nerves. The only baseness possible in such a case would not be in making such an imputation, or even in making it erroneously; but in making it knowing it to be erroneous. The idea that Mr. Froude, whom Sir James admits to have been an honourable man in the ordinary affairs of life, was guilty of this conduct, is an idea too absurd to require refutation or discussion.'

[2] *The Truth about Carlyle*, pp. 10–11.

the wild incursion into the matter of perhaps the most injudicious writer of the present day.' The *British Medical Journal* in its issue of July 4, 1903, expresses the opinion editorially that Froude's children 'cannot fairly be blamed for seeking to vindicate the character of their father.' The writer points out that Sir James relies largely upon gossip, some of which seems irrelevant. One skilful thrust is aimed at his inconsistency. 'Sir James complains that Froude did not test Miss Jewsbury's statement, and points out that "many medical men who had attended Mrs. Carlyle were accessible." This strikes one as a somewhat remarkable suggestion from a writer who a little further on makes a fine display of indignation at the mere thought of Sir Richard Quain having committed an act infamous in a professional respect by divulging a secret confided to him by a patient.' In this same issue the *British Medical Journal* published extracts from the letters of four physicians in regard to Sir James's article, all of them hostile. The *Medical Press* of July 8, 1903, objects to his 'peculiarly bitter and in many ways unfortunate and unsatisfactory reply to Froude's imputation.' [1]

Froude's enemies have always vehemently asserted that the stories about the sexual relations of the Carlyles originated with Geraldine Jewsbury and rest upon her authority alone. They have written many unkind and unjust things about her in their attempts to discredit her testimony. She need not, however, remain longer under the opprobrium of being an irresponsible and neurotic gossip. From a source quite independent of Miss Jewsbury came corroboration of her story as nearly equivalent to absolute proof as can now perhaps ever be expected. The corroboration came from John Ruskin, whose veracity cannot be questioned. Froude himself was surprised

[1] The articles from the medical journals are printed among the illustrative documents on pp. 340–352 of this volume.

to find that Ruskin knew all about the matter. It is now permissible to say that W. J. Richardson, M.D., of Tunbridge Wells, while attending Mrs. Carlyle during one of her serious illnesses, suspected upon examination that the usual marital relations had not occurred. She admitted the fact to him, and spoke of the distress it was to her to be denied the happiness of motherhood. This information Dr. Richardson, in confidence, imparted to his aunt Mrs. Margaret Cox Ruskin and her son John, his own first cousin. His doing so, even to near relatives, was doubtless a breach of medical etiquette; but there were circumstances which made the communication excusable. Froude, out of deference to Ruskin's kinsman, generously refrained from using the information, although his doing so would have silenced his enemies. When the matter came again to public attention in 1903, Mrs. Joan Ruskin Severn verified Ruskin's statements over her own signature.

When the 'Reminiscences' were published and Mary Carlyle attacked Froude in *The Times*, Ruskin wrote Froude one of his most characteristic notes, hitherto unpublished. It follows:

'You were ABSOLUTELY right to publish the Reminiscences, and Miss Aitken was a mere selfish and proud and cowardly Scotch Molly Foulservice. I had quarrelled with her myself long before *you* did. Ever your *un*repentant RUSKIN.'

'It has often seemed to me strange,' wrote Mrs. Joan Ruskin Severn to Margaret Froude, June 28, 1903, 'that we never had any communication with Mary Carlyle after her uncle's death; possibly he (J. R.) may have spoken strongly to her!' That he did, the little note to Froude now makes certain. Ruskin's knowledge of the facts is the clue to his strong championship of Froude's work, and his hostile attitude towards Charles Eliot Norton. It enables us to understand, too, the remarks of Sir Edward Cook in his 'Life of Ruskin' and in the Library Edition of Ruskin's 'Works,' as well as the statements of W. G. Collingwood in his biography of Ruskin.[1]

In the autumn of 1886 Froude visited Ruskin at Brantwood.

'They had much talk about Carlyle [writes Cook], for the storm which Froude's "Life" and subsidiary publications had caused was then raging. Ruskin was in the difficult position of being the attached friend both of Froude and of his antagonist in this matter, Professor Norton. His sympathies were, as has been said already, with Froude, whose picture of Carlyle was, he held, in the main true, and therefore what the subject of it would have desired. In some respects, however, he thought there was still something more to be said, and he proposed to write on the subject himself—partly to vindicate, and partly to supplement Froude. "You are the only person," Froude had written, "to whom I can talk about Carlyle, or from whom I could either seek advice or expect it." And at a later time he said: "Your assurance that on the whole the selection which I made from Carlyle's letters is a good one, has given me more pleasure than anything which I have yet heard on that subject. . . . I cannot tell you how I feel your own willingness to clear the sky for me in my own lifetime." And again, "Your proposal to bring out a small volume on Carlyle simply delights me." This was in 1889, and Ruskin's working days were then almost at an end. The little volume was

[1] Collingwood writes: 'It added not a little to the misfortunes of the time [of Ruskin's failing health in the latter 1880's] that two of his best friends in the outside world were disputing over a third. By nobody more than by Mr. Ruskin was Carlyle's reputation valued, and yet he acknowledged that Mr. Froude was but telling the truth in the revelations which so surprised the public; and much as he admired Mr. Norton he deprecated the attack on Carlyle's literary executor, whose motives he understood and approved.' *Life of Ruskin*, p. 387, Houghton Mifflin Company's one-volume edition of 1902.

never to be written, and the personal mention of Carlyle in " Præterita " is only incidental.' [1]

Ruskin did attempt to write something in defence of Froude's intimation that to Mrs. Carlyle marriage never brought happiness and the fulfilment of her wishes. He even proceeded so far as to have an article put into type. 'I remember seeing a proof sheet,' wrote Mrs. Joan Ruskin Severn to Margaret Froude, June 28, 1903, 'which was so violent that it was destroyed with the intention of saying his say in calmer language.'

The evidence presented to disprove Froude's position is doubtful. In 1903 a statement was made to the effect that the two unmarried daughters of Carlyle's sister Jean, who were then living at Dumfries, recalled 'that twice whilst at Craigenputtock Mrs. Carlyle consulted their mother, the late Mrs. Aitken, about her maternal hopes, which alas ! came to nought ; and the late Mrs. Alexander Carlyle, when, on her aunt's death, she became her uncle's companion, was much touched to find in a drawer at Cheyne Row a little bundle of baby clothes made by Mrs. Carlyle's own hands.' [2] It is important to

[1] Ruskin's *Works*, Library edition, xxxv. pp. xxiv.–xxv. See also xxxiii. p. lii. and xxxvi. pp. xcii.–xciii. of the same edition. January 31, 1883, Ruskin wrote as follows to Miss Jessie Leete : 'Nobody has any business with Carlyle's ways to his wife—or hers to him ;—but you may depend on it—whatever Froude says, or does, about him will be right ; in the meantime, the faultless public had better enjoy its own domestic bliss in peace. As for depreciating Carlyle because he had faults, the little phosphorescent polypes might as well depreciate the Dog Star because it wasn't the Polestar.' Library edition of *Works*, xxxvii. p. 436.

[2] *Nemesis*, pp. 63–64. This is repeated by David Wilson in *The Truth about Carlyle*, p. 47. The report originated with Sir James Crichton-Browne, who wrote in the *British Medical Journal*, June 27, 1903, as follows : 'Miss Annie Aitken and Miss Margaret Aitken, now living in Dumfries, inform me that upon two separate occasions Mrs. Carlyle when at Craigenputtock intimated to their mother, the late Mrs. Aitken, that she was in the family way, and consulted her about her preparations. Carlyle, Mrs. Aitken used to add, took it very quietly and seemed grieved when nothing came of it. Miss Mary Aitken, afterwards Mrs. Alexander Carlyle, when on her aunt's death she became her uncle's housekeeper, was much touched to find in a drawer at Cheyne Row a little bundle of baby clothes made by Mrs. Carlyle's own hands.' For some reason, the two Misses Aitken did not communicate their information to their cousin Alexander Carlyle, but chose rather to give it to Sir James.

remember that in the matter of this evidence three persons stand between the public and Jane Carlyle. It should hardly be necessary to call attention to the fact that to consult one about 'maternal hopes' need not by any means be taken as evidence of pregnancy. Thousands of sterile women, and women with impotent husbands, annually consult physicians and others about 'maternal hopes.' So far as 'the bundle of baby clothes' is concerned, they were in all likelihood a portion of Jane's own infant wardrobe, some of the articles mentioned by Carlyle in the 'Reminiscences' as 'memorials of her infant self,' among them 'her own christening cap.'[1] Elizabeth Drew recognises the uncertainty of such evidence, and thinks that it does not amount to actual proof.[2]

Similarly doubtful is Sir James Crichton-Browne's report of Madame Venturi's interview with Sir Richard Quain, when the latter physician was in attendance upon Mrs. Carlyle.[3] 'I know not,' writes David Wilson, 'how Sir James was informed of what was said to Mrs. Venturi, but I have myself heard it from a gentleman unwilling to be named, who said to me that Mrs. Venturi told it to his wife, from whom he heard it. He added that Mrs. Venturi said Dr. Quain replied that he did not dare to speak to Carlyle himself about it, and she rejoined: "Then how can you expect me to do it, being a woman?" She was an English lady of superior intellect and character, and on very intimate terms with the Carlyles. The story is quite a likely one, and may safely be believed on her word alone.'[4] That is the kind of evidence

[1] See Norton edition, i. 210.

[2] See her *Jane Welsh and Jane Carlyle*, pp. 139–140.

[3] See Crichton-Browne's article in the *British Medical Journal*, June 27, 1903.

[4] *The Truth about Carlyle*, pp. 54–55. Sir James refers the interview to 'sometime' in the 1860's. A note by Carlyle himself in *Letters and Memorials*, iii. 271, identifies the beginning of the acquaintance with the Venturis with the middle of the year 1865. Carlyle was then in his seventieth, Mrs. Carlyle in her sixty-fourth year and in feeble health! As Mrs. Carlyle died in April 1866, her acquaintance with Madame Venturi could not have become 'very intimate.'

which David Wilson, lawyer and judge, asks intelligent people to believe. Nevertheless, he does not hesitate to find fault with Froude for giving credence to Geraldine Jewsbury, or refrain from discrediting the manner in which Froude makes use of correspondence.[1]

The most important evidence bearing upon the sexual relations of the Carlyles is that brought forward by Alexander.[2] 'In the summer of 1831,' he writes, 'her [Jane's] sister-in-law Miss Jean Aitken[3] staid with her during Carlyle's absence, in London, and helped her to prepare a tiny wardrobe for the expected little new-comer. But the hardships of Mrs. Carlyle's journey to London, and in London, induced a relapse to her former condition. Just before she started on this trip to London Carlyle wrote to her, with anxious solicitude, these impressive and significant words: "Take every care of thyself, Wifekin: there is more than thy own which thou carriest with thee."' One observes that since the publication of 'The Nemesis of Froude' in the preceding year, Alexander has added a detail to Mrs. Aitken's testimony. The account in the 'Nemesis' informs us only that Mrs. Aitken was 'twice consulted' by Mrs. Carlyle about her 'maternal hopes'; nothing is said about Mrs. Aitken's helping to make an infant wardrobe. Such an important bit of evidence should not have been omitted. Moreover, one of Alexander's phrases attracts attention. Instead of saying plainly that the hardships of the journey to London brought on a miscarriage, he says that they 'induced a relapse

[1] See Wilson's *Carlyle*, I. p. 392, *note*. Wilson is in error about the letters. According to Charles Eliot Norton, *Early Letters of Carlyle*, ii. 370, the letter which Froude has summarised in *Thomas Carlyle*, I. pp. 305–306, is dated July 3, 1825. The letter which Wilson represents Froude as having summarised is postmarked July 20, 1825. The public has not been favoured, I believe, with the text of Mrs. Montagu's letter to Jane Welsh of July 3, 1825.

[2] *Love Letters*, i. 318–319, *note* 2. The letter of Carlyle's from which Alexander quotes is in *Letters of Carlyle*, i. 344.

[3] Alexander should have written 'Miss Jean Carlyle.' Jean did not marry James Aitken until November 1833. See *Letters of Carlyle*, ii. 129, *note* 2.

to her former condition.' What is the purpose of such a roundabout expression? What was the former condition to which she relapsed? It is not customary to say that a woman who has had a miscarriage relapses to her former condition.

In discussing the matter Sir James Crichton-Browne involves himself, as usual, in contradiction. After asserting that Mrs. Carlyle was twice pregnant he suggests that she was sterile. 'The history of the Carlyle and Welsh families,' he writes, 'leaves little doubt that the infertility was on her side. All Carlyle's brothers and sisters who married had families, most of them large families. Mrs. Carlyle was an only child, born prematurely, and during her life her family became extinct, so that when Carlyle came to make his will there was no Welsh left to whom he could bequeath Craigenputtock. . . . Darwin has remarked that the last surviving members of a dying-out family are likely to be barren.' [1] Little help is to be derived from such contradictory statements. If Sir James really believes that Mrs. Carlyle was twice pregnant, why does he maintain that she was sterile or barren? I believe that physicians apply the terms sterile and barren to women who are incapable of becoming pregnant. If Sir James does not use the words in this sense, he is at least open to the charge of using language loosely.

If the Carlyles had been expecting a child in 1831 it does not seem probable that they would have gone to London away from their kindred and intimate friends. The fact is that no trustworthy evidence has yet been brought forward to prove that Mrs. Carlyle suffered a miscarriage in that year. If she did, is it likely that written evidence of it should have remained hidden until 1904, or, when such alleged evidence is produced, that it should be so indefinite? The Carlyles were a letter-writing people who were in

[1] *British Medical Journal*, June 27, 1903.

the habit of recording minute details of their everyday life. Carlyle, in particular, was in the habit of writing very specifically. In any correspondence which has yet been given to the public the fact of any such miscarriage seems to have escaped record.

Jane's own correspondence for the period reveals that she discussed her health in detail, but she makes no mention of pregnancy.[1] In a letter of September 1, 1831, she reports a rash on her face, but says 'indeed my health is improved.' On September 3 she informs Carlyle that she has ridden, presumably on horseback, from Craigenputtock to Dumfries, a thing which a pregnant woman whose health was normally uncertain would not be likely to do. On September 11 she again writes to Carlyle: 'I was seriously afraid when I last wrote that I was going to be laid up with some fever or other violent disorder: no *safe* quantity of paregoric did me either ill or good; and one of my cheeks (not the diseased one) was frightfully swelled.' According to Alexander she arrived in London about October 1, 'and except for some falling off in her health, enjoyed the winter beside her husband.'[2] In a letter dated October 15, 1831, Carlyle informed his brother at Craigenputtock that Jane had 'arrived safe' in London.[3] Within ten days after her arrival she was offering to nurse Francis Jeffrey, who at that time was suffering from the effects of a surgical operation.[4]

Quite apart from the truth or falsity of the reports about the sexual relations of the Carlyles, some people condemn Froude utterly for writing 'My Relations with Carlyle.' They shift the argument from matters of fact to matters of good taste. Of course, there is no arguing with such people. They refuse to recognise the virulence with which Froude

[1] The three of her letters quoted herewith are printed in the *Nineteenth Century* of August 1914, pp. 344, 345, and 347 respectively.
[2] *Nineteenth Century*, August 1914, p. 348.
[3] *Letters of Carlyle*, i. 352.
[4] Wilson's *Carlyle*, 2. p. 256.

was attacked ; they do not take into account his regard for his faith as a friend and his honour as a gentleman ; they close their eyes to the fact that it was his strong desire to suppress the material which the persistence of his enemies finally made it necessary to publish.[1] Left to himself Froude would have given the world no more than he gave it in the four volumes of the 'Thomas Carlyle.' The nature of the attacks upon him left him with the feeling that his enemies would pursue his good faith and honour beyond the grave, and to furnish his representatives with some means of defending him he wrote the story of his relations with Carlyle. His children were goaded into publishing it. It is not strange that a disinterested editor should write that they 'cannot fairly be blamed for seeking to vindicate the character of their father.' My own opinion is that Froude erred in not making a brief but final statement in the biography about the sexual relations of the Carlyles. What is of utmost consequence, however, is that Froude cannot be condemned for saying what he did say in biography and pamphlet when he had such foundation for his statements as I have here presented.

[1] In the *Fortnightly Review*, lxxx. 190, William H. Mallock wrote thus : 'After the event it is proverbially easy to be wise ; and my own opinion, formed in this easy way, is that Mr. Froude would have been better advised had he told the whole truth at once. But the fact is now made evident that his error, if error it was, was due to those very qualities of loyalty and over-sensitive friendship in which his ignorant traducers declare him to have been so scandalously and conspicuously wanting.' Mr. Mallock was writing in 1903 shortly after the publication of *Relations*.

CHAPTER XXII

THE WILSON BIOGRAPHY

As David Wilson is writing his biography of Carlyle with the avowed intention of superseding Froude, his work should be examined in the light of that purpose. Five of the six promised volumes are now (1929) in print, a fact which reminds one of Carlyle's remark when he undertook to review Lockhart's 'Scott' in 1837. At that time the seventh and last volume of Lockhart's work had not yet appeared. 'The physiognomy of Scott will not be much altered for us by that seventh volume ;—the prior six have altered it but little,' wrote Carlyle ; 'and, in the *mean* while,' he continued, 'study to think it nothing miraculous that seven biographical volumes are given where one had been better.' The five volumes which Wilson has already published foreshadow the nature of the one which is yet to appear. The completed work will stand as an eloquent commentary upon Wilson's criticism of Froude for having written Carlyle's life in four volumes.

As I have already pointed out, Wilson's 'Carlyle' is the culmination of more than thirty years of active propaganda. Ever since the publication of his 'Mr. Froude and Carlyle' his Froudophobia has grown upon him, until now it is chronic and incurable. In setting about to supersede Froude he is under the necessity of being both advocate and biographer, a tight-rope feat not easy even for a man of the highest genius. A biographer with confidence in his subject-matter and in his own integrity should be willing to allow facts to speak for themselves. If one wishes to present an argument, one should call it such, and not send it forth under the guise of biography. Wilson has chosen, however, to enter the lists as a champion of Carlyle against the world.

It is evident to one who is familiar with Wilson's previous attacks upon Froude that he has shifted his ground and altered his tone. His mood is no longer fierce and destructive. He does not bring charges so confidently against Froude. Much has happened since 1898 to vindicate Carlyle's chosen biographer, and of this Wilson seems to be aware. At the same time it is clear that he takes for granted the effect of his earlier books, and those of Norton, Alexander Carlyle, and Crichton-Browne. He believes in the efficacy of iteration. 'What's oft said is at last believed,' he quoted in 1898, and now, confident that the repeated charges against Froude have been accepted wholesale, he proceeds to his biographical labours with the assumption of victory.

Throughout the five volumes his intention is clear. When he does not refer to Froude in a patronising manner he does so in a pitying or belittling fashion. It is now 'the foolish Froude,' or 'Froude poor fellow,' or 'Froude the dupe of a knave,' whom the public is asked to commiserate. In a burst of enthusiasm he dismisses Froude once and for all. 'He was an English-clerical variety of Tartarin of Tarascon, a very English compromise or blend of Don Quixote and Sancho Panza, living in illusions. But he is also a bore, and it is needless to do more than look at him and pass.' [1] Wilson's purpose is to impress upon his readers the conviction that Froude is insignificant, that he needs only to be brushed aside with a gesture. What is the use, he suggests, of

[1] *Carlyle*, I. p. 6.

looking longer into a biography of Carlyle written by such an insignificant fool and bore as Froude?

Wilson claims to have undertaken a full-length biography on his own initiative, and contrary to the advice of Alexander Carlyle and Gavan Duffy.[1] He has admitted, however, that Charles Eliot Norton instigated him to write 'Mr. Froude and Carlyle,'[2] and the influence of Norton upon the biography is evident. The most charitable judgment that can be passed upon Wilson is to say that he is a Carlyle zealot, almost a Carlyle fanatic, and that his work is marked by the characteristics of fanaticism. Anything that detracts in the slightest from Carlyle's reputation is anathema to him. Such unrestrained partisanship does not make for unbiased judgment or truthful representation. Thus we find Wilson intimating[3] that the Squire Papers are genuine, although as long ago as 1904 the Lomas and Firth edition of Carlyle's 'Cromwell' settled that matter finally. It is unfortunate too, I think, that Wilson's method obliges him to interpret Jane Welsh's young womanhood unjustly. It is easy to see that he shades that part of the story as unfavourably as he possibly can. Froude has been accused of deliberately championing Mrs. Carlyle. It is difficult to read Wilson's account of Jane Welsh without feeling that he has deliberately set himself to construct a narrative which makes her appear to have been before marriage 'an impudent baggage.'[4] We are given to understand that both Jane and her mother made a pretence of having more money than they really possessed, that all along they

[1] *Carlyle*, 1. pp. x–xi.

[2] See *The Truth about Carlyle*, p. 28, and *East and West*, pp. 270–272. In *East and West* note especially Wilson's report of Norton's remarks about Froude on pp. 269–270. According to Wilson, *Mr. Froude and Carlyle* pleased Norton. If it did, we have a means of forming an estimate of Norton's taste. In 1895, says Wilson, Norton 'spoke throughout in the noble spirit of an old man planting seeds whereof he never expects to see the growth.' In Wilson's *Carlyle* the seeds have come to full fruitage.

[3] *Carlyle*, 3. pp. 402–403.

[4] *Ibid.*, 1. p. 276.

played a clever game to see how fortunate a catch Jane could make. We are assured that the gossips of Haddington could have told Froude a thing or two if he had only taken the trouble to inquire. Froude has been severely criticised for accepting Geraldine Jewsbury's statements on behalf of Mrs. Carlyle. Wilson introduces anonymous small-town gossip as evidence against her conduct in courtship.[1] Indeed, throughout the five volumes, as in the 'Mr. Froude and Carlyle,' Wilson relies to a surprising extent upon anonymous testimony, as the footnotes reveal. The introduction of anonymous witnesses begins with the preface of the first volume, where Wilson asserts that a 'clever Scotch maid of hers whom she treated confidentially told me Mrs. Carlyle showed her a letter from Froude and scoffed at him as hollow, and bade her observe him for the fun of the thing.'[2] One wearies of such childishness, and longs for open and competent testimony. Who cares for the whispering of clever maids? They are capable of telling anything.

In his open letter to Frank Harris, Wilson forecast the essential nature of his own projected biography of Carlyle. 'I confess to you frankly, in advance of the "Life" I may not be spared to complete,' he wrote to Harris, 'that I have no fine new theory at all. Anecdotes and dialogues which can be believed shall be the substance of that work, if ever it is finished.'[3] There he spoke truly. However voluminous his work, Wilson tells us nothing new about Carlyle. He is little more than an industrious compiler of materials which he has striven laboriously but rather unsuccessfully to condense.[4] Neither in style nor in structure does he achieve distinction. His volumes are mosaics

[1] *Carlyle*, I. p. 427.
[2] *Ibid.*, I. p. vii.
[3] *The Truth about Carlyle*, p. 85.
[4] In *Carlyle*, I. pp. v–vi, Wilson says: 'The method of composition has been like that of the artist who began by elaborately drawing everything, and then struck out the most of it. When I retired in 1912, the materials available about the European Confucius would have filled fifty volumes of the common kind; and I allowed myself ten years to reduce it all to a readable size.'

of quotations, anecdotes, scraps of correspondence, *obiter dicta* of David Wilson. As all know who have ever undertaken the preparation of a biography, anecdotes and dialogues are always the most treacherous materials with which to deal. Letters are contemporary facts. Even letters, however, are scarcely to be trusted in the hands of a man who has deliberately set out to discredit an earlier biographer.

Not content with his rather sorry account of Jane's early life, Wilson asserts that Miss Welsh was unattractive in appearance as well as in character. The familiar Macleay miniature, which Froude had used as representative of her young womanhood, Wilson dismisses as 'merely a standard type of beauty.' [1] In short, he wishes to prove that Froude was as mistaken in his portraits as in his facts. To this end, misled by his own gross misinterpretation of one of Francis Jeffrey's letters, he selected a portrait which he took to be like Jane as a young woman, and published an alleged etching of it in the first volume of the biography.[2] He succeeded only in falling into his own snare. Before the publication of his second volume he had discovered his error. The fact is that the alleged etching is a hideous caricature of the portrait of Mrs. Carlyle by Gambardella. It is impossible to believe that the publication of this caricature was not a part of Wilson's method of representing Miss Welsh in an unattractive light. If any one thinks otherwise let him compare the etching and the original portrait. It would have been necessary for him to do in the first volume only what he did in the second—print a half-tone engraving of Gambardella's rather attractive painting of Mrs. Carlyle. To have done that, however, would not have been in keeping with his attitude toward Jane Welsh.

[1] Read all of the two paragraphs under the etching opposite *Carlyle*, I. p. 176. These paragraphs, which are to be suppressed in the future, are of unusual importance to students of Wilson's methods.

[2] The etching faces p. 176.

I protested against Wilson's conduct in this matter. 'I find it very difficult to understand your procedure with reference to the portrait of Mrs. Carlyle by Gambardella,' I wrote on February 7, 1926. 'How could you present the public with the caricature facing page 176 of your first volume and assure your readers that it is an "etching" (which should be in some degree a faithful copy) of the original? The "etching" facing page 176 is hideous; the half-tone of the portrait by Gambardella facing page 328 of your second volume shows an attractive, really good-looking woman. Why did you not give a half-tone reproduction in volume one? It seems to me that the same fidelity should be practised in presenting portraits as in giving the contents of letters. In your own judgment, has Froude ever reproduced the substance of a letter with as little faithfulness to the original as is evidenced in Susan Crawford's so-called etching of the portrait by Gambardella?' In reply Wilson said only that the picture in volume one would be replaced in future editions by the half-tone of the Gambardella. 'It would take too long to explain everything,' he wrote in conclusion. His explanation at the close of the preface to the second volume of the biography is awkward, and does not touch the heart of the matter.[1] Why should a hideous travesty have been used in place of a good photographic reproduction, if not to support his assertions in regard to Jane's unattractive appearance?

A similar spirit permeates the entire biography. Wilson says, for example, that Froude had no commission to write an account of Carlyle's life. The biography, he maintains, 'was volunteer work, undertaken long afterwards.'[2] He repeats the stories in

[1] *Carlyle*, 2. p. vii.

[2] *Carlyle*, 1. p. viii. Wilson's phrase 'long afterwards' is rather indefinite. I understand him to mean that Froude undertook the biography long after he had been charged with 'the task of condensing further a voluminous mass of selections from Mrs. Carlyle's later letters.' The first two volumes of the

regard to Mrs. Carlyle's pregnancy, yet offers no proof that she ever had a miscarriage.[1] He reports that Alexander Carlyle declines to believe that Jane said she married for ambition.[2] He should have remembered that Alexander never saw Jane, and is not qualified to speak for her. He professes to know just how Edward Irving's remark about Jane's making a Paradise wherever she was should be interpreted.[3] He represents the period of residence at Craigenputtock as restorative of Mrs. Carlyle's health.[4] He continues his belittling and misrepresenting of Geraldine Jewsbury.[5] Whenever any matter does not agree with his preconceived notions he refuses to believe it. Such are a few of the characteristics of the volumes which are presented as an authoritative biography of Carlyle.

The biographer is confident. 'There is not the slightest chance,' he wrote to me under date of February 22, 1926, 'of any documents or anything else ever clearing Froude from the only charge I have made against him, utter unreliability in his statements about Thomas Carlyle and Mrs. Carlyle, in regard to a great many matters, especially sexual matters, wherein he was obsessed by a number of obscene delusions mainly caught from Miss Jewsbury, apparently, but, however caught, fatal to his work as a biographer. He was a very loose and inaccurate writer in general, deficient in humour, and incapable, I fear, of judicial impartiality, or reverence for facts;

biography were written by Froude before Carlyle's death in 1881, two years before the *Letters and Memorials* were published. Wilson seems to forget that Alexander Carlyle and his coadjutors criticise Froude sharply for doing just what is here admitted he was commissioned to do, that is, condense the voluminous mass of Mrs. Carlyle's correspondence. He seems, likewise, to forget that Alexander Carlyle in *Nemesis*, p. 85, recognises that the writing of the biography was imposed upon Froude by Carlyle. These are only examples of the many contradictions in which Wilson involves himself.

[1] *Carlyle*, 2. pp. 198, 220, 247. Wilson seems to say, 2. p. 198, 'that a baby was twice at least expected' in 1831.

[2] *Ibid.*, 1. p. 300, *note*.

[3] *Ibid.*, 2. p. 371.

[4] *Ibid.*, p. 301.

[5] *Ibid.*, 3. pp. 140–141, 213–217.

but these are matters of opinion. His unreliability in respect to Thomas Carlyle is not really a matter on which there is room for two opinions.' Such note of confident authority has carried conviction to certain readers who have evidently forgone investigation.

Wilson is eager to have his work widely circulated and accepted as authoritative. As in the case of his former books on Carlyle, he offers the biography freely to every tongue and nation. 'All or any part of it,' he writes, 'may be translated into any language without payment. The sooner that is done, the better.'[1] Foreign scholars now have an opportunity to judge for themselves as between Wilson and Froude. They can be trusted to separate truth from error.

[1] Wilson's *Carlyle*, I. p. xi.

CHAPTER XXIII

FROUDE AS EDITOR

CHARLES ELIOT NORTON, following the lead of Freeman and other critics of Froude's historical work, began the attack upon Froude as editor of the Carlyle documents at the point of inaccuracy. He deviated from Carlyle's punctuation, insisted Norton ; he misread words ; he mistook dates ; he sometimes abridged instead of giving the exact words of Carlyle's text. Having once determined his course as laid down in the issue of the *New Princeton Review* of July 1886, Norton steadily held to it through the seven volumes of material which he edited, and thus pointed the way for Alexander Carlyle and David Wilson. The work accomplished by these three men bulks large. Charles Eliot Norton's name gave it standing in the scholarly world. The attack has been prosecuted almost without opposition. Froude's slender pamphlet of eighty pages is small beside the twenty-six volumes with a total of 9,123 pages which make up the work of his detractors.[1] It is not to be wondered at, perhaps, that even intelligent people have been decoyed into attaching to such a volume of work greater value than it merits. The worth of the criticism directed against Froude's editorial work can be estimated properly only when we understand what the nature of that work is.

[1] This estimate does not include magazine articles, or books not directly hostile to Froude.

First of all, let us keep in mind the age at which Froude undertook to carry out Carlyle's commission. He was fifty-three years old in 1871 when Carlyle first suggested the matter to him. He was sixty-three years old when Carlyle died. He was, moreover, worn by a long life of hard literary labour, having completed twelve volumes of the 'History of England' and three volumes of 'The English in Ireland,' in addition to several minor volumes, and his work as editor of *Fraser's Magazine* from 1860 to 1875. A large portion of this work, particularly that on the 'History of England,' was based upon original documents in difficult handwritings and in several different languages. His eyesight was no longer keen. He was a worn veteran turning to another heavy task of editing original manuscripts, and upon the foundation of thousands of original documents constructing a biography.

It is doubtless true that the creative and the technical moods are ill to combine. We need only turn to the first drafts of the work of some of our greatest poets and prose writers for evidence of this. In many cases they are almost innocent of details of punctuation. It is undoubtedly true, also, that as a man grows older, he has less interest in the minutiæ of composition—in capitals and commas, colons and semicolons—and a great deal more interest in the thought behind the conventional symbols. From details his interest has turned to substance.

In the next place, we must remember that Froude always worked alone. He could not adapt himself to secretaries. He made his own transcripts, read his own proofs, did everything single-handed. True enough such a method is not conducive to literal accuracy. Anyone who has ever had anything to do with proof-reading knows how dangerous it is to read proof by turning from proof sheets to original copy. Froude was an old-fashioned country-gentleman scholar, who worked in the leisurely manner of the eighteenth century. I am quite sure that the modern method of making books, the method by which a score of clever young women work under the direction of a chief, and manipulate a complicated card-index system, would have been repulsive to him. He could work only in his own way. What he did must be done so or not at all, as far as he was concerned. He made that clear in his inaugural lecture as Regius Professor of Modern History at Oxford. 'In conclusion,' he said, 'I have only to add that if I am to be of any use in my present office I must follow my own lines. I cannot at my age work in harness with the athletes of the new studies.' Work so done has at least the stamp of one mind upon it, and is doubtless worth more than work put together by secretaries following the card-index system. And, it may be added, its accuracy is sometimes not less by the one method than by the other.

Froude has told us something of his work as editor of the Carlyle material. 'I copied out the greater part of the "Reminiscences" myself. A large part of them I copied twice ; I had to work at them with a magnifying glass, and in many hundred instances I was at a loss to know exactly what particular words might be. My own hand is not a good one, and there was a further source of error in the printer's reading of this. At least I was not careless, except perhaps that I had found the manuscript so difficult that in reading the proofs I trusted too much to my own transcript. The "Memoir" of Mrs. Carlyle was printed directly from the copy which Carlyle gave me. If there were mistakes in this the fault did not rest with me.' [1] The fact that Froude submitted the proofs of the Scottish portions of the 'Reminiscences' to John Skelton to

[1] *Relations*, pp. 35–36. The copy of the 'Memoir of Mrs. Carlyle' from which Froude printed was made by Mary Carlyle under the direction of her uncle.

revise with reference more particularly to the Scots names and idioms is one indication of the care which he took to be accurate.[1]

I make no claim that either as editor or biographer Froude is free from errors ; this claim cannot be made even on behalf of his severest critics, as has been abundantly demonstrated. Let it be said once and for all that Froude was not a good proof-reader. As Charles Sears Baldwin once remarked to me, not many great writers are. I have examined Froude's published works from 'Shadows of the Clouds' onward, and have gathered a collection of curious typographical errors. In 'Shadows of the Clouds' the following occur : 'Machrynnleth' for 'Machynlleth'; 'the boys was sitting awkwardly in their chairs'; 'I could not doubt it was him'; 'They could not stay in a place which were crowded with such recollections'; 'proved their theories form the constitution of the soul'; 'I may not lay beside them in their grave'; 'and departed to search of the lady's sister'; 'persuming on a general order'; 'extacy' for 'extasy'; 'scissons' for 'scissors.'[2] There is an error in the Greek quotation on the title-page of 'The Nemesis of Faith.' The 'Thomas Carlyle' is freer from typographical errors than either 'Shadows of the Clouds' or the 'Reminiscences,' but it contains many. One sentence reads thus : 'He was far enough from desiring insurrection, although a conviction did lay at the very bottom of his mind that incurably unjust societies would find in insurrection and conflagration their natural consummation and end.'[3] A typographical error, also, or it maybe a slip of the pen originally on Froude's

[1] See Skelton's *Shirley*, p. 172.

[2] These occur in order on pp. 10, 98, 134, 180, 203–204, 212, 226, 231, 260, 276.

[3] *Thomas Carlyle*, 2. p. 136. Another annoying error occurs in the preface (1. p. xiv.) : 'A few weeks before Mrs. Carlyle's death, he asked me what I meant to do.' Of course the 'Mrs.' should be 'Mr.' This error is repeated in the American edition.

part, is the substitution of the word 'mother' for 'brother' in the following sentence: 'I do not expect,' he told his mother, 'that he will be able to accomplish anything for me.'[1] Froude was copying from one of Carlyle's letters to his brother John, and nothing could have been easier than inadvertently to write 'mother' for 'brother.' Charles Eliot Norton has seized upon this slip of the pen or error in typography to make a point against Froude. He and Alexander Carlyle have made other charges of inaccuracy and misrepresentation against Froude which can be explained in the same way. They have made similar errors themselves.[2]

One feels that the publishers should have taken more pains to eliminate some of these typographical errors. We must remember, however, that it is only in recent years that publishers have made determined efforts to produce error-proof texts, and, even at the present time, only the greatest publishing houses make such efforts. Those who are in the habit of looking for typographical errors know how far from perfect most of the books issued even by the greatest presses are. At any rate, all such errors are errors of

[1] *Thomas Carlyle*, 2. p. 155.

[2] Wilson confesses that his version of one of Carlyle's letters is unlike that of Alexander Carlyle in two places as a result of different readings of the same manuscript! See his *Carlyle*, 2. p. 317, *note*. Norton in his edition of *Reminiscences*, i. 69, makes Carlyle say of Geraldine Jewsbury's anecdotes of Mrs. Carlyle's early life, that 'there is a certain mythical truth, in all or most parts of the poor scribble, and it may wait its doom, or execution.' Carlyle actually wrote 'examination' instead of 'execution.' I am making a list, which I may print in the future, of hundreds of similar errors in the books sponsored by Froude's enemies. The examples which I give are typical. Those who point out misprints and misreadings in Froude frequently fall into worse error with less excuse. For example, in Chambers's *Cyclopædia of English Literature*, iii. 502–503, P. Hume Brown writes: 'To take but one example of his [Froude's] negligence—surely Froude should have laid his hand on his heart when he made Carlyle speak of his friend Sir Henry Taylor's "morbid vanity," when the words he actually wrote were "marked veracity."' Froude's version is not 'morbid vanity' but 'morbid vivacity.' See his edition of *Reminiscences*, ii. 312. Carlyle himself was frequently in error. Thus, he says his wife's grave is in 'the nave of the old Abbey Kirk' at Haddington. See *Reminiscences*, Norton edition, i. 254. The grave is in the chancel.

the press, and as such they may be charged to carelessness, indifference, or what not on the part of either author or publisher. What should be insisted upon is that such errors must not be used as proofs of deliberate intention on the part of an author to deceive. Nor should they be used as proofs of ignorance on the part of the author. If it is permissible to use them for such a purpose, it could be proved, on the strength of two errors which I have previously quoted, that Froude was ignorant of the distinction between the verbs 'to lay' and 'to lie.'

In judging Froude as editor we must also take into consideration methods of transcribing manuscript material. There is the *verbatim et literatim* method, which leads to the reproduction of every word, every letter, every mark of punctuation with most punctilious accuracy. Such a method has value. In these days of so-called scientific scholarship it has become more or less a fetish. Except in the case of the very greatest men—men whose every peculiarity of penmanship and composition reveals something of character which is worth knowing—one may be permitted to doubt its value. On the other hand, there is the method which results in the conveyance of the thought of the writer as apart from the conventional symbols in which it is expressed. For example, when a man dates a letter '2 Feb'y '84' there is no doubt that he means 'February 2, 1884.' When he writes 'Yrs affy' there can be as little doubt that he means 'Yours affectionately.' When he writes, 'I shall look on the Houses he built with a certain proud interest: they stand firm and sound to the heart, all over his little district: no one that comes after him will ever say, Here was the finger of a hollow Eye-servant,' as Carlyle often did write, to what extent does the original differ in fundamental meaning from the following form? 'I shall look on the houses he built with a certain proud interest. They stand firm and sound to the heart, all over his little district. No one that comes after him will ever say, Here was the finger of a hollow eye-servant.'

Froude chose to follow the second method—that of delivering in the clearest possible way the thought which Carlyle meant to impart. He had ground, too, for his choice of method. So far as Carlyle was concerned the public had in his already published writings an ample quantity of his idiosyncrasies of capitalisation, punctuation, and such like. One who has made a study of Carlyle's punctuation knows that its principal variation from that of the present is the frequent use of a colon or a semicolon where now a period is employed. His colons are for the most part equivalent to periods, his semicolons frequently so, and it is noticeable that Froude, who was himself a believer in short, effective sentences, and who was making an attempt to edit Carlyle's manuscripts in conformity with modern methods of punctuation, usually substitutes a period for a colon. In order to emphasise the point I have in mind I shall give a few lines from the two texts of the 'Reminiscences.'

'As for the departed we ought to say that he was taken home "like a shock of corn fully ripe." He "had finished the work that was given him to do" and finished it (very greatly more than the most) as became a man. He was summoned too before he had ceased to be interesting—to be loveable. (He was to the last the pleasantest man I had to speak with in Scotland.) For many years too he had the end ever in his eye, and was studying to make all preparation for what in his strong way he called often "that last, that awful change."[1]

'As for the Departed, we ought to say that he was taken home "like a shock of corn fully ripe:" he "had finished the work that was given him to do," and finished it (very greatly more than the most) as

[1] Froude's edition, i. 4–5.

became a man ; he was summoned too before he had ceased to be interesting, to be lovable (he was to the last the pleasantest man I had to speak with in Scotland) ; for many years too he had the End ever in his eye, and was studying to make all preparation for what in his strong way he called often " that last, that awful change." '[1]

A comparison of these passages will enable a reader to understand how Charles Eliot Norton and David Wilson were able to amass so vast a number of errors in Froude's volumes. The heart of the matter, however, does not lie in the deviation of Froude's printed versions from Carlyle's original manuscripts in points of punctuation and capitalisation ; it lies more properly in whether Froude's versions depart from the meaning expressed in those manuscripts. A careful collation of Froude's text of Carlyle's sketches of James Carlyle and Jane Welsh Carlyle reveals thirty-nine errors of fact which affect the sense.[2] The small number of such errors in Froude's edition of the ' Reminiscences ' is indeed surprising to one who turns to the book after reading the charges made by Norton and Wilson. One may emphasise the matter in this way. Suppose we had a text of ' Hamlet ' or ' Othello ' or ' King Lear ' of which we could be certain that it followed the sense of the original manuscript as accurately as Froude's edition of the ' Reminiscences ' follows Carlyle's manuscripts. We should be justified in feeling a sense of high satisfaction in the knowledge that we were so close to the actual words which Shakespeare wrote. Yet all this accuracy on the part of Froude is ignored by Norton, Wilson, Alexander Carlyle, and their followers. As a matter of fact, Froude was attacked at his weakest point—the point of minor details of transcription, proof-reading, and the like—and without taking into consideration methods of editing ; and because it could

[1] Norton's edition, i. 2–3.

[2] See pp. 352–358 of this volume.

be shown that he was vulnerable at this one point, he was represented as in error at all points.

I must emphasise once more the fact that Froude made no effort to conceal anything. I have already said that he returned the manuscripts intact to Mary Carlyle ; there was no tampering with them on his part to suit his purposes. When new material came to light, he welcomed it. When David Ritchie applied to him, as an executor of the Carlyle estate, for permission to print the 'Early Letters of Jane Welsh Carlyle,' he granted it freely. He was always willing to have his errors corrected, always ready to welcome new light. It was only reflections upon his honesty and good faith which he flung from him indignantly.

In this connection it is important to examine Froude's method of dealing with the material which Geraldine Jewsbury collected in regard to Mrs. Carlyle. His handling of this is of utmost value in estimating his intentions as editor. Investigation shows that he was scrupulously honest in conveying the truth of the matter. He introduced the material in this fashion : 'On these anecdotes, when Miss Jewsbury gave him as much as she was able to give, Mr. Carlyle made his own observations, but he left them undigested ; still for the most part remaining in Miss Jewsbury's words ; and in the same words I think it best that they shall appear here, as material which may be used hereafter in some record more completely organised, but for the present serving to make intelligible what Mr. Carlyle has to say about them.'[1] In addition, he mentions in a note that Miss Jewsbury's work is 'described by Mr. Carlyle as Geraldine's mythic jottings.'[2] Moreover, Froude's version of Carlyle's remarks is to the effect that 'few or none of these narratives are correct in details,'[3]

[1] *Reminiscences*, Froude edition, ii. 70–71. [2] *Ibid.*, 71.
[3] *Ibid.*, 91.

whereas Norton gives Carlyle's version literally: 'Few or none of these narratives are correct in all the details.'[1] It is noticeable that Froude's version is more emphatic than Carlyle's actual words.

Observe also that Froude takes care to speak of 'a certain mythical truth in all or most of them,' in referring to Carlyle's remarks about Geraldine's anecdotes. It would appear from this that his understanding of what Carlyle meant by 'mythical' differs very widely from that of Alexander Carlyle and Charles Eliot Norton. Indeed, it is important to know what the word meant to Carlyle himself. Fortunately it is not necessary to guess. Alexander himself quotes this passage from Carlyle: 'Mythically *true* is what *Sartor* says of his schoolfellows.' Upon which comment Alexander proceeds to remark: 'There are besides these many other instances in which Carlyle has referred to *Sartor* as giving facts in his own life.'[2] We are, indeed, justified in understanding Carlyle to mean by 'mythical' something which embodies much truth. What he really means to say is that, at bottom, Miss Jewsbury's anecdotes of Mrs. Carlyle convey the substantial truth. 'The Geraldine accounts of her childhood are substantially correct,' he affirms.[3] 'Geraldine's account of *Comley Bank* and life at Edinburgh, is extremely mythic; we did grow to "know everybody of mark," or might have grown; but nobody except Jeffrey seemed to either of us a valuable acquisition.'[4] And further: 'Geraldine's *Craigenputtock* stories are more mythical than any of the rest. Each consists of two or three, in confused exaggerated state, rolled with new confusion into one, and given wholly to *her*, when perhaps they were mainly some servant's in whom she was concerned.'[5] Carlyle's

[1] *Reminiscences*, Norton edition, i. 68.
[2] *Love Letters*, ii. 365.
[3] *Reminiscences*, Norton edition, i. 72.
[4] *Ibid.*, 79.
[5] *Ibid.*, 80.

'perhaps' is important. It indicates that after the lapse of many years he is himself uncertain as to many details of the life at Craigenputtock. The fact is that he was engrossed in his work there, and knew little of many things that were going forward. Miss Jewsbury received her information as to Mrs. Carlyle's activities directly from Mrs. Carlyle herself. That they do not harmonise with Carlyle's account does not make them untrue. In the memoir of his wife Carlyle interprets the life at Craigenputtock from his own point of view. We must not forget that his wife also had a point of view, which she expressed in unmistakable language. 'The *second* ride, in Geraldine, is nearly altogether mythical; being in reality a ride from Dumfries to Scotsbrig,' says Carlyle. Nevertheless, it was a ride; there is the foundation of fact. The remainder of Carlyle's paragraph reveals only that he himself was uncertain of the exact facts in the case.[1]

David Wilson, in commenting upon the manner in which Froude edited the 'Letters and Memorials,' says that 'it must be obvious that he failed to appreciate the correct limits of an editor's and an executor's functions.'[2] Alexander Carlyle and Crichton-Browne express their views in these words: 'The Letters and Memorials of Jane Welsh Carlyle were absolutely Froude's property, given and bequeathed to him to do his best and wisest with, and to publish when made ready for publication, after what delay, seven, ten years, he might in his discretion decide. The only questions that arose regarding them were whether they were not published prematurely and whether they were wisely edited. Instead of waiting for seven years after Carlyle's death—and most people will, we think, accept that as the plain meaning of the will, they were out within two years of that event, and

[1] *Reminiscences*, Norton edition, i. 90.
[2] *Mr. Froude and Carlyle*, pp. 155–156.

"fit editing" there was none.'[1] These statements require examination.

First, then, let us consider the time of publication. I believe it will be generally admitted that a man makes a will in order to have his wishes carried out irrespective of the date of his death. If it should happen that he died the next day after his will was legally executed, it would be the duty of those upon whom the task devolved to carry out the expressed wishes of the testator. Carlyle's will was written February 6, 1873. Let us suppose he had died within the year. Then the limit of seven or ten years which he mentions as elapsing before the publication of the 'Letters and Memorials' would bring us to 1880 or 1883. It happens that 1883 was the date of publication. Carlyle prepared his will in anticipation of his death, and it is well known that he was expecting, even hoping, to die at any time. Mary herself admits this. 'My uncle,' she testified in May 1881, 'during many years spoke of his death as near at hand.'[2] Froude says that when Carlyle went to Mentone in December 1866 'he was expecting that in all probability he would never see England again.'[3] When Carlyle brought the first lot of material to Froude in 1871, Froude says there was no mention of any limit of time. 'I was to wait only till he was dead, and he was then in constant expectation of his end.'[4] By what authority can anyone claim that Carlyle in his will meant that nothing was to be published until seven or ten years after February 5, 1881? Carlyle could not fix the date of his death. His will was written to take care of matters irrespective of the time of death.

The strictures upon the manner in which Froude edited the material leave one in perplexity. Froude's critics would deprive him of editorial privileges;

[1] *Nemesis*, p. 93.
[2] *Ibid.*, p. 139.
[3] *Thomas Carlyle*, 4. p. 333.
[4] *Ibid.*, p. 409.

they would demand that in carrying out his duties he should conform to their notions of what constitutes fit editing. They blame Froude for omitting any of the material which Carlyle had annotated, as well as for including any which Carlyle had not specifically marked for inclusion. And yet Carlyle explicitly states that the manuscript of the 'Letters and Memorials' was 'by no means ready for publication,' and adds that the questions of how or when it or any portion of it should be published were still dark to him, 'but on all such points James Anthony Froude's practical summing up and decision is to be taken as mine.' Carlyle knew something about the duties of an editor of unfinished material. He also knew Froude and all about Froude's methods of work. With respect to all the documents Froude performed the duties laid upon him to the best of his understanding and ability. He made a selection of correspondence for the 'Letters and Memorials' and arranged the matter with such explanations as the exigencies of the case seemed to require. For the 'Reminiscences' he cast the manuscript of the sketch of Jane Welsh Carlyle into the form of connected and finished narrative by omitting Carlyle's irrelevant observations and questionings and by shifting the position of some of the material in regard to Mrs. Carlyle's family. Alexander Carlyle is not satisfied with Froude's work. It was not Alexander, however, that Froude was under obligation to please. Froude performed his task as under the eye of Thomas Carlyle, who had solemnly commissioned him to do his wisest and best. Had Carlyle wished Alexander or any other person than Froude to perform the task he would doubtless have indicated his desire. Froude was the man of Carlyle's choice, and it is to Carlyle alone that Froude, both as editor and biographer, is answerable. In carrying out a commission such as Carlyle entrusted to Froude one is sure to be criticised. Many questions in regard to taste and judgment arise. An honest man is not required to concern himself with what his enemies may say ; the one ideal he should keep before himself is to do his wisest and his best. Froude was ever confident that he had worked in the spirit of such an ideal.

CHAPTER XXIV

FROUDE AS BIOGRAPHER

MANY reasons have been advanced to prove that Froude was constitutionally disqualified to act as biographer of Carlyle. Having done their best and failed to prevent him from performing the work, Mary and Alexander Carlyle and their sympathisers resorted to the method of attempting to destroy confidence in him. Froude, we are told, was hopelessly inaccurate ; he had no sense of humour ; he could not understand a Scotchman ; between him and Carlyle ' there flowed both Tweed and Trent and the history of the whole world ' ; he was insincere, incapable of telling the truth, malicious, ' a continental liar.' The difficulties under which he had to work are apparent to all who have read thus far. I have tried to show the manner in which he confronted and overcame all obstacles. I have yet to tell something of the spirit in which he went about his task and to summarise briefly his achievement as biographer.

I have already called attention to the fact that Froude was about sixty years old when he turned to the actual composition of the biography. Those who are inclined to find fault with him for haste should keep this fact in mind. Already his health was uncertain, and he was haunted by the fear that he might not live to finish the task. ' I am writing quietly at Carlyle's " Life," ' he informed Olga

Novikoff, April 11, 1880, 'and I hope I may live to complete it.' He was then near the end of his sixty-second year. After Mary Carlyle began attacking him publicly, he had further dread of not living to carry through the entire task. 'I have a wonderful faculty for worrying myself, but it will be all right,' he wrote to his daughter Margaret, from Fowey, July 11, 1883. 'I have had a fuss on me that I might not live to finish Carlyle's life, and then I should be at the little girl's mercy.[1] Therefore I thought and think that I ought to draw up a clear statement of the way in which Carlyle left his papers, and how I came to have to do with them. There will be no end to the lies she will tell if I do not put it out of her power.' The genesis of 'My Relations with Carlyle' is revealed in those last sentences.

From first to last Carlyle's commission was a source of anxiety to Froude; the questions involved at almost every stage of its composition were among the most baffling that ever confronted him. The obstacles which Mary placed in his way were not more troublesome than the questions of how much to tell and the manner of relating what was to be told. May 4, 1883, Froude, writing of the recently published 'Letters and Memorials' and of the biography which he was then completing, confided to Skelton some of his difficulties: 'In Carlyle's will the manuscript is described as *not yet fit for publication* and as *put into my hands to complete*. He leaves me all other documents elucidatory of the letters to be used as I please, and desires that my judgment shall be taken as his own. I mean to rest entirely on these words. I will give no explanation, for I cannot give any without showing that something is concealed.'

A portion of discarded manuscript reveals Froude's state of mind with respect to the publication of the 'Reminiscences.' 'In the discharge of the first part

[1] That is, at the mercy of Mary Carlyle. See p. 28, *note*.

of my duty I have laid myself open to misconstruction. I ought perhaps to have realised more clearly how impossible it was for the world to comprehend, or make allowance for, so singular a commission. The English people, who owe so much to Carlyle, will not fail to judge him generously. My claim for indulgence is nothing. They will be sorry for much which they have read, and " the first bringer of unwelcome news Hath but a losing office." Yet I too feel sure that I shall not ask in vain for a fair construction of a service itself so sad, a service perhaps the most unwelcome which ever was required in the name of friendship. In this as in all things he desired to be true.' Ashley Froude, who was in his eighteenth year when Carlyle died, tells me that as a boy he knew his father was to take charge of Carlyle's papers and write his biography, and that matters connected with the life formed the usual topic of conversation when Carlyle and Froude were together. 'It had a very depressing effect on my father, who told me that he was to be made Carlyle's " whipping boy." My sisters and I thought it hard that Carlyle would not expiate his sins while he was alive, instead of leaving the task to be performed vicariously by my father. The effect of the whole affair on my sisters and me was that we hated the name of Carlyle and everything connected with him. The conclusion that I came to was that Carlyle's remorse was genuine and that the history of his married life gave ample grounds for it ; that if it was not genuine, he was an arrant humbug, and this, much as I disliked him, I could not believe. I could never understand the veneration, respect, and affection with which my father regarded his memory, but this was the ignorance of extreme youth.' [1]

As biographer Froude is criticised for not reporting Carlyle's personal talk more fully. David Wilson

[1] Personal information from Ashley Froude, July 23, 1925.

expresses the point of view in this way: 'When Mr. Froude had decided to write the Life of Carlyle he did not assiduously note Carlyle's conversation, as Boswell did Johnson's. Of all the reporters of it, he is perhaps the worst, although his opportunities were the best. He speaks vaguely of its high qualities, but shows us almost none . . . Ten pages of Sir C. G. Duffy's "Conversations with Carlyle," are worth more than Mr. Froude's four volumes.' [1] It was not from any desire to do injustice to Carlyle that Froude abstained from reporting his conversation. He had considered the matter carefully and had come to much the same conclusion as had Lockhart before him. 'To report correctly the language of conversations, especially when extended over a wide period, is almost an impossibility. The listener, in spite of himself, adds something of his own in colour, form, or substance.' [2] It is well known that Boswell converted into 'Johnsonese' his notes of the Doctor's conversation; although he reports with amazing accuracy the substance and manner of Johnson's talk, he does not give the exact words.

Charles Eliot Norton himself has explained why it was unwise to attempt to report Carlyle's conversation. 'The essential quality,' he writes, 'of his talk and Ruskin's alike is not so much in the words of it as in the manner and expression. If repeated—if even reported word for word—it is likely to produce a different effect from that which it made when first spoken, owing to the loss of the incommunicable look, the evanescent air, the qualifying and inimitable tone.' [3] Norton published a portion of his record of Carlyle's conversation only to have it pointed out by Alexander Carlyle that the report 'does not reproduce his uncle's speech with phonetic accuracy.' [4] Froude, it seems, was wise not to undertake the task. Had he

[1] *Mr. Froude and Carlyle*, p. 88.
[2] Froude's *Thomas Carlyle*, 4. p. 443.
[3] *Norton Letters*, i. 441.
[4] *Ibid.*, 323, *note*.

done so, he would only have laid himself open to further criticism.

To be sure, Froude did give a few brief fragments of Carlyle's talk, but he made no effort to imitate the inimitable. He knew that his long and intimate acquaintance with Carlyle needed no show of cleverness such as he might possibly have exhibited in reporting some of Carlyle's racy talk. He simply explained that his fullness of knowledge precluded any necessity of such effort. He would vouch only for the general purport of his material. 'I knew Carlyle . . . so long and so intimately,' he writes, 'that I heard many things from him which are not to be found under his hand; many things more fully dilated on, which are there only hinted at, and slight incidents about himself for which I could make no place in my narrative.[1] I have already noticed the general character of his talk with me. I add here some few memorabilia, taken either from notes hastily written down, or from my own recollection, which I believe in the main to be correct.'[2]

That Froude as biographer did not take pains to be accurate is false. I have already shown how as editor he struggled for accuracy, and have given some of the reasons which prevented his fully achieving it. The charge is especially emphasised that he made no attempt to familiarise himself with the circumstances of Carlyle's life in Scotland, or the scenes of his activities there. The truth is that Froude made special journeys to Scotland in 1876[3] and 1880 to visit the scenes of Carlyle's early life, in company with Mr. George Howard, later Earl of Carlisle, who under

[1] Let those who are disposed to doubt Froude dwell upon the implications of this sentence.

[2] *Thomas Carlyle*, 4. p. 443.

[3] Sir James Crichton-Browne asserts that Froude 'had no personal knowledge of' Craigenputtock. See his *Stray Leaves from a Physician's Portfolio*, p. 331. Isaac W. Dyer, in his recent *Bibliography of Carlyle's Writings*, p. 348, repeats Crichton-Browne's statement. In September 1876 Froude, who was visiting the Howards at Naworth Castle, went to Craigenputtock with Mr. Howard and his sister-in-law, Miss Stanley.

Froude's eye, made the sketches which were reproduced in the original edition of the biography. On October 26, 1880, he wrote to Margaret Froude: 'We made our Ecclefechan expedition yesterday with great success. The day was fine, the air not bitterly cold. We saw the house where Carlyle was born, the farm in the hills where was he bred up, the other farm to which his father and mother removed in 1826, and where they both died. We saw the tomb in the Ecclefechan churchyard. Mr. Howard made three sketches. It was all extremely interesting, but the details will keep.' Again, on the occasion of Carlyle's funeral, Froude visited the Mainhill farm. In addition, he had visited Scotland on numerous other occasions.

The same careful investigation is evident in matters of text and interpretation. Froude's correspondence with Max Müller in regard to the printing of Goethe's letters throws light upon his methods of striving for the best possible expert opinion.

'I will thank you . . . for your assistance with the accompanying letter [he wrote to Müller, October 28, 1881]. I send you Carlyle's copy and my own *transcript*, which I should like you to correct for the press. If Georgie will send me a translation guaranteed by yourself, so much the better, as the passage about the *Prachtmütze* fairly beats me. Carlyle, I think, must have made a mistake in writing it out. The original is unhappily mislaid and cannot be found. I should not wonder if it had been long ago given away as an autograph. On second thought I do *not* send Carlyle's copy, for fear of possible accidents. I have transcribed it as it stands correctly. It was written with evident haste, and here and there are pencil marks indicating error, I think in his brother's hand. What can Goethe mean by calling himself *obgesagt*?

'My very best thanks [he wrote again, December 23, 1881]. I knew that "worthiest Sir" could not possibly be right, but in every language words acquire a secondary meaning when worked into the phraseology of conventional politeness, and the correct equivalents are the last which a foreigner learns. I cannot say whether Goethe dated this letter. I have only Carlyle's copy of it hastily transcribed into the letter of his brother, and on this there is no date, nor can I tell whether Goethe used the *von* before his name. *I* have not omitted it. Had I better put it in?

'You have not answered my question as to the relative position of the translation and the original. My own instinct says that the actual words of such a man as Goethe ought to be in the most honourable place, and ought not to be relegated to a note. From your silence, however, I conclude you to be satisfied to leave it as it is.

'I will send you another proof; rather I will return you this one when I have transferred the corrections to a clear sheet. (No, I find a spare clean one which I can let you have conveniently.)

'There are three more letters complete—two of them very long—and fragments of one or two more. The wise old man took alarm at Carlyle's radicalism, and earnestly cautioned him against it.

'Carlyle writes *bey*, *frey*, etc. My dictionary says *bei*, *frei*. Which is right?

'My very warmest thanks [he wrote finally, January 8, 1882]. You have recovered and replaced the subtle shadings of Goethe's. Even without your help, I suppose I should have myself mended the translation somewhat, but you will see that I have adopted every one of your suggestions . . . You will have a proof on Wednesday morning.

'As to the verses, the grace depends so entirely on the form that (subject to your better judgment) I think it will be best to let the German lines stand in the text, and not attempt a translation. I had been beaten altogether by the *augenblicklich aufzuwarten*.

I had considered (on looking at it again) that the point lay in the contrast between *augenblicklich*, in sense of face to face (if it could mean that) and the remoteness of the friend to whom he was writing ; and I suppose there is in the original some suggestion of the kind, but I do not see how it can be preserved in another language.

'Goethe was an *artist* ; verses by him were specimens of art, and therefore may fitly stand in their own form. If they set a few people puzzling their brains, what harm ? I send—not this time to give you any trouble, but for your own amusement merely—the proofs of the first chapter of the second volume. They are uncorrected, but the mistakes are not many, and nowhere affect the sense. I suppose they will set the dogs all barking again.'

In order to bring the biography within reasonable compass Froude's method for the most part was that of using portions of letters quoted directly, other portions incorporated within his own text, and abstracts or abridgments.[1] Otherwise his book would

[1] It would seem that Froude is far more accurate than John Gibson Lockhart, if we are to believe Davidson Cook, whose article on 'Lockhart's Treatment of Scott's Letters' is in the *Nineteenth Century*, September 1927. Mr. Cook says : 'It was not only with letters addressed to himself that Lockhart tampered, and the text of the whole mass of Scott's family correspondence, as vouched for by the responsible writer of the official biography, is more than suspect. For instance, on the authority of the original manuscripts, I can testify that Lockhart made pencilled scribblings through lengthy passages of the letters written by Sir Walter to his son and namesake ; and with seldom a hint of such excisions published the letters with these and other mutilations in his *magnum opus*. Similar liberties were taken with the rest of the family correspondence.' I cannot speak with authority in regard to Lockhart's work, but a careful reading of Cook's article along with the text of the biography of Scott leads me to believe that nothing essential has been suppressed. The fact is that Lockhart was simply following the custom of his day, when, in Cook's words, 'textual purity had not been exalted as a literary virtue.' To-day the emphasis is on marks of omission, brackets, capitalisation, and punctuation. I should not fail to add that David Wilson's recent biography offends most seriously against the canons of the present. He fails to mark omissions and does not distinguish between marks of parenthesis and brackets. The point, it seems to me, is whether Lockhart understood Scott. If he did, then I shall read what he wrote about Scott in preference to what any present-day author writes, especially an author who lacks the first-hand information and the insight of Lockhart. Technical accuracy, while highly desirable, cannot make up for essentials.

have been swollen to enormous size. As it is, he has been criticised for making so large a work. 'That Mr. Froude meant to tell the public whatever facts about his [Carlyle's] life it concerned the public to know, he [Carlyle] was aware; but his natural reserve and modesty prevented him from suspecting on what a scale the would-be Boswell was about to write,' remarks David Wilson.[1] The remark is worth while if only for the pleasant admission on Wilson's part that Carlyle was aware of what Froude was about. It seems, though, a peculiar criticism for one to make who has written the story of Carlyle's life at so much greater length than did Froude. If, however, Carlyle's authorised biographer had not followed the method of reducing his material, to what lengths his biography might have gone it is hard to say. Froude used the method which Carlyle himself followed in 'Cromwell' and 'John Sterling.' And with such an example as Carlyle had set in 'Frederick,' Froude could hardly be blamed had he written about his subject at even greater length. That Carlyle, after reading Froude's article on Trevelyan's 'Macaulay' in *Fraser's Magazine* of June 1876, knew thoroughly well how his biographer would proceed is entirely clear. And if Carlyle was satisfied, why should others complain?

Froude's honesty of purpose is apparent throughout the biography. He speaks freely not only about Carlyle but about himself. Indeed, he was always mercilessly honest in speaking of himself. One example is the account of his relations with the Eyre Committee, with which Carlyle was so prominently connected. 'I was myself one of the cowards,' writes Froude.[2] Again, in speaking of the manner in which he has written the biography he plainly remarks: 'It may be said that I shall have thus

[1] *Mr. Froude and Carlyle*, p. 319. Wilson's own scale is that of a six-volume biography as against Froude's of four volumes!

[2] *Thomas Carlyle*, 4. p. 329.

produced no "Life," but only the materials for a "Life." That is true. But I believe that I shall have given, notwithstanding, a real picture as far as it goes; and an adequate estimate of Carlyle's work in this world is not at present possible.' Those are the words of a great, modest, and truthful man, who is not overwhelmed by a sense of the importance of his own work. He makes no claim for the biography beyond the fact that it is the embodiment of the best he can do. 'What object could I have in misrepresenting the most intimate friend I had in the world?' he asked Skelton. His communings with himself in his private journals are in the same strain. In looking forward to a time of accounting he kept a clear conscience. 'The biographer himself will soon end, and go where he will have to answer for the manner in which he has discharged his trust, happy so far that he has been allowed to live to complete an arduous and anxious undertaking.'[1] There is a ring of sincerity in the words. Carlyle wished himself and his work to be forgotten if his message were of no value; 'his own desire for himself would be the speediest oblivion both of his person and his works.' There can be no doubt that Froude's attitude toward his own work as biographer of Carlyle was the same; if there were no truth in it, he would wish for it speedy oblivion.

Froude's own deliberate summary of the matter is found in a paragraph of the twelfth chapter of 'Oceana.'[2] 'In writing the biography of a great man you are to tell the truth so far as you know it. You are not to trouble yourself with the impression which you may produce on the rank and file of immediate readers. You are to consider the wise, and in the long run the opinion of the wise will be the opinion of the multitude. Carlyle was the noblest and truest man that I ever met in this world.

[1] *Thomas Carlyle*, 4. p. 460.

[2] *Oceana*, p. 177.

His peculiarities were an essential part of him, and if I was to draw any portrait of him at all, I was bound to draw a faithful portrait. His character is not likely to please his average contemporaries, of whom he himself had so poor an estimate. Had I made him pleasing to such as they are, I should have drawn nothing which in any trait could resemble the original.' Those sentences contain the essence of what as biographer Froude kept before himself from the beginning.

One error Froude did make, and for that he has had to pay dearly. He did not make a full revelation of what he knew. It was perhaps natural and inevitable that he should not. He had undertaken the task in the spirit of Carlyle's review of Lockhart's 'Scott.' Carlyle's opinion, as there expressed, and as we have previously explained it, seems to be that a biographer should 'keep all his charities about him, but all his eyes open.' He has a difficult road before him. 'Far be it from him to set down aught *untrue*; nay, not to abstain from, and leave in oblivion, much that is true.' What Froude did tell was sufficient to arouse the wrath of Mary and Alexander Carlyle. It does not appear, however, that any other members of the Carlyle family were offended. It now seems clear that Froude erred not so much in what he revealed as in what he did not reveal. In his desire to pass lightly over the sexual question he left the matter dark, wrote in a way that gave opportunity for wrong inferences. Had he expressed fully and clearly, as far as he knew the truth, what he later told in his posthumous pamphlet, his work would have been less vulnerable. He did, however, exactly what Sir Edward Cook later did in writing of Ruskin. Nothing is ever gained by giving just enough to whet curiosity and then leaving a matter dark. Froude has suffered the penalty of his omission. His error has been balanced, however, by the mistaken zeal of the attack by Alexander Carlyle, which forced Froude's children to publish the account which their father had left behind in self-defence.

It is not easy to see how the criticism that Froude was seriously deficient in humour can be justified in the case of the man who wrote those two delicately ironic sketches 'The Cat's Pilgrimage' and 'A Siding at a Railway Station.' His quiet humour reveals itself at many points. 'Eternal punishment is reserved, we hope, only for mortal sins,' he once wrote. 'To publish a bad poem and be praised for it is at least a venial sin, for which purgatory may suffice.'[1] It is not likely that Carlyle would have chosen for an intimate friend a man with no sense of humour, one who always had the air 'of a man driving a hearse.'[2] Froude was a man with a keen sense of humour, as his works and his letters abundantly attest. He was a good conversationalist, and his talk was pointed with many good stories. His intimate friends knew him as a pleasant and humorous companion. It was not to everyone, however, that he revealed himself.[3]

Like the biographer himself, Froude's 'Thomas Carlyle' has been grossly misrepresented. One thing that has helped to forward the misrepresentation is the fact that most of those who read hostile criticism fail to read the four volumes of the biography itself.

[1] See article 'Lord Macaulay' in *Fraser's*, June 1876.

[2] See Wilson's *Carlyle*, 2. p. 49, and Masson's *Carlyle Personally and in his Writings*, p. 17. For a good estimate of Froude's sense of humour see Paul's *Life of Froude*, pp. 436–442.

[3] Leslie Stephen has made this fact clear in his *Life of Sir James Fitzjames Stephen*, p. 200. 'No one could be blind to Froude's great personal charm whenever he chose to exert it; but many people had the feeling that it was not easy to be on such terms as to know the real man. There were certain outworks of reserve and shyness to be surmounted, and they indicated keen sensibilities which might be unintentionally shocked. But to such a character there is often a great charm in the plain, downright ways of a masculine friend, who speaks what he thinks without reserve and without any covert intention. Froude and Fitzjames, in any case, became warmly attached; Froude thoroughly appreciated Fitzjames's fine qualities, and Fitzjames could not but delight in Froude's cordial sympathy.'

To do so is salutary. Accurate readers find that the presentation of Carlyle is not one-sided. They find that Froude sees and portrays Carlyle from many points of view. One of the most difficult things for the average or commonplace mind is to see a man from more than one—and that the narrow and personal—point of view. That a man can be kind and at the same time savage and irritable is beyond the comprehension of many. And when a man is a paradox, when he is ' not one but many men,' there is little wonder that most people have difficulty in compassing him. Froude fairly and with unusual skill portrays the Carlyle who was not one man but many. Hence came the outcry, almost inevitable at the time. The contemporary misjudgment on the part of those who were prejudiced, ignorant, or incapable of comprehension is sure to pass.

So evident is Froude's fairness of portrayal to any one who reads the biography with open mind that it should be unnecessary to insist upon it. So commonly is the contrary asserted, however, that I feel constrained to give examples. The closing paragraph of ' The Nemesis of Froude ' gives the following summary of Carlyle :

' Intellectually fulfilling one's ideal of greatness, a man made in the noblest human mould, in originality, in range of historical knowledge, in breadth of literary culture, in command of language, in lustre of imagination, in grasp of judgment, unsurpassed in his century, Carlyle will yet be recognised, through the mists and miasms that Froude has drawn around him, and through the gloom of his own moodiness and melancholy, as morally as well as intellectually great. He was, verily, one of the kindliest, most generous, true-hearted, humane, and upright of men, in whom, under a rugged exterior, were great depths of tenderness and comprehensive sympathy, who with intense earnestness combined quaint pleasantry and genial humour. When his shallow and ribald critics are forgotten, his memory will be cherished by the world.'

Among Froude's remarks upon Carlyle, written about ten years before the previously quoted paragraph, are the following :

'Carlyle exerted for many years an almost unbounded influence on the mind of educated England. . . . It may be, and I for one think it will be, that when time has levelled accidental distinctions, when the perspective has altered, and the foremost figures of this century are seen in their true proportions, Carlyle will tower far above all his contemporaries, and will then be the one person of them about whom the coming generations will care most to be informed. . . . In the grave matters of the law he walked for eighty-five years unblemished by a single moral spot . . . In no instance did he ever deviate even for a moment from the strictest lines of integrity. . . . Tender-hearted and affectionate he was beyond all men whom I have ever known. His faults, which in his late remorse he exaggerated, as men of noblest natures are most apt to do, his impatience, his irritability, his singular melancholy, which made him at times distressing as a companion, were the effects of temperament first, and of a peculiarly sensitive organisation ; and secondly of absorption in his work and of his determination to do that work as well as it could possibly be done. Such faults as these were but as the vapours which hang about a mountain, inseparable from the nature of the man. . . . The more completely it is understood, the more his character will be seen to answer to his intellectual teaching. The one is the counterpart of the other. There was no falsehood and there was no concealment in him. The same true nature showed itself in his life and in his words. He acted as he spoke from his heart, and those who have admired his writings

will equally admire himself when they see him in his actual likeness.' [1]
The concluding chapters of the last volume of the biography are even more laudatory.

A comparison of summaries of the married life of the Carlyles is still more illuminating. David Wilson, always enthusiastic, wrote in 1898 that Carlyle, 'seems to have never spoken harshly' to his wife.[2] In his recent biography of Carlyle he declares that 'Their married life was one long honeymoon of forty years, with hardly enough of a breeze to vary the monotony.' [3] His own 'Mr. Froude and Carlyle,' to be sure, contains plenty of evidence to the contrary. Alexander Carlyle and Crichton-Browne sum up the matter in this way :

'The Carlyles lived on a higher plane than Froude conceived. Their married life of forty years' duration was essentially beautiful. It was not blessed with offspring. It was chequered, as all married lives are, with cares, anxieties, and sorrows, it was ruffled by angry breezes, it was shadowed by sickness, which at one time gathered into a thunder-cloud, but it was irradiated throughout by the pure white light of wholesome human love.' [4]

Charles Eliot Norton writes of it in this fashion :

'The lives of Carlyle and his wife are not represented as they were, in this book of Mr. Froude's. There was much that was sorrowful in their experience ; much that was sad in their relations to each other. Their mutual love did not make them happy, did not supply them with the self-control required for happiness. Their faults often prevailed against their love, and yet "with a thousand faults they were both," as Carlyle said to Miss Welsh (25th May 1823), "true-hearted people." And through all the dark vicissitudes of life love did not desert them. Blame

[1] *Thomas Carlyle*, 3. pp. 4–7.
[2] *Mr. Froude and Carlyle*, p. 243.
[3] *Carlyle*, 2. p. 21.
[4] *Nemesis*, pp. 60–61.

each of them as one may for carelessness, hardness, bitterness, in the course of the years, one reads their lives wholly wrong unless he read in them that the love that had united them was beyond the power of fate and fault to ruin utterly, that more permanent than aught else it abided in the heart of each, and that in what they were to each other it remained the unalterable element.' [1]

What does Froude say?

'The married life of Carlyle and Jane Welsh was not happy in the roseate sense of happiness . . . For the forty years which these two extraordinary persons lived together, their essential conduct to the world and to each other was sternly upright. They had to encounter poverty in its most threatening aspect. . . . If he ever flagged, it was his wife who spurred him on; nor would she ever allow him to do less than his very best. She never flattered anyone, least of all her husband; and when she saw cause for it the sarcasms flashed out from her as the sparks fly from lacerated steel. Carlyle, on his side, did not find in his marriage the miraculous transformation of nature which he had promised himself. He remained lonely and dyspeptic, possessed by thoughts and convictions which struggled in him for utterance, and which could be fused and cast into form only (as I have heard him say) when his whole mind was like a furnace at white heat. . . . Though the lives of the Carlyles were not happy, yet if we look at them from the beginning to the end they were grandly beautiful. Neither of them probably under other conditions would have risen to as high an excellence as in fact they each achieved; and the main question is not how happy men and women have been in this world, but what they have made of themselves. I well remember the bright assenting laugh with which she once responded to some words of mine when the propriety was being

[1] *Early Letters of Carlyle*, ii. 382.

discussed of relaxing the marriage laws. I had said that the true way to look at marriage was as a discipline of character.'[1]

The outcry against the biography upon its publication, so far as it was not engineered by Mary Carlyle and her adherents, must be interpreted in the light of the time. We must remember the *Zeitgeist* of the period. There was then more reserve, more prudishness, if you will, than now. Tennyson's attitude towards biography is typical. He would have all details of a writer's life concealed from the public. He felt that 'Merlin and the Gleam' was sufficient as a biography of himself. The result is that his own biography is colourless. It fails to portray the man as he was; it does not present the gruff and human Tennyson. Such an attitude is almost directly opposite to that of the present. The modern spirit is well summarised by Carlyle himself.

'He [the biographer] is found guilty of having said this and that, calculated not to be entirely pleasant to this man and that; in other words, calculated to give him and the thing he worked in a living set of features, not leave him vague, in the white beatified-ghost condition. Several men, as we hear, cry out, "See, there is something written not entirely pleasant to me!" Good friend, it is pity; but who can help it? They that will crowd about bonfires may, sometimes very fairly, get their beards singed; it is the price they pay for such illumination; natural twilight is safe and free to all. For our part, we hope all manner of biographies that are written in England will henceforth be written so. If it is fit that they be written otherwise, then it is still fitter that they be not written at all: to produce not things but ghosts of things can never be the duty of man.'[2]

Froude himself feared at times that, in the biography, he was portraying his subject in too favourable

[1] *Thomas Carlyle*, I. pp. 364–367. [2] Carlyle on 'Sir Walter Scott.'

a light.[1] In view of the savage criticism directed against his work during so many years, it is amusing to consider that the prevalent opinion to-day is that Froude very greatly over-estimated Carlyle. Certainly the man who wrote the last paragraph of 'Thomas Carlyle' cannot justly be accused of having tried to malign his subject.

At present the searchlight is directed into every remotest corner of a man's life. Carlyle would be no safer than any other man. Fortunately, Froude anticipated the microfiers and the scandal-mongers. He boldly presented Carlyle as he was, and thus took the wind out of the sails of later biographers. It is significant that Carlyle has not been made the subject of a fictionised or a defamatory biography. The trend is rather in the other direction. Now that the worst has been told, the world is beginning to see or at least is beginning to attempt to see Carlyle in proper perspective. The progress of his biographical history has been thus singular. Whereas the lives of most other literary men have been at the first ideal portraits—Wordsworth's conspicuously so—and then human portrayals, with all discoverable details included, Carlyle's has been the other way. The flurry of gossip which arose when undue attention was centred upon Carlyle's frailties has subsided. On the foundation of Froude's work there will some day be constructed a short and properly proportioned interpretation of Carlyle. Then we shall know that the Carlyle whom Froude portrayed was neither a god nor a devil, but a man—a being subject to the same frailties as we ourselves, yet also a spirit which in its aspiration uttered some thoughts which the world will not willingly allow to die.

If there is something of paradox in the life as portrayed by Froude, it must be remembered that

[1] 'I fear that in my work there is too much of the idol.' Froude to Max Müller, January 16, 1882.

there was paradox in the nature of Carlyle himself, as there was in that of Jane Welsh. 'There is something *demonic* both in him and in her which will never be adequately understood,' wrote Froude to Fanny Kingsley. In the matter of their personal relations, for example, Froude is criticised for saying that they had serious domestic differences, and their letters are offered as proof of the falsity of such a statement. Could differences exist between people who in absence wrote to each other as the Carlyles wrote? we are asked. The two facts are by no means irreconcilable. Many can perhaps recall a similar state of affairs among certain of their friends who are husbands and wives. The case of Anna Murphy and Robert Jameson is on record. It was seemingly impossible for Jameson to live with his wife, and yet when he was separated from her he was always eager to have her join him. 'Nothing could be better or kinder in expression than the repeated letters which called her to his side,' we are told. Those who have read Gerardine Macpherson's account of Mrs. Jameson's life will never forget the story of the wife's solitary journey from England to Toronto, Canada, in mid-winter, to join her husband, only to be rebuffed and in the end defrauded of her portion of her husband's property. 'Mr. Jameson seems to have been one of those strangely constituted persons to whom absence is always necessary to reawaken affection, and who prize what they are not in possession of, and habitually slight and neglect what they have. At a distance he was the most devoted and admiring of husbands, but in the privacy of the domestic circle, cold, self-absorbed, and unsympathetic, and his most affectionate phrases evidently inspired no confidence in the bosom of the woman who had already believed and trusted and been disappointed over and over again.' [1]

[1] *Memoirs of Anna Jameson*, p. 98.

There, *mutatis mutandis*, is a clue to the paradox of Carlyle's home life and his correspondence.

When the weary task was completed Froude wrote with unusual freedom to Fanny Kingsley, the sister of his first wife, what is perhaps his own best word about the biography. After asking her to tell him what impression she derived from reading the volumes he said :

'Only remember this : that it was Carlyle's own determination (or at least desire) to do justice to his wife, and to do public penance himself—a desire which I think so noble as to obliterate in my own mind the occasion there was for it. *I* have long known the worst, and Charles knew it generally. We all knew it, and yet the more intimately I knew Carlyle, the more I loved and admired him ; and some people, Lord Derby, for instance, after reading the "Life," can tell me that their opinion of him is rather raised than diminished. There is something *demonic* both in him and her which will never be adequately understood ; but the hearts of both of them were sound and true to the last fibre. You may guess what difficulty mine has been, and how weary the responsibility. You may guess, too, how dreary it is to me to hear myself praised for frankness, when I find the world all fastening on Carlyle's faults, while the splendid qualities are ignored or forgotten. Let them look into their own miserable souls, and ask themselves how *they* could bear to have their own private histories ransacked and laid bare. I deliberately say (and I have said it in the book) that Carlyle's was the finest nature I have ever known. It is a Rembrandt picture, but what a picture ! Ruskin, too, understands him, and feels too, as he should, for *me*, if that mattered, which it doesn't in the least.' [1]

'A Rembrandt picture'—the notion was firmly fixed in Froude's mind ; he had used the same phrase

[1] Quoted from Paul's *Life of Froude*, pp. 330–331.

in a letter to Olga Novikoff of a year previously. 'I get on with Carlyle; a sort of Rembrandt portrait will come out at last, not unlike; and if I can make others feel as I do, intensely lovable.' That is the truth of the matter. Froude's 'Thomas Carlyle' is a Rembrandt portrait. If the work of a great portrait painter is of value at all, it is as a record of what the painter saw in the subject; the painter is one of the three factors concerned. If the work of a great biographer is of value it is as a portrayal of the subject as the biographer sees him, an interpretation from the biographer's point of view. Even a critic none too friendly to Froude bears witness to the greatness of his achievement. 'Working with consummate skill upon magnificent materials, Froude has constructed a character and has left a picture of life enthralling in its interest,' writes Hugh Walker.[1]

The whole superstructure of hostile criticism rests upon slight foundation, notwithstanding statements to the contrary. 'The view of Mr. Carlyle's character presented in this biography,' wrote Charles Eliot Norton in 1886, 'has not approved itself to many of those who knew Carlyle best.'[2] That is the kind of statement which has been deceiving the public for almost fifty years. The fact is that the immediate reception of Froude's books on Carlyle was favourable except in a few quarters where personal interests or prejudices were affected. Apart from Mary and Alexander Carlyle only a few persons, such as Julia Wedgewood, Margaret Oliphant, William E. H. Lecky, and J. Cotter Morison, disapproved. David Masson, often referred to as hostile to Froude, voiced generous if reluctant approval. 'Nor must we forget,' wrote Masson, 'the prodigious interest and impressiveness, all in all, of those nine volumes, or the fact that they themselves contain, whether in the

[1] *Literature of the Victorian Era*, p. 875.
[2] *Early Letters of Carlyle*, i. p. vi.

autobiographical letters and extracts or in Mr. Froude's own comments and narrative, so much in direct contradiction and rebuke of the paltry misjudgment of Carlyle which many readers of the volumes have carried away from them that the persistence of such readers in their misjudgment can be accounted for only by the radical smallness of the average mind, its inability to grasp or appreciate anything very uncommon.' [1]

Richard Garnett, whose 'Life of Carlyle' appeared in 1887, wrote under the influence of Mary Carlyle and Charles Eliot Norton. It was impossible for Lecky, disliking as he did 'The English in Ireland,' to do justice at the moment to Froude's biographical and editorial labours. In an unpublished letter to Froude of June 20, 1874, Carlyle dismissed Lecky's criticism of 'The English in Ireland' in these words: 'Poor Lecky is weak as water—bilge-water with a drop of formic acid in it: unfortunate Lecky, he is wedded to his Irish idols; let him alone.' Criticism motivated by such strong political feeling as Lecky exhibited cannot be taken seriously.[2] At heart, however, Lecky recognised and admired the value of Froude's work and the greatness of his character. On the day of Froude's death he wrote: 'Few men, indeed, have won more affection, or lived down more animosity, or borne themselves (as I have had much reason to know) amid grave differences of opinion with such a complete absence of personal bitterness.' [3]

Among those who approved of Froude's work may

[1] *Carlyle Personally and in his Writings*, pp. 9–10. As for Margaret Oliphant, Froude, in a letter of March 2, 1884, to his daughter Margaret, wrote: 'her antipathies to me are many years old, and whatever I had done with the Carlyle papers she would have found ill done. It lies in the nature of the case. Half the world would have it one way and half another. Both quarrel with me, as they were sure to do. I shall stand clear in my own eyes when these last volumes [of *Thomas Carlyle*] are published, and the rest may say what they please.'

[2] See his review of Froude's *English in Ireland* in *Macmillan's Magazine*, June 1874.

[3] *Memoir of the Right Hon. William Edward Hartpole Lecky*, p. 261.

be mentioned John Ruskin, Edward FitzGerald, John Skelton, Sir James Stephen, Lord Derby, and John Nichol, a really impressive group. Of Ruskin's championship of Froude enough has been said. It is well to remember that Ruskin was one of Carlyle's most intimate and valued friends. Edward FitzGerald was delighted to find that Froude had revealed to him a new Carlyle. Writing in August 1882 to Fanny Kemble, he said: 'The Carlyle "Reminiscences" had long indisposed me from taking up the biography. But when I began, and as I went on with that, I found it one of the most interesting of books: and the result is that I not only admire and respect Carlyle more than I ever did: but even love him, which I never thought of before.'[1] Again, in September 1882, he wrote: 'Yes; you must read Froude's Carlyle above all things, and tell me if you do not feel as I do about it. Professor Norton persists . . . that I am proof against Froude's invidious insinuations simply because of my having previously known Carlyle. But how is it that I did not know that Carlyle was so good, grand, and even loveable, till I read the letters which Froude now edits? I regret that I did not know what the book tells us while Carlyle was alive; that I might have loved him as well as admired him.'[2]

The remarks of Sir John Skelton are important: 'How far the outcry that arose on either side of the Atlantic was spontaneous, how far due to the direct initiative of unfriendly "friends," it is hard to say. It appeared to me at the time to be due in the main to political feeling. Neither Carlyle nor Froude had flattered the democracy, and their contempt for its idol [Gladstone] had been perhaps too openly expressed. "He is omnipotent as ever. Nothing will disenchant the English public with him till the mischief comes home to themselves. . . ." Carlyle always

[1] *Letters of Edward FitzGerald to Fanny Kemble*, p. 245. [2] *Ibid.*, p. 248.

said that it would be his [Gladstone's] fate to break the Constitution to pieces. But I was not behind the scenes (as Sir Fitzjames Stephen was—who strenuously vindicated his friend and colleague), and it would seem, to say the least, that other motives had been at work. So far however as Edward FitzGerald was concerned the appeal to passion and prejudice failed. No doubt it impressed him at first ; but his native good sense and English love of fair play quickly asserted themselves ; and his final judgment was eminently favourable to Mr. Froude. . . . That this judgment will be affirmed by " the best literary opinion of the future " (to use the words of *The Spectator*), I have no doubt whatever. Froude himself never doubted that this would be the ultimate verdict. " Mrs. Skelton's judgment," he wrote in 1889, " about the Carlyles is quite sound. When the dogs have done barking and the thing is steadily looked at, it will be found that Carlyle as I have represented him is a much greater figure than the painted doll which the idolaters looked for. The form which his remorse took is so infinitely beyond the measure of the fault that it not only does away with it, but is itself an evidence of the tenderness and beauty of his character. So at least it appears, and from the first has appeared, to me." '[1]

On October 20, 1884, Lord Derby wrote to Froude the following letter :

' I hope you do not object to be told that you have written the most interesting biography in the English language ; for that is what you will hear very often, and in my poor judgment it is the truth. What you will probably care for more, I think you have finally silenced the foolish talk about indiscretion and treachery to a friend's memory. It is clear that you have done only, and exactly, what Carlyle wished done : and to me it is also apparent that he and you

[1] *Shirley*, pp. 347–349.

were right: that his character could not have been understood without a full disclosure of what was least attractive in it: and that these defects—the product mainly of morbid physical conditions—do not really take away from his greatness, while they explain much that was dark, at least to me, in his writings. You will not thank me for adding, what nevertheless I firmly believe, that fifty or one hundred years hence the memoir will have ten readers for every one of the "Frederic[k]" or "French Revolution." What a relief to your mind to have got this work off it!'

'Lord Derby's opinions,' remarks Herbert Paul, 'were not lightly formed, and he was as much guided by pure reason as mortal man can be.'

John Nichol's opinion agrees with that of Lord Derby. He pronounces Froude's account of Carlyle's life 'the most eminent, and, in the main, the most reliable.' He was writing eight years after the completion of Froude's 'Thomas Carlyle.' 'Every critic of Carlyle,' he continues, 'must admit as constant obligations to Mr. Froude as every critic of Byron to Moore or of Scott to Lockhart. The works of these masters in biography remain the ample storehouses from which every student will continue to draw. Each has, in a sense, made his subject his own, and each has been similarly arraigned.' Nichol was not satisfied with this expression of approval, but paid his respects to Froude's critics. 'I must here be allowed to express,' he writes, 'a feeling akin to indignation at the persistent, often virulent, attacks directed against a loyal friend, betrayed, it may be, by excess of faith and the defective reticence that often belongs to genius, to publish too much about his hero. But Mr. Froude's quotation, in defence, from the essay on Sir Walter Scott requires no supplement: it should be remembered that he acted with explicit authority; that the restrictions under which he was at first entrusted with the manuscripts of the "Reminiscences" and the "Letters and Memorials" (annotated by Carlyle himself, as if for publication) were withdrawn; and that the initial permission to select finally approached a practical injunction to communicate the whole. The worst that can be said is that, in the last years of Carlyle's career, his own judgment as to what should be made public of the details of his domestic life may have been somewhat obscured; but, if so, it was a weakness easily hidden from a devotee.'[1]

Crichton-Browne cites the testimony of Tennyson and Browning as to the domestic happiness of the Carlyles.[2] As I have already indicated, Tennyson was disqualified as a critic of biography. Moreover, he has nowhere spoken definitely in contradiction of the accuracy of Froude's narrative. His remark that 'Mr. and Mrs. Carlyle on the whole enjoyed life together, else they would not have chaffed one another so heartily'[3] is a slender foundation upon which to base refutation of Froude. Browning, also, because of his dislike of Mrs. Carlyle, was inclined to be too favourable in judging Carlyle.[4] Even Crichton-Browne admits that Browning 'went too far in describing her as a hard, unlovable woman.'[5] Emerson is often cited as a witness to the happy married life of the Carlyles, but anyone who has ever estimated the number of days Emerson was in the presence of the couple will not be misled by such testimony. In determining the relative value of such evidence against that of Froude we must always keep in mind the extent of close personal acquaintance and contact. Those who do keep such facts in mind cannot be deceived.

It is clear that, for the most part, those who were

[1] Nichol's *Thomas Carlyle*, pp. v–vi.
[2] *New Letters and Memorials*, i. p. lxvii.–lxviii.
[3] Hallam Tennyson's *Tennyson*, ii. 233.
[4] See Mrs. Sutherland Orr's *Robert Browning*, p. 366, *note*.
[5] *New Letters and Memorials*, i. p. lxviii.

dissatisfied with the biography at the time of its publication were chiefly those who for personal reasons were hostile to Froude. The others were unable to form a correct estimate of its value because they did not know how to distinguish between small and great. 'What ought to have struck all readers of these volumes,' remarks Herbert Paul, 'was the courage, the patience, the dignity, the generosity, and the genius of the Scotch peasant. What chiefly struck too many of them was that he did not get on with his wife.'[1] Even to-day there are too many readers of the latter class. In spite of all criticism, however, the biography has held its place. Even hostile critics have recognised its greatness. Right well did Charles Eliot Norton add the following remarks to the very preface in which he expressed disapproval : 'For the present, at least, it appears impracticable to prepare another formal biography. The peculiar style of Mr. Froude's performance, already in possession of the field, might perhaps put a portrait of Carlyle drawn by a hand more faithful to nature, and less skilled in fine artifices than his own, at a temporary disadvantage with the bulk of readers.'[2] Mowbray Morris wrote : 'It would be an ill compliment to Mr. Froude to suppose him hurt by the hard words that have been flung at the great mausoleum he has now completed to the memory of Carlyle. For great it assuredly is, nor in substance only. Whatever be our feelings for the relics it is intended to enshrine, whatever even we may think of the style of the building, we must all respect the pious care and industry of the architect. Our language is not rich in biographies of this high class. . . . It seems hard to doubt the truth of the portrait. The man that many, perhaps, who never set eyes on him in the flesh have fashioned out of his works, it may not be ; but that this is the true and theirs the counterfeit likeness, is surely writ

[1] *Life of Froude*, p. 319.

[2] *Early Letters of Carlyle*, I. p. vi.

large on every page, and with the man's own hand.' [1]

When Alexander Carlyle published the 'New Letters of Thomas Carlyle' in 1904 he offered them as a kind of autobiography of his uncle, for the reason, as he said, that 'no life of Carlyle, satisfactory to those who knew him intimately, has yet appeared.' The very small number of Carlyle's friends who were not satisfied is now clear. The 'New Letters,' moreover, contain nothing to show that Carlyle's life was essentially different from Froude's portrayal of it. To-day Froude's 'Thomas Carlyle' stands with no rival. The biography which David Wilson is completing, quite apart from its fundamental defects, is not happy from the single point of view of style in having to endure comparison with the great work of Froude. It is as though Edward Augustus Freeman should have rewritten the 'History' of Herodotus.

Gladstone has suggested what this last word should be. 'What we want in a biography,' he writes, 'and what, despite the etymology of the title, we very seldom find, is *life*. The very best transcript is a failure, if it be a transcript only. To fulfil its idea, it must have in it the essential quality of movement; must realise the lofty fiction of the divine shield of Achilles, where the upturning earth, though wrought in metal, darkened as the plough went on, and the figures of the battle-piece dealt their strokes and parried them, and dragged out from the turmoil the bodies of their dead. . . . But neither love, which is indeed a danger as well as an ally . . . nor forgetfulness of self, will make a thoroughly good biography, without this subtle gift of imparting life.' To him who attains unto such 'lofty fiction' much may be forgiven. And Froude has attained. To those who read with open, unprejudiced minds, the story of Carlyle's life unrolls itself with a power not unlike that of the greatest Greek dramas. We see, before

[1] *Quarterly Review*, 159. pp. 76–79. The date of the magazine is January 1885.

our very eyes, the pilgrimage of Carlyle from birth to death ; we see his Titanic struggle with life ; we see him go down into the darkening shadows. We feel ourselves growing old with the hero as we proceed to the end of the volumes. Of such a biography it is little wonder that P. Hume Brown, Historiographer Royal of Scotland, and a critic not disposed to be lenient towards Froude, expressed the opinion that ' the eminence and distinctiveness of its subject and the skill of the biographer combine to make it a representative book of an epoch, and as such it has its only companion in Boswell's " Life of Johnson." '

CHAPTER XXV

THE VERDICT

THE circumstances under which Froude received and fulfilled his commission have now been narrated. The charges under which he has rested for almost half a century have been explained. The evidence on both sides has been presented. In conclusion it is only necessary to summarise the findings and render a verdict.

The evidence appears conclusive that Carlyle, after an acquaintance of twenty-two years, placed in Froude's hands in 1871 the correspondence of Jane Welsh Carlyle, and requested him to do with it what he thought best. It appears further that in 1873 Carlyle again charged Froude with the editing of Mrs. Carlyle's letters, and at the same time gave him a large collection of material bearing upon his own life with the understanding that it was to be used as the foundation of a biography. There can be no manner of doubt that in his will of 1873 he legally empowered Froude with full authority to act as his literary executor and do as he thought fit in regard to a biography. It is certain that, in spite of all that Mary could do, Carlyle until his death continued to keep Froude supplied with materials for the work which he had entrusted to him.

On the other hand, the evidence appears equally conclusive that about 1877 Mary Carlyle awoke to a realisation that the papers which her uncle had given to Froude were valuable and that the books to be compiled from them would yield a large return in money. It appears that, although she was unable to influence Carlyle to revoke his commission to Froude, she did succeed in securing his promise that Froude would be requested to give the papers to her when the work for which they were needed was done. It seems that at this point Carlyle was dilatory and evasive, at times impatient, and in the end satisfied to allow the matter to rest upon oral statements. As long as he lived, however, he saw to it that Froude went forward with the work. The 'Reminiscences' were in type and the first part of the biography was written before Carlyle's death.

It appears that Mary Carlyle's claims to the proceeds from the 'Reminiscences' grew out of a misunderstanding occasioned by Moncure Conway's suggestion of an immense sum from Harper and Brothers for an American edition which never materialised. Mary always maintained that Froude had no rights in the 'Reminiscences,' yet she claimed the profits on the ground that he had promised them to her. It is difficult to understand how he could promise what never belonged to him.

After Carlyle's death Mary publicly attacked Froude as soon as he began to carry out his commission. In the long controversy which followed, it gradually became evident that the law supported Froude, and in the end he carried his task to completion. To Mary Carlyle and her supporters there remained only the hope of destroying confidence in Froude and his work. The story of their efforts requires no further elaboration.

In the whole history of English biography perhaps no other work has been the object of such organised, long continued, and bitter criticism, or enmeshed in such a tissue of misrepresentation. Every page of the material about Carlyle edited or written by Froude has been subjected to microscopic examination. Thwarted in their efforts to prove that Froude was uncommissioned, his enemies shifted their attack to questions of taste and propriety. It was certain from the beginning that Mary and Alexander Carlyle would resent and repudiate whatever Froude did. Their hostility was inevitable. Had they been able to work their will, Froude would have been dispossessed of all materials except the manuscripts of Mrs. Carlyle which had been specifically bequeathed to him. Family pride and the desire to have the proceeds no doubt motivated their action. Carlyle, however, had taken care to put the matter beyond the control of relatives, choosing Froude apparently because he could write as an outsider, unhampered by family considerations.

Froude's work emerges from the fires of controversy unscathed. It contains errors, to be sure; errors in such tasks are inevitable. But as Froude himself has said, when errors are found they can be corrected. He was intent chiefly upon establishing the correct general features of his subject, confident that if these were correctly drawn they could not be greatly altered by time. Lights and shadows might shift, as the lights and shadows shift over the Great Stone Face, but the general outlines would remain unaltered. Ruskin expresses the matter admirably when he says that 'it is perfectly possible to protect oneself against small errors, and yet to make great and final error in the sum of work: on the other hand, it is equally possible to fall into many small errors, and yet be right in tendency all the while, and entirely right in the end.' That is the final word. *Froude is right in tendency all the while, and entirely right in the end.*

Froude's place is secure. In spite of Wilson's repeated ejaculations of 'foolish Froude' and 'Froude poor fellow,' Carlyle's biographer is in no need of pity. He was a stalwart pioneer who hewed his way through unexplored regions ; a man of courage, who refused to allow himself to be thwarted by virulent and unfair opposition. His biographical and historical work was based upon original documents. As historian he was one of the first great Englishmen to work upon original documents in many different languages. Such errors as may rightly be charged against him are largely the errors of pioneer work. They may be corrected, but the fact of their existence cannot deprive him of the honour due to a pioneer. Not less significant is his work as biographer. Here again he made no claim of having produced errorless work ; he maintained only that his work was right in motive and in its general features. He offered his 'Thomas Carlyle' as the material upon which future biographers might draw. So well did he do his work, however, that there seems little hope of superseding it. He endeavoured to present a truthful portrayal of Carlyle, and in doing so, if he did not inaugurate a new era in biography, he at least brought an era to completion. He made an end of the incredible panegyric. More even than Boswell he portrayed his subject at full length. His errors of judgment were such as are inevitable when an intimate friend acts as biographer. In attempting to shield Carlyle he laid himself open to malicious attack. Fortunately, however, for both Carlyle and himself he revealed enough to insure that the truth would be ultimately established.

What is needed at present is not such a biographical medley as David Wilson is producing, but a carefully revised edition of Froude's 'Thomas Carlyle.' It is one of the world's greatest biographies, a work whose place for many reasons is most assuredly next to Boswell's 'Life of Johnson.' In importance of subject, in skill of presentation, in prominence of authorship, Froude's 'Carlyle' must always occupy a high place. It is a faithful record, a striking portrait, a moving narrative, a great mausoleum to the memory of Carlyle. Were Carlyle here to pass judgment upon the manner in which Froude has fulfilled his commission, who can doubt that his verdict would be that his chosen representative wrought with no other fear before him than the fear of God ?

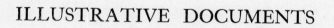

ILLUSTRATIVE DOCUMENTS

ILLUSTRATIVE DOCUMENTS

[Documents printed for the first time are marked *. Those which have hitherto been printed in part are marked †.]

I

WILL AND CODICIL OF THOMAS CARLYLE

'I, Thomas Carlyle, of 5 Great Cheyne-Row, Chelsea, in the County of Middlesex, Esquire, declare this to be my last Will and Testament Revoking all former Wills. I direct all my just debts, funeral and testamentary expences to be paid as soon as may be after my decease. And it is my express instruction that, since I cannot be laid in the Grave at Haddington, I shall be placed beside my Father and Mother in the Churchyard of Ecclefechan. I appoint my Brother, John Aitken Carlyle, Doctor of Medicine, and my Friend, John Forster of Palace Gate House, Kensington, Esquire, Executors and Trustees of this my Will. If my said Brother should die in my lifetime, I appoint my Brother, James Carlyle, to be an Executor and Trustee in his stead; and if the said John Forster should die in my lifetime, I appoint my friend, James Anthony Froude, to be an Executor and Trustee in his stead. I give to my dear and ever helpful Brother, John A. Carlyle, my Leasehold messuage in Great Cheyne-Row in which I reside, subject to the rent and covenants under which I hold the same, and all such of my Furniture, plate, linen, china, books, prints, pictures and other effects therein as are not hereinafter bequeathed specifically. My Brother John has no need of my money or help, and therefore, in addition to this small remembrance, I bequeath to him only the charge of being Executor of my Will and of seeing everything peaceably fulfilled. If he survives me, as is natural, he will not refuse. My poor and indeed almost pathetic collection of books (with the exception of those hereinafter specifically given) I request him to accept as a memento of me while he stays behind. I give my Watch to my Nephew Thomas, the son of my Brother Alexander, "Alick's Tom," as a Memorial of the affection I have for him and of my thankful (and also hopeful) approval of all that I have ever got to know or surmise about him. He can understand that of all my outward possessions this Watch is become the dearest to me. It was given me on my Wedding, by One who was herself invaluable to me; it had been her Father's, made to her Father's order; and had measured out, into still more perfect punctuality, *his* noble years of well-spent time; and now it has measured out (always punctually, *it*!) nearly forty-seven years of mine, and still measures, as with an everloving solemnity, till time quite end with me: and may the new Thomas Carlyle fare not worse with it than his two Predecessors have done. To Maggie Welsh, my dear Cousin (and *Hers*), One Hundred Pounds. To my House servant, Mrs. Warren, if in my service at the time of my decease, Fifty Pounds. Having with good reason, ever since my first appearance in Literature, a variety of kind feelings, obligations and regards towards New England, and indeed long before that, a hearty good-will, real and steady, which still continues, to America at large, and recognising with gratitude how much of friendliness, of actually credible human love, I have had from that Country, and what immensities of worth and capability I believe and partly know to be lodged, especially in the silent classes there,—I have now, after due consultation as to the feasibilities, the excusabilities of it, decided to fulfil a fond notion that has been hovering in my mind these many years ; and I do therefore hereby bequeath the Books (whatever of them I could not borrow, but had to buy and gather, that is, in general, whatever of them are still here) which I used in writing on "Cromwell" and "Friedrich," and which shall be accurately searched for, and parted from my other Books, to "The President and Fellows of Harvard College, City of Cambridge, State of Massachusetts," as a poor testimony of my respect for that *Alma Mater* of so many of my Trans-Atlantic Friends, and a token of the feelings, above indicated, towards the Great Country of which Harvard is the Chief School. In which sense I have reason to be confident that the Harvard Authorities will please to accept this my little Bequest ; and deal with it, and order and use it, as, to their own good judgment and kind fidelity, shall seem fittest. A certain symbolical value the Bequest may have ; but of intrinsic value, as a collection of old Books, it can pretend to very little. If there should be doubt as to any Books coming within the category of this Bequest, my dear Brother John, if left behind me, as I always trust and hope, who already knows about this Harvard matter, and who possesses a Catalogue or List drawn up by me, of which the Counterpart is in possession of the Harvard Authorities, will see it for me in all points accurately done. In regard to this, and to all else in these final directions of mine, I wish him to be regarded as my Second Self,—my Surviving Self. My Manuscript entitled "Letters and Memorials of Jane Welsh Carlyle" is to me naturally, in my now bereaved state, of endless value, though of what value to others I cannot in the least clearly judge ; and indeed for the last four years am imperatively forbidden to write farther on it, or even to look farther into it. Of that Manuscript, my kind, considerate and ever-faithful friend, James Anthony Froude (as he has lovingly promised me) takes precious charge in my stead; to him therefore I give it with whatever other fartherances and elucidations may be possible; and I solemnly request of him to do his best and wisest in the matter, as I feel assured he will. There is incidentally a quantity of Autobiographic Record in my Notes to this Manuscript; but except as subsidiary, and elucidative of the Text I put no value on such: express Biography of me I had really rather that there should be none. James Anthony Froude, John Forster and my Brother John, will make earnest survey of the Manuscript and its subsidiaries there or elsewhere, in respect to this as well as to its other bearings; their united utmost candour and impartiality (taking always James Anthony Froude's practicality along with it) will evidently furnish a better judgment than mine can be. The Manuscript is by no means ready for publication; nay, the questions, How, When (after what delay, seven, ten years) it, or any portion of it, should be published, are still dark to me; but on all such points James Anthony Froude's practical summing up and decision is to be taken as mine. The imperfect Copy of the said Manuscript which is among my papers with the original letters I give to my Niece Mary Carlyle Aitken; to whom also, dear little soul, I bequeath Five Hundred Pounds for the loving care, and unwearied patience and helpfulness she has shown to me in these my last solitary and infirm years. To her also I give, at her choice, whatever Memorials of my Dear Departed One she has seen me silently preserving here,—especially the table in the Drawing-Room at which I now write and the little Child's-Chair (in the China-Closet), which latter to my eyes has always a brightness as of Time's Morning and a sadness as of Death and Eternity, when I look on it; and which, with the other dear Article, I have the weak wish to preserve in loving hands yet awhile when I am gone. My other Manuscripts I leave to my Brother John. They are with one exception of no moment to me; I have never seen any of them since they were written. One of them is a set of fragments about James First, which were loyally fished out for me from much other Cromwellian rubbish, and doubtless carefully copied more than twenty years ago by the late John Chorley who was always so good to me. But neither this latter, nor perhaps any of the others, is worth printing. On this point however my Brother can take Counsel with John Forster and James Anthony Froude, and do what is then judged fittest. Many or most of these Papers I often feel that I myself should burn; but probably I never shall after all. The "one exception," spoken of above, is a Sketch of my Father and his Life hastily thrown off in the nights between his Death and Burial, full of earnest affection and veracity;—most likely *un*fit for printing; but I wish it to be taken charge of by my Brother John, and preserved in the Family. Since, I think, the very night of my Father's Funeral (far away from London and me!) I have never seen a word of that poor bit of writing.—In regard to all business matters about my Books (of which not only the Copyrights but all the Stereotype plates from which the three several collected Editions have been respectively printed, and which are at present deposited with my Printers, Messrs. Robson and Son, belong exclusively to me), Copyrights, Editions, and dealings with Booksellers and others in relation thereto, John Forster's advice is to be taken as supreme and complete, better than my own ever could have been. His faithful, wise and ever punctual care about all that has been a miracle of generous helpfulness, literally invaluable to me in that field of things.

Thanks, poor thanks, are all that I can return, alas! I give the residue of my personal Estate to my Trustees, before named, In trust to convert into money, such part of my Estate as shall not consist of money, or securities for money, and Upon trust to invest, in such securities as they shall think fit, the moneys to arise from such conversion and the moneys and securities of which my personal Estate shall consist at the time of my decease: With power to change investments from time to time, And to stand possessed thereof In trust as to one-fifth part thereof for my Brother Alexander, absolutely; And as to one-fifth part, In trust for my Brother James, absolutely; And as to one other fifth part thereof, In trust for my Sister Mary, Wife of James Austin, Farmer at Gill, Cummertrees, Dumfriesshire, absolutely, for her separate use independent of the debts, control or engagements of her present or any future Husband; And as to one other fifth part thereof, In trust for my Sister Jean, the Wife of James Aitken of Dumfries, absolutely, for her separate use independent of the debts, control or engagements of her present or any future husband; And as to the remaining fifth part thereof, In trust for my Sister Janet, Wife of Robert Hanning of Hamilton, Canada, absolutely, for her separate use independent of the debts, control or engagements of her present or any future husband. Provided always that, if my said Brothers Alexander and James, or my said Sisters, or any, or either of them shall die in my lifetime, the share or shares of him, her or them, so dying, shall be In trust for the Children of my Brothers or Sisters respectively, so dying, who shall attain the age of Twenty-one years, or being Daughters shall marry, in equal shares; but if there shall be no such Child, then such share or shares shall go to the others, or other, of my said Brothers and Sisters in equal shares, but so that the shares which may thus accrue to my Sisters shall be for their separate use in the same manner as their original shares. I direct all legacies to be paid free of duty. I direct that, notwithstanding the trust for conversion hereinbefore contained, my Trustees shall have absolute authority to postpone the conversion, for any period not exceeding two years after my death, of all or any part of my personal Estate ; and I say this with especial reference to my Copyrights. And the income to be derived from my Estate, previous to its conversion, shall be applied in the same way as the income of my Estate, if converted, would be applicable. To my dear friends, John Forster and James Anthony Froude (Masson too, I should remember in this moment, and perhaps some others), I have nothing to leave that could be in the least worthy of them ; but if they, or any of them, could find among my reliques a Memorial they would like, who of Men could deserve it better !—No Man at this time. If no such choice be made by themselves, I leave to Forster Faithorne's Print of Cromwell between the Pillars, now in the Drawing-Room here, and to Froude Pesne's Portrait of Wilhelmina with the Fontange on her brow, now in the same Room. In witness whereof I, the said Thomas Carlyle, the Testator, have to this, my last Will and Testament, set my hand this sixth day of February, One thousand eight hundred and seventy-three.

'Signed and Declared by the said Thomas Carlyle, the Testator, as and for his last Will and Testament, in the presence of us both present at the same time, who in his presence at his request, and in the presence of each other, hereunto subscribe our names as Witnesses.

'T. Carlyle.

'William Hares,
'Butler,
'Palace Gate House.

'Frederic Ouvry,
'66 Lincoln's Inn Fields, Solicitor.'

'This is a Codicil to the last Will and Testament of me, Thomas Carlyle, of No. 24 Cheyne-Row, Chelsea, in the County of Middlesex, Esquire, which said Will bears date the Sixth day of February, One thousand eight hundred and seventy-three. Whereas by my said Will I have appointed my Brother, John Aitken Carlyle, Doctor of Medicine, and John Forster, Esquire, Executors and Trustees thereof, and appointed and directed that, if my said Brother should die in my lifetime, my Brother, James Carlyle, should be an Executor and Trustee in his stead. And that, if the said John Forster should die in my lifetime, my friend, James Anthony Froude, should be an Executor and Trustee in his stead. And whereas, my dear and ever faithful friend, the said John Forster has been taken from me by death, and I am desirous of revoking the said appointment of Executors and Trustees contained in my said Will, and of appointing my said Brother, John Aitken Carlyle, the said James Anthony Froude and Sir James Fitz-James Stephen, of No. 24 Cornwall Gardens, South Kensington, in the said County of Middlesex, K.C.S.I., Q.C., to be Executors and Trustees of my said Will. Now, therefore, I do hereby revoke the above recited appointment of Executors and Trustees contained in my said Will, and do hereby appoint my said Brother, John Aitken Carlyle, the said James Anthony Froude and the said Sir James FitzJames Stephen to be Executors and Trustees of my said Will. I hereby revoke the gift in my said Will of the Writing-table, belonging to me, which stands in the Drawing-Room at No. 24 Cheyne-Row, aforesaid, and hereby give and bequeath the same Writing-table to the said Sir James FitzJames Stephen. I know he will accept it as a distinguished mark of my esteem. He knows that it belonged to my honoured Father-in-Law and his Daughter, and that I have written all my Books upon it except only "Schiller" and that, for the fifty years and upwards that are now past, I have considered it among the most precious of my possessions. I give and bequeath the Screen which stands in the Drawing-Room at No. 24 Cheyne-Row aforesaid, to my dear Niece, Mary Carlyle Aitken, who best knows the value I have always put upon it, and will best take care of it to the end of her life when I am gone. She knows by whom it was made, and I wish her to accept it as a testimony of the trust I repose in her, and as a mark of my esteem for her honourable, veracious and faithful character, and a memorial of all the kind and ever-faithful service she has done me. The Faithorne Portrait of Oliver Cromwell, which I had intended for my loving and ever-faithful friend, John Forster,—the only bequest he would accept of from me,—I now give and bequeath to his Widow, Mrs. Forster, and I beg her to accept it in memory of him and of me. I give and bequeath to my dear friend, David Masson, my photographically printed, folio copy of Shakespeare's Works, in memory of me. The two pictures of Luther's Father and Mother, which were a gift to me from Mr. Robert Tait of Queen Anne Street, Cavendish Square, in the said County of Middlesex, I give back to him. The large oil painting which hangs in the Drawing-Room at No. 24 Cheyne-Row, aforesaid, and which has been engraved under the title of "The little Drummer," I give and bequeath to Louisa Caroline, the Dowager Lady Ashburton, for her life, and after her death, to her Daughter, The Honourable Mary Florence Baring, absolutely. And, whereas, by my said Will I have given to my said dear Brother, John Aitken Carlyle, my Leasehold messuage No. 24 Cheyne-Row, aforesaid, in which I reside, subject to the rent and covenants under which I hold the same, and all such of my Furniture, plate, china, linen, books, prints, pictures and other effects therein as are not by my said Will bequeathed specifically. And whereas I am desirous of revoking such gift, and of making such bequest of the said messuage, property and effects as hereinafter appears. Now therefore I do hereby revoke the said gift of the said messuage, property and effects and hereby bequeath the said last mentioned leasehold messuage and all such of my Furniture, plate, linen, china, books, prints, pictures and other effects therein as are not by my said Will and this my Codicil bequeathed specifically, unto my said Brother John Aitken Carlyle for his life, he paying the rent and all rates, taxes and outgoings payable in respect of the same messuage and performing the covenants and conditions under which I hold the same, and after his death, I give and bequeath the same messuage, Furniture, plate, linen, china, books, prints, pictures and other effects unto my said Niece, Mary Carlyle Aitken, absolutely. In all other respects I confirm my said Will. In witness whereof I have to this Codicil to my said Will set my hand this Eighth day of November, One thousand eight hundred and seventy-eight.

'Signed and Declared by the said Thomas Carlyle, the Testator, as and for a Codicil to his last Will and Testament, in the presence of us who in his presence, at his request, and in the presence of each other (both being present together at the same time) have hereunto subscribed our names as Witnesses.

'T. CARLYLE.

'VICTOR H. DEACON, Sol^{r}. 'C. ERNEST BOWLES.	Clerks to Messrs. Farrer Ouvry & Co., Sol^{rs}. 66 Lincoln's Inn Fields, London.'

II

FROUDE'S LETTER OF FEBRUARY 14, 1881

To the Editor of *The Times*.

'SIR,—Will you allow me to say a few words on a subject about which some general interest is felt?

'Ten years ago Mr. Carlyle placed in my hands a collection of his wife's letters with directions to publish them, if I should think fit, after he was gone. It was his wish at that time that no biography of himself should be written or attempted to be written: his life was in his works; his private history, he said, was his own—a thing with which the world had no concern; nor did he think that I or anyone was likely to give a true version of it. On subsequent reflection, however, he considered that a life or lives of him would certainly appear from some hand or other, and, since it must be so, he made over to me all his correspondence, his journals, private papers, and unfinished manuscripts, with permission to use them or destroy them as I might think fit. The materials thus at my disposition I found extremely voluminous, several thousand letters among them: his own letters to members of his family, and letters from the most eminent of his contemporaries to himself. Besides these were "Reminiscences" of his father and mother, of Edward Irving, of Lord Jeffrey, with whom in early life he had been extremely intimate, and the materials for a memoir of Mrs. Carlyle, intended to form an introduction to the letters of hers which he had prepared for publication. These "Reminiscences" appeared to me to be far too valuable to be broken up for purposes of biography. I therefore told Mr. Carlyle that I thought that before anything else was done they ought to be published as they stood. He assented, and 18 months ago I proposed to him that they should be printed while he was still alive, that he might himself revise them. For a time he thought that this might be possible, but he found that it would agitate and excite him. He left me, therefore, to follow my own judgment, and to bring them out myself, if I thought proper, after his death.

'These sketches will appear in a few weeks: sketches of his father, James Carlyle, of Ecclefechan; of Edward Irving, of Lord Jeffrey, and of Jane Welsh Carlyle. The first three will be printed exactly as Mr. Carlyle left them. The account of Mrs. Carlyle is fragmentary; it contains many things obviously not intended for publication, and Mr. Carlyle himself directed in strong terms that it was not to appear without careful examination and revision. I have, therefore, used my discretion in making large omissions.

'The mass of matter remaining on my hands is so extensive that I have not yet decided in what way to deal with it. Mr. Carlyle's own letters are so uniformly admirable that none of them ought to be lost. The same may be said of the letters to him from Goethe, Mill, Jeffrey, Sterling, Emerson, Leigh Hunt, Dickens, Thackeray, Varnhagen von Ense, and many other famous persons. Paper and ink, it is said, should least be spared over the biography of a remarkable man. I must try to discover the fit limit between the too much and the too little.

'J. A. FROUDE.'

III

FROUDE'S LETTER OF FEBRUARY 25, 1881

To the Editor of *The Times*.

'SIR,—As some misapprehension may possibly have arisen from the words which I addressed to you a few days since on the subject of Mr. Carlyle's papers, I wish to add that in saying that Mr. Carlyle gave me these papers, I do not mean that he gave them to me as my property, but that he intrusted me with the use of them and the discretionary power of destroying those which I might think ought not to be preserved.

'The papers belong to his niece, Mrs. Alexander Carlyle, to whom he directed me to return them.

'Your obedient servant,

'J. A. Froude.

5 Onslow-gardens, S.W.'

The foregoing letter was written as a result of Mary Carlyle's objection to Froude's letter to *The Times* of February 14. In 'The Nemesis of Froude,' p. 88, the following portion of a letter from Froude to Mary Carlyle, dated February 23, 1881, is printed: 'As to the *Times*, I think I had better write a little note to Chinery [the Editor] to say that by "gave" I only meant "gave in charge to make use of," and that the MSS. belong to you.'

IV

MARY CARLYLE'S LETTER OF MAY 5, 1881

This is printed on pp. 34–35 of this volume.

V

FROUDE'S LETTER OF MAY 6, 1881

This is printed on pp. 35–36 of this volume.

VI

MARY CARLYLE'S LETTER OF MAY 7, 1881

To the Editor of *The Times*.

'SIR,—I have no wish to enter upon any controversy with Mr. Froude. It was due to the memory of my uncle that those who read his private note-book should know what his wishes (as they are there expressed) were.

'As to Mr. Froude's reference to hidden reasons and explanations, he has awakened curiosity which he can hardly now refuse to satisfy.

'On one point in Mr. Froude's letter it is necessary to say something. He wrote to me on February 8, 1880, in reference to letters of my uncle, as to which I had reminded him that they were to be returned to me when he had done with them,—

"I cannot read such a mass of letters and decide at a single glance what is necessary to the purpose and what is not. . . . I would sooner replace everything in your hands at once and let you do the editing yourself, as you easily could do, if I am not to be left to work at my leisure and to bear the responsibility."

'This is the only communication of the kind I had with Mr. Froude, and this referred to the whole collection of letters and papers sent to Mr. Froude, and not merely to those note-books, which, in fact, were not in my mind at the time. My reply to this was that I did not expect to have the letters returned to me until he had finished with them. Neither then nor afterwards had I any notion that Mr. Froude was going to publish the note-book called "Jane Welsh Carlyle." The other note-books I never read till I read them in print.

'If Mr. Froude would but surrender the papers now, to be examined and decided upon by three friends of Carlyle, it would be in accordance with his obvious intention as he has expressed it in his will, and it would be joyfully accepted by every member of Mr. Carlyle's family.

'I am, Sir, your obedient servant,

'MARY CARLYLE.

24 Cheyne-row, Chelsea, May.'

VII

FROUDE'S LETTER OF MAY 9, 1881

To the Editor of *The Times*.

'SIR,—I am reluctant to occupy your columns with further discussion about Mr. Carlyle's papers. If I ask space for a very few words, it is that the public may be under no misapprehension as to my position with respect to them. The memoir of the late Mrs. Carlyle and the collection of her letters, made by Mr. Carlyle and partially prepared by him for publication, are my personal property, given to me to make such use of as might seem good to me. I am the sole judge what parts of them should or should not be printed, and neither Mrs. Alexander Carlyle, nor any one else has a right to call in question the discretion which Mr. Carlyle left with me alone. These papers, which are mine, I shall keep. The memoir is published. The letters will be published. I decline to allow any person or persons, whether friends of Mr. Carlyle or not, to be associated with me in the discharge of a trust which belongs exclusively to myself. The remaining papers, which I was directed to return to Mrs. Alexander Carlyle as soon as I had done with them, I will restore at once to any responsible person whom she will empower to receive them from me.

'I have reason to complain of the position in which I have been placed with respect to these MSS. They were sent to me at intervals, without inventory or even numerical list. I was told that the more I burnt of them the better, and they were for several years in my possession before I was even aware that they were not my own. Happily, I had destroyed none of them, and Mrs. Alexander Carlyle can have them all when she pleases.

'Apologising for the trouble which I am giving you, and assuring you that this is the last notice which I shall take of anything which is said upon the subject,

'I remain your obedient servant,

'J. A. FROUDE.'

VIII

'TIMES' EDITORIAL OF MAY 9, 1881

'Our columns have been occupied for the last few days with a controversy between Mr. J. A. Froude and Mrs. Alexander Carlyle. It is painful that the literary legacies of a great man should so soon become matter of wrangling.

'We do not pretend to fathom any private circumstances which may have provoked this unhappy difference between Mrs. Carlyle and her uncle's literary executor. But from an outside view of the question, we find it impossible to concur in this attack on Mr. Froude. Apart from the instructions, subsequent to 1866, which Mr. Froude affirms were given to him as to the publication of the memoir, and which no one has a right to call in question, the quality of Thomas Carlyle's temper and his manner of talking of his own unpublished manuscripts as fit for nothing but to be burnt seem to afford a strong presumption that the prohibition was not meant to be final. We cannot but think that Mr. Carlyle was not at the bottom of his heart averse to the publication of the memoir of his wife. Lastly, we have the authority of Mr. Carlyle's will itself, in which the testator says that he gives the manuscript in question into the charge of Mr. Froude, "with whatever other fartherances and elucidations may be possible, and I solemnly request of him to do his best and wisest in the matter, as I feel assured he will."

'But though, strictly interpreted, Mrs. Alexander Carlyle's letters would seem to imply that Mr. Froude ought not to have published the manuscript at all, they no doubt suggest a wider question. We cannot go far behind the terms of Mrs. Carlyle's remarks, but they seem to have been prompted by a conviction on her part and of her friends that Mr. Froude has not performed his office of editorship with discretion. Mr. Carlyle's pen was satirical and scolding. He recorded bluntly and roundly his impressions of those whom he met. To publish them in the form in which they were found was to wound often the living, often the descendants of the dead. Mr. Froude it has been said, ought to have used the scissors more unsparingly. We are not concerned to dispute that among very many penetrating and just judgments of men which are to be found in the "Reminiscences" are sprinkled not a few estimates that seem ill-conditioned and ungenerous. Homer himself is sometimes caught napping, and Carlyle occasionally lets impetuosity get the better of fairness. No one, for instance, will be disposed to accept the portrait of Charles Lamb for one moment as anything but superficial and savouring of prejudice. Mr. Froude, however, in the exercise of his discretion, came to the conclusion that the greater part of the memoirs ought to be published as they came into his hands. In so doing he aroused remonstrances all round—from the representatives of the dead as well as from the living. It is easy, indeed, to understand the annoyance of one whom Carlyle, perhaps, has met once, a young man, at a dinner-table, and who now finds that he has been dashed off in a couple of uncomplimentary epithets. But in these days of multitudinous criticisms a thick skin is the most valuable commodity that one can have. It is perhaps more essential to ambition than genius or industry. The aggrieved in this case are not so badly off as most public men in any position. And if the living ought to take the sallies in good part, the same attitude may fairly be asked from the champions of deceased progenitors, whose memories may be trusted to take care of themselves. But to be satirised by Thomas Carlyle ! Well, after all, great philosopher as Carlyle was, the world is not bound by his decisions, especially as to the abilities or character of those about him. Carlyle had as strong prejudices as any man ever had. All the world knows that, and makes allowances for it. The man possessed a crotchetty, imperious, whimsical way of looking at things and persons. People are not misled by these little extravagances, and, indeed, nothing is easier in Carlyle's writings than to distinguish the perpetual humour from the well-considered utterances of his soul. There is far less that can be justly taken exception to in the "Reminiscences" as edited by Mr. Froude, than there is in many works of notoriety. Boswell's "Life of Johnson" roused a hubbub of protest from the susceptible. Moore's "Life of Byron" provoked hardly less controversy. The relentlessness of the revelations contained in "Greville's Memoirs" throws all such gentle satire as is contained in the Autobiography completely into the shade. Whatever hasty things Carlyle may have said, he has made no aspersions on the character of those whom he has ridiculed. He has grouped two or three peculiarities of intellect or of manner into a sentence or a word.

No satire upon men, as distinguished from their acts, could well be more harmless. It was a question for Mr. Froude's own discretion whether he should draw these talons, and it may be doubted whether, on the whole, he did not do wisely in maintaining the integrity of the composition, leaving it to the public to make the allowance, which, judging from the context and colour of each personal criticism, they will well know how to do.

'For these reasons, and because it is for the interest of the public that they should have Mr. Carlyle's productions unmutilated, we are disposed to think those wrong who challenge Mr. Froude's taste or wisdom. Mr. Froude has performed a valuable service in giving us at so short notice the materials which were needed for obtaining a greater insight into the genius of a master-life. The records of Carlyle's reverence for his father and of his affection for his wife will be as widely read and as widely appreciated as anything else from the same pen. The "Reminiscences" are not only deeply interesting but in Carlyle's best style. Instead of the signs of dotage which many pretend to detect in them, they are written in a more sober, more natural tone and phraseology than, say, his "Frederick the Great." We are fairly entitled to read them as a whole. If they contain a few rash personalities, these afford no valid reason for outcry against the editor. Their elimination would have been in the result more pleasant to Mr. Froude. But we are attached even to Carlyle's errors, and we cannot help being glad that few of these oddities of thought, of those concentrated outbreaks of spleen have been withdrawn from us. Each is an element in the study of the Carlylean mind—a mind interesting even in its extravagance. It must always be remembered that Mr. Froude is the sole depositary of the discretion bequeathed by Mr. Carlyle in the publication of his manuscripts.

Even now we do not know how much that is exceptionable he may have cut out. We are tolerably confident that there is still more to come, and we are anxious that no terrorism should fetter his judgment in the future.'

IX †

STEPHENS'S STATEMENT OF JULY 5, 1881

This is printed on pp. 65–68 of this volume.

X *

FROUDE TO STEPHEN

The Molt, Salcombe,
October 12, [1881].

'My dear Stephen,—I have read Benson's letter, and this is my answer:

'1. As to the profits of the "Reminiscences."

'(*a*) There was *no* agreement between Carlyle and myself. He never mentioned the subject to me. The offer was purely voluntary on my part.

'(*b*) It was meant by me when first made to extend only to the American profits, which were then expected to be considerable. Mrs. Carlyle took it to mean the whole profits, and I allowed her interpretation.

'(*c*) It did not imply that I was not to deduct something from the sum paid by the publishers for my own labour.

'(*d*) It applied only to the profits of two-thirds of the book, which at the time the offer was made was not intended to include the account of Jane Welsh

Carlyle. This is my own distinct property by Mr. Carlyle's will.

'2. As to his biography, Mr. Carlyle put his remaining papers in my hands in order that I should write it, with directions to *burn*. This I understood to imply that they were my own, and it was not till after several years that he desired me to return them to his niece when I had done with them. I inferred from this that they were her eventual property, and that I was no longer at liberty to burn.

'My offer to return them *at once* was made in a moment of irritation at the unworthy treatment which I had received from Mrs. Carlyle. I conceived, however, at that time that the long labour which I had undergone over these papers would enable me to write the biography without further use of them. Mrs. Carlyle had disclaimed any wish to interfere with me in the use which I might make of the materials which I had already selected, and I was unwilling to remain in any relations to Mrs. Carlyle whatever. *I withdraw that letter and that offer. The greater part of the biography is written.* The first part of it will be published in the spring. Mr. Carlyle's family, his surviving brothers and sisters, have earnestly protested against my abandoning the trust which Mr. Carlyle himself committed to me, and I mean to fulfil it unless I am otherwise ordered by a court of law.

'I myself individually and also in my capacity as executor am willing to carry out Mr. Carlyle's wishes in giving over such of his papers as are properly to be eventually hers, but it must be first determined which of them are bequeathed to me as illustrative of the Letters and Memorials of the late Mrs. Carlyle. If the whole collection be demanded immediately I must first be satisfied that Mrs. Carlyle has *now* a right to be put in possession of them.

'I have offered to fulfil every claim which can be made upon me as a gentleman and a man of honour in the proposals which have been submitted to Mr. Benson, subject only to my being able to carry out Mr. Carlyle's personal instructions to me relating to his biography ; but I find that I cannot do that duty adequately without retaining the papers until the book is finished.

'The question has become so complicated that I wish for myself that it should be properly sifted in a court. I can therefore make no further concessions, and I adhere to my resolution that unless the proposals are accepted before the end of the present month, they will be regarded as withdrawn.

'Yours faithfully,
'J. A. FROUDE.'

XI *

FROUDE'S MEMORANDUM OF OCTOBER 16, 1881

'My recollection of what passed relating to the gift of the profits of the "Reminiscences" to Mary Carlyle :

'About a year before Mr. Carlyle's death it was proposed that the reminiscences of Edward Irving, Lord Jeffrey, *old* Mr. Carlyle of Scotsbrig, Southey, and Wordsworth should be prepared for publication, and Mr. Carlyle thought of revising them himself. An American publisher hearing of this sent word to me that he was willing to give a large sum for the right of publishing this book, *with the author's sanction*, in the United States. Mr. Carlyle, after reflection, abandoned his intention of revision and left the whole duty of publishing his papers, *where he had before placed it*, in my hands.

'I considered that under these circumstances this

provisional *large sum from America* ought not to belong to me. I thought that Mary Carlyle had been inadequately provided for in Mr. Carlyle's will, and therefore I would give it to *her*. I told her this. She said the money would be mine and not hers. To relieve her scruples and to prevent her from feeling under any obligation to me, I said that this book would be her uncle's and not mine, and that I should not touch this money. Nothing was said about the English profits, nor were they in my mind at the time; but I always intended that she should share liberally in the profits of any book about Mr. Carlyle which I might publish.

'I never spoke to Mr. Carlyle himself on the subject of the profits, nor he to me. It was never once mentioned between us. That there was any *agreement* between us is totally without foundation. I did not know, till Mary Carlyle informed me of it, that she had told him of my promise to her.

'Mr. Carlyle had many conversations with me about the "Reminiscences." It was agreed between us that, as much would probably be written about him as soon as he was gone, this book should be published at once that the world might have something authentic to go upon. A few weeks before he died, he spoke to me very solemnly about the Letters and Memorials of Jane Welsh Carlyle, which he had given to me in 1871, and had bequeathed to me in his will. He asked me what I meant to do about it. I had told him from the first, ten years ago, that *if* the letters were to be published, his own memoir of his wife must be published first, and he had directed me to act entirely on my own judgment. On the occasion I speak of, I answered that I thought the reminiscences of his father, of Irving, Jeffrey, Southey, and Wordsworth should be published immediately on his death; that the memoir of his wife should be also published, and that *then* I could publish the letters.

He entirely agreed. He said not a word in objection, and this was the final arrangement.

'About the same time I found that for various reasons the profits to be expected from America would fall far short of what had been at first promised. I therefore decided in my own mind that Mary Carlyle should share the profits of the English edition, *what share* I reserved to myself to consider when I knew what the profits would be. The memoir of Jane Welsh Carlyle increased the size of the intended book by *one-third.* There were two volumes instead of one, and this third I regarded as properly my own in a different sense from the rest, as it was part of Mr. Carlyle's special gift to me.

'When the book was published the Americans sent £100, with a promise of a share of the profits on the sale in the States, which was not likely to be less than £300 or £600. *Longman* paid me for the first edition £650. I wrote to Mary Carlyle to say that of the present sum of £750 she should have £450, with all that might come hereafter from America. I thought that she might feel scruples in taking so much, so I added that she had well deserved it by her long service to her uncle in copying his manuscripts. I was surprised and disturbed to find that she was greatly disappointed ; that either I had not expressed myself clearly, or that she had entirely misunderstood me ; that she demanded the whole profits both English and American and refused to take less.

'I explained her mistake to her ; but she would not accept my explanation, and put herself in lawyers' hands. I was very unwilling that there should be a dispute between me and her uncle's niece on the subject of money. I thought that perhaps I might not have spoken clearly enough. The English sale was rapid, and the £750 rose in a week to £1800. I pointed out to her that since my original promise was made the book had been increased by the added publication of a third to which that promise had no reference, but that in addition to the entire profits of the original *two-thirds* she should have half the profits of the remaining third; that is, £1500 out of the £1800, and all the profits hereafter, whatever they might be.

'Mary Carlyle then wrote to her solicitors saying that if I had forgotten the letter of my promise, I had entirely fulfilled the spirit of it. She sent me a copy of this. She then came to me. She said [I was] too generous, that I was giving too much, that I was heaping coals of fire on her head, etc. I really thought that I *had* in some degree misled her through want of care in my expressions. I accepted her version of them. She in turn admitted that those expressions could have had no reference to the memoir of the late Mrs. Carlyle, and I supposed the matter was settled. Afterwards, however, Mary Carlyle sent me word through her solicitors that she would receive *nothing* from me. It appeared that she thought she had a *right* to the money and would not therefore take it as a favour. He [one of the solicitors] hinted to me that perhaps she might take it from him, and I at once placed £1500 in his hands to be held in trust for her.

'A question was next raised about Mr. Carlyle's papers in the use of which she wished to interfere with me. Mr. Carlyle had placed them in my hands with direction *to give them to her when I had done with them.* She insisted that he had given them absolutely to her. She attacked me in the London press in a very offensive manner. I had been for many years at work over Mr. Carlyle's papers, and had extracted sufficient material for the history *of his early life.* It was painful to me after what had passed to remain in any sort of relation to Mary Carlyle, and I therefore said in a letter to *The Times* that she should have the papers at once.

'But I was one of Mr. Carlyle's executors. I was

at once warned that before I parted with property of so much consequence, I must ascertain who were the legal owners of these papers *at this present moment* ; for according to Mr. Carlyle's instructions to me they were to be given to his niece only when the trust with which he had charged me was completed. By the terms of the will they might form part of the general estate. I was warned also that questions would rise, if Mary Carlyle was *not* the *present* legal owner, as to the profits of the "Reminiscences," and that if the £1500 was paid to her I might have to pay it again to someone else ; also that I could have no security in the use of the materials for the biography which I had extracted.

'And again it is to be noticed that Mr. Carlyle in his will had specially bequeathed to myself a certain part of these papers as "elucidatory of the letters and memorials of his wife." These, apparently, I was at liberty to select for myself. Counsels' opinion was taken which was unfavourable to Mary Carlyle's claims, and the solicitors then declined to pay over the £1500 to Mary Carlyle, pending a settlement either by arrangement or by a court of law, and there at present the matter stands.

'I, as executor of Mr. Carlyle, and having been entrusted by him with an important duty, am anxious only to carry out what I know to have been his wishes. I have offered for myself to give Mary Carlyle the £1500, with all further profits on the book, "Reminiscences" (provided it is not claimed as a *right*, which I cannot regard it as being), and to incur any risk which there may be of the money being claimed hereafter by others, and also to give her all the manuscripts, except the letters and memorials of Mrs. Carlyle, as soon as I have completed her uncle's life, I feeling on reflexion that I was too hasty in thinking of abandoning any part of this trust, and that I ought, if I live, to finish it.

'Mary Carlyle has fallen back on her original demand for the entire profits of the "Reminiscences," with a demand for the immediate surrender of her uncle's papers, and she requires me to transfer to her, or to someone else, the duty of writing her uncle's life. I cannot comply with her demands, and I prefer that the whole matter shall be investigated and settled in a court of law.

'J. A. FROUDE.'

Salcombe,
October 16, 1881.

XII*

BENSON TO LEMAN

No. 1 Clements Inn, Strand,
London, April 3, 1886.

'DEAR SIR,—Mrs. Carlyle would be glad to have the copyright of the "Reminiscences" assigned to her as arranged.

'Perhaps under the circumstances mentioned in your recent letter Mr. Froude no longer desires to reserve the literary control in the sense expressed in the correspondence.

'If Mr. Froude should still desire to make this reservation Mrs. Carlyle cannot object to his doing so.

'Mrs. Carlyle would, however, be quite willing to prepare a new edition of the work if Mr. Froude will authorise her to revise it as suggested by you.

'I am,
'Yours faithfully,
'JAS. BOURNE BENSON.

'J. C. LEMAN, ESQ.'

XIII*

FROUDE TO MARY CARLYLE, APRIL 20, 1886

This is printed on p. 93 of this volume.

XIV*

MARY CARLYLE TO FROUDE, APRIL 25, 1886

This is printed on p. 94 of this volume.

XV

FROUDE'S LETTER OF NOVEMBER 1, 1886

To the Editor of *The Times*.

'Sir,—As an edition of Mr. Carlyle's early letters by Mr. Charles Norton is attracting some attention, and as Mr. Norton has been pleased in an appendix to make severe reflections upon my own conduct, I venture to ask you to let me say a few words for myself in *The Times*. You may be the more willing to grant me this opportunity as, if I can help it, I shall never return to the subject again.

'Mr. Norton, like most of my critics, has overlooked the important consideration that I never wished to write Carlyle's life; that I never sought it; that I consented only at Carlyle's own urgent request. I undertook it at the sacrifice of all the arrangements which I had made for my future work, at the sacrifice of time and money which I could ill spare and, as it has turned out, of the peace and comfort which at my age become precious. Had I chosen the subject for myself, I might be supposed to have some private interest to further, some view to defend, some aim or other of my own which I wished to arrive at. I did not choose it. It was chosen for me.

'I am charged with having disregarded instructions to suppress particular papers. I had no such instructions. Mr. Carlyle placed in my hands such letters, journals, &c., as he desired me to see. He left me with absolute discretion to do what I pleased with them. The only limitation which he ever made was at my own instance, when I remonstrated with him about certain passages which he had himself prepared for publication. If persons now professing to represent his wishes are to produce prohibitions given at an earlier time and before his commission to myself, and have authority to pretend that they were binding upon me, I have been treated with an unfairness to which it would be hard to find a parallel. In his will, as well as in his conversations with myself, he left me entire freedom, and desired all whom it might concern to regard my judgment as his own.

'Under these conditions I accepted my commission. I have no respect for idealising biographies. I considered it my duty to draw as faithful a picture of Carlyle as I could from my own knowledge and from the materials with which he supplied me. I have done this to the extent of my ability. If there are errors of the press in my version of his letters, I did my best to avoid them. His handwriting was small and often difficult to read. I worked through his manuscripts with a magnifying glass. As the different portions of my work were published I restored the papers which I had done with to Mr. Carlyle's niece, as he directed. As I could no longer refer to them, it would have been courteous, I consider, if, when she discovered mistakes, she had communicated them to me—with the "Reminiscences" especially, where, I am told, the mistakes are most numerous. In that case I was in such haste to let her have the originals that I trusted to my own transcripts, and did not allow myself time for a final revise before the book was republished. She was herself receiving the profits of this book as a gift from myself, and, had I not heard accidentally that the text required correction, I might have continued to bring out new editions for her benefit without a word of warning.

'If there are mistakes in the letters and memorials of Mrs. Carlyle, they are not due to me. These volumes were printed directly from copies with which Carlyle furnished me. It has been over this publication that the chief irritation has arisen, and here I confess I think some blame attaches to Carlyle himself. If, in remorse for real or imagined faults of his own, he thought it right to put together these memorials, he should have himself decided whether they were to be printed or not. The responsibility should not have been left to a friend. He told me often that he ought to do penance like Johnson; but, as a fact, he has left me to stand in the pillory for him, and I am tired of the situation.

'The greater part of his papers are now beyond my reach. Those who, like Mr. Norton, pretend to be most zealous for Carlyle's honour, have disregarded absolutely the words in his will which were intended for my protection. Originally, I suppose, he meant these papers to remain in charge of myself or of his executors, for he left them without inventory for six years in my keeping, with instructions to burn freely, and without a word on their future disposition. In the last year of his life he desired me to give them to his niece. She now says that they had been hers long before the time when he spoke to me. If it was so, I ought to have been informed of it. When

I was told that she was to have them, I was told also that of course she would make no use of them without consulting me. If she had been intended to use them independently of me, again I ought to have been made aware of it, that I might have the option—which unquestionably I should have chosen—of relinquishing any share in the undertaking. I make no complaint. I merely say these things that the world may understand why for the future I must remain entirely silent under any attacks which may be made upon me, and take no part for the future in any controversy of which Carlyle is to be the subject.

'The four volumes of the "Biography" I revised carefully before returning the originals. The few faults which I found are corrected, and these volumes will be republished if a new edition is called for. The manuscript of the letters and memorials annotated by Carlyle is mine, and remains with me. The copyright of the "Reminiscences" I have made over to the present holder of the originals of these; and now with my own will I shall neither write nor read another word upon a subject which has been the torment and perplexity of too large a portion of my life.

'Your obedient servant,

'J. A. Froude.'

5 Onslow Gardens,
Nov. 1, [1886].

XVI

MARY CARLYLE'S LETTER OF NOVEMBER 3, 1886

To the Editor of *The Times*.

'Sir,—Will you kindly allow me to say a few words, which I, too, hope may be the last, in reply to Mr. Froude's letter in *The Times* of yesterday?

'Mr. Froude says, "I am charged with having disregarded instructions to suppress particular papers. I had no such instructions." Even if this were literally true, it is certain that Mr. Froude received from Mr. Carlyle, both verbally and in writing, repeated and earnest injunctions to use the utmost caution and reticence in dealing with the papers entrusted to him. Mr. Froude goes on, "In his will, as well as in his conversations with myself, he left me entire freedom." In the will it is distinctly stated that Mr. Froude, as to the writing of the Life as well as to the editing of "The Letters and Memorials of Jane Welsh Carlyle," is to act only in conjunction with Dr. Carlyle and Mr. John Forster, and I can myself avouch that Dr. Carlyle was strongly averse to the papers being placed in Mr. Froude's hands, and on more than one occasion expressed this opinion to Mr. Carlyle. As to conversations, the only evidence is that of Mr. Froude's memory, which has hardly proved itself an infallible witness, and the obvious comment on the whole statement is that Mr. Froude was at least as free to abstain from publishing any of the papers as to publish them.

'Mr. Froude says that he was in such haste to return the original manuscript of the "Reminiscences" to me that he did not allow himself time for a final revise before the book was republished; and that it would have been courteous to him (Mr. Froude) when I discovered mistakes to have communicated them to him. I need only say that I did nothing to hurry Mr. Froude, who, unasked, returned the manuscript to me seven days before he left home for Madeira, and eight days before the "Reminiscences" was published. At that stage, when I had read the books and noted errors in them, matters were in the hands of our lawyers. There has, in fact, up to the present time been no republication of the "Reminiscences." The mistakes in the "Reminiscences" are not more abundant than in the "Life"; nor can Carlyle's handwriting account for many of these, for in an extract from a letter ("Life in London," i., pp. 304–5), where Mr. Froude says, "The handwriting, even for Carlyle, who at this time wrote most beautifully, is exceptionally excellent," there are in one page of print over thirty deviations from the text, and in a quotation from "Sartor Resartus" (given in "Life," 1795–1834, i., pp. 101–4) there are in the first eight lines over twenty deviations from the printed text. Many of Mr. Froude's deviations cannot come under the head of errors in copying or printing. For example (a very noteworthy one), a passage in the "Reminiscences" (1881, ii., p. 91, "Jane Welsh Carlyle") is thus given by Mr. Froude: "Mr. Carlyle now continues: few or none of these narratives are correct in details, but there is a certain mythical truth in all or most of them." This in the original (as shortly to appear in the corrected version of the book) is as follows, being a letter to Miss Jewsbury: "Dear Geraldine,—Few or none of these Narratives are correct in all the details; some of them, in almost all the details, are incorrect. I have not read carefully beyond a certain point which is marked in the margin. Your recognition of the character is generally true and faithful; little of portraiture in it that satisfies me. On the whole, all tends to the mythical; it is very strange how much of mythical there already here is! As Lady Lothian set you on writing, it seems hard that she should not see what you have written; but I wish you to take her word of honour that no one else shall; and my earnest request to you is that, directly from her ladyship, you will bring the Book to me and consign it to my keeping. No need that an idle, gazing world should know my lost Darling's History, or mine; nor will they ever, they may depend upon it! One fit service, and one only, they can do to

Her or to Me: cease speaking of us through all eternity, as soon as they conveniently can.—Affectionately yours, T. Carlyle (Chelsea, May 22, 1866)." The words, "There is a certain mythical truth," &c., are transferred and altered by Mr. Froude from a subsequent passage.

'The assertion that I received the proceeds of the "Reminiscences" as a gift from Mr. Froude I simply deny, and can, if necessary, produce my lawyer's statement on the point.

'I am, sir, your obedient servant,

'Mary Carlyle.'

3 Chalcot Gardens, Haverstock Hill. N.W.,
Nov. 3, [1886].

XVII*

FROUDE TO LEMAN

5 Onslow Gardens, S.W.,
November 18, 1886.

'My dear Leman,—Mary Carlyle having denied that she received the profits of the "Reminiscences" as a gift from me, it remains my duty as Carlyle's executor to ascertain from a competent court to whom this money belonged or belongs. I paid it to Mr. Farrer in her behalf, believing it to be my own. If it was not my own, I had no right to pay it to Mr. Farrer for such a purpose.

'It is pretended that some bargain or arrangement was made. I entered into none. I should have violated my duty as executor if I had done so. What Mr. Farrer may have done or said, I do not know. I from the first said that I would do what I had from the outset said that I would do, make her a present of the money, and let her have the papers when I had done with them.

'I must ask you to take at once the necessary steps for an interpretation of Mr. Carlyle's will and for a decision as to ownership of the property. I think too that you had better see Mr. Farrer and tell him what I say. I am now acting simply as executor, and not as a private person.

'Yours faithfully,
'J. A. Froude.'

XVIII

FROUDE TO STEPHEN

5 Onslow Gardens,
November 30, 1886.

'My dear Stephen,—The question of my action in connection with Carlyle's biography having been again raised with some acrimony, I venture to ask you to put in writing your own impressions on a part of the matter with which you, as my fellow-executor, were immediately concerned. I am unwilling, for many reasons, to prolong a personal controversy, as if I thought that my own conduct required defence; but life is uncertain; it will be more satisfactory to me to know that there is an authoritative statement in existence, to which, if circumstances make it necessary, an appeal may hereafter be made. I am not now speaking of the larger contention, whether I made a right use of the discretionary powers which were entrusted to me as to the publication of Mr. Carlyle's letters. A subsidiary question was raised, as you know, on the ownership of the materials which I used for the "Reminiscences" and for the "Biography." Claims were put forward, as a matter of right, on the profits arising from the former of these publications; and where I had supposed myself to be acting liberally (I might almost say with generosity) of my own free will, I was met with threats of a legal action. You are aware of everything that took place. You are in a position which no one else occupies, or can occupy, to relate all the circumstances completely and impartially. I am not asking for a report which can be published, but for a narrative and a judgment, to which I, or my friends after me, may be able to refer should a continuance of the controversy seem to make such a reference desirable. I hope that you will consider my request a reasonable one, and will not refuse to comply with it.

'Yours faithfully,
'J. A. Froude.'

XIX

STEPHEN TO FROUDE

32 De Vere Gardens,
December 9, 1886.

'My dear Froude,—At your request I put into writing what I know of your connection with the papers of Mr. Carlyle which formed the materials of your works about him and his wife. The story is long and intricate, but the facts can for the most part be ascertained beyond dispute, as most of them are stated in three voluminous correspondences, one between Messrs. Farrer, the solicitors to Mr. Carlyle's executors, and myself, on one side, and Messrs. Benson, Mrs. Alexander Carlyle's solicitors, on the other ; the other two between your solicitor (Mr. Leman) and Mrs. Alexander Carlyle's solicitors (Messrs. Benson). All these and many other papers I have carefully examined before writing this letter. Parts of it rest on what you at various times have told me. Some of the papers are in the possession of Messrs. Benson, and these I have not seen since they were written.

'The story is this.

'Mrs. Carlyle died in April 1866. Mr. Carlyle, after her death, passed much of his time in writing and arranging papers relating to her. In particular he wrote in a memorandum book an account of her which formed the principal material for the sketch of her life published in the second volume of the "Reminiscences." To this he added a note saying in solemn terms that it was not in case of his death to be published as it stood. This you tell me was written in 1866 or soon afterwards. I call it the Sketch.

'After this Mr. Carlyle put together a number of letters and other matters which he called a "Memorial of Jane Welsh Carlyle." Mrs. Alexander Carlyle made by his directions a fair copy of both the Memorial and the Sketch. This fair copy was placed in your hands in 1871. The original letters and draft remained with her, with the exception of the original Sketch just mentioned, which was delivered to you.

'On February 6, 1873, Mr. Carlyle made his will. He left the Memorial to you absolutely, "with whatever other fartherances and elucidations may be possible," which words you regarded as covering the Sketch. He added elaborate provisions as to your consulting his brother Dr. Carlyle and Mr. Forster as to the publication of these matters. The three he said "will make earnest survey of the MS. and its subsidiaries there or elsewhere." He adds: "The manuscript is by no means ready for publication; nay the question, How, when (after what delay—seven, ten years) it or any portion of it should be published are still dark to me, but on all such points James Anthony Froude's practical summing up and decision is to be taken as mine."

'The direction as to Dr. Carlyle and Mr. Forster

became inoperative by the fact of their dying in Mr. Carlyle's lifetime, and in your view both the Memorial and the Sketch became under these provisions yours absolutely, with an express direction to use your discretion as to publication, overruling the note appended to the Sketch.

'The "imperfect copy" and the original letters which Mrs. Alexander Carlyle had copied were bequeathed to her. The rest of his MSS. Mr. Carlyle bequeathed to his brother Dr. Carlyle, directing that one of them, a sketch of his father should be "preserved in the family." On Dr. Carlyle's death this bequest lapsed, and the documents not specially bequeathed in the will or otherwise disposed of during his lifetime passed to the executors of the will by the general bequest of all personal property.

'Dr. Carlyle, you, and I were made executors by a codicil dated November 8, 1878, and Dr. Carlyle having died in his brother's lifetime, you and I took out probate.

'So far as the will was concerned no difficulty arose, at least no legal difficulty, but after the making of his will Mr. Carlyle dealt with his papers in a way which caused much embarrassment. The will says, "Express biography of me I had really rather that there should be none." Upon this point Mr. Carlyle changed his mind, and not very long after the will, either in the course of the year 1873, or at all events not later than the beginning of 1874, he sent to you as materials for his biography a great mass of papers and MS. books without any sort of inventory or written directions of any sort. Verbally, he told you to do as you pleased with them, adding in particular that you were to "burn freely." The sketch of his father and the other papers used as materials for the "Reminiscences" were amongst these, or were sent afterwards.

'Mrs. Alexander Carlyle informed us through her

solicitors, some months after her uncle's death, that in 1875 he made a verbal gift to her of all his papers, and gave her his keys. Of this gift neither you nor I had any notice till we were informed of it by Mrs. Alexander Carlyle's solicitors in June 1881.

'About a year before his death Mr. Carlyle told you that after you had done with the papers to be used for his biography you were to give them back to Mrs. Alexander Carlyle.

'All this afterwards gave rise to three distinct views as to the property in the papers not disposed of by the will. You considered that they were yours by a gift accompanied by delivery, but you admitted yourself to be bound, morally at least, to give them to Mrs. Alexander Carlyle after you had written the biography. Mrs. Carlyle claimed them as hers in virtue of the gift which, as she said, was made to her in 1875. Lastly, the executors were advised that, notwithstanding the delivery of the papers to you, those which were not specifically bequeathed passed to the executors under the general bequest of personal estate. The effect of this upon the right of the residuary legatees to the proceeds and copyright of the works was a separate question of much delicacy.

'There was a further distinct question, or set of questions, about the "Reminiscences." Your account to me of what took place is that not long before Mr. Carlyle's death it occurred to you that it would be well to publish in a separate form his accounts of his father, of Irving, and of Lord Jeffrey. Your first plan was that he should edit them, but this he was unable to do; you also meant to publish in America, being led to believe that a very large profit would be made there, and you promised to give the whole profits of the American edition to Mrs. A. Carlyle, but owing to circumstances these profits became very small. You then formed an intention, which you believe you afterwards expressed in a letter to her, to give her half the profits of your " Biography " as well as the " Reminiscences " ; but her view on the other hand appeared to be that she was entitled to the whole of the profits of the " Reminiscences," wherever published, by your promise, and further that she was entitled by Mr. Carlyle's gift to the whole of the papers necessary for writing his life, but this last claim was never known either to you or to me till June 1881.

'Apart from this, before publication and after your promise, whatever it was, you altered the plan of the " Reminiscences " and included in it the sketch of the life of Mrs. Carlyle, entitled " Jane Welsh Carlyle," which formed a third of the whole work.

'Mr. Carlyle died on February 5, 1881. On February 21, 1881, I called on Mrs. Alexander Carlyle and had a long conversation with her, of which I there and then made a memorandum, which is now before me. I showed it to her and her husband, and I sent her a copy of it next day. I never received from her any disclaimer of its correctness. Mr. Ouvry (Mr. Farrer's late partner), who was then acting as solicitor for all parties, and Mr. Alexander Carlyle were present on the occasion. At the time when the memorandum was made I was very superficially acquainted with these matters. The memorandum is as follows :

'Memorandum of Mrs. A. Carlyle's understanding of the facts relating to Mr. Carlyle's papers.

'1. Papers relating to the late Mrs. Carlyle bequeathed to Mr. Froude by the will of Mr. Carlyle. These papers Mrs. A. Carlyle considers to be Mr. Froude's absolutely.

'2. The papers relating to Mr. Carlyle's father, Mr. Irving, and Lord Jeffrey, intended to be published under the title of " Reminiscences," Mrs. A. Carlyle also understands to have been given to Mr. Froude after the death of Mr. Forster, though she does not know what may have passed between Mr. Carlyle and Mr. Froude on the subject. She, however, says that Mr. Froude some time ago promised to give to her the whole of the proceeds of the "Reminiscences" when published, and that she informed her uncle of this intention, and that he approved of it, and under these circumstances she declines to receive any share of the proceeds less than the whole.

'3. The papers relating to Mr. Carlyle and intended to serve as materials for his biography. These papers Mrs. A. Carlyle understands to have been given to Mr. Froude, so that the property in them passed to him. She also understands that her uncle intended that any profit to be derived from the book, for which they are to be materials, was to go to Mr. Froude, and she has no wish to interfere in any way with Mr. Froude's discretion as to the use to be made of these papers; on the other hand, Mrs. A. Carlyle considers that Mr. Froude ought not to burn or otherwise destroy any of these papers, but to return them to her (Mrs. A. Carlyle) after the biography for which they are to be used as materials is published.

February 21, 1881. 'J. F. STEPHEN.'

'This was written in the presence of Mr. and Mrs. Carlyle and Mr. Ouvry, and was accepted by Mrs. Carlyle as a full statement of her views. I sent her a copy of it this day, February 22, 1881.—J. F. S.'

'This memorandum gives no hint of the gift of papers afterwards alleged to have been made to Mrs. A. Carlyle in 1875. It states as to the "Reminiscences," that, as you had promised her the whole of the proceeds of the "Reminiscences," she would not take less. I was not at that time aware that you had made any proposal to her about the profits of any other work about Mr. Carlyle, nor did I know the precise details of what you have since told me till very lately. I had told her that you proposed to give her half, and you afterwards told me that the original promise was to give her the whole profits of an edition not comprising the Sketch, to be published in America, and that your offer of half of the proceeds of the English edition including the Sketch was regarded by you as equivalent to the falling short on the American edition excluding the Sketch. The probable proceeds of the American edition had, you told me, been originally represented to you as likely to be much greater than you found they would actually be. However this may be, it is obvious that Mrs. A. Carlyle at the time of the memorandum thought that your promise, whatever it was, had reference to an edition exclusive of the Sketch, as the memorandum enumerates all the papers contained in the " Reminiscences " except the Sketch and the appendix entitled " Reminiscences of Southey."

'With regard to the materials for the biography the memorandum says : " These papers Mrs. Carlyle understands to have been given to Mr. Froude, so that the property passed to him." I have a distinct independent recollection of the words which are here recorded. She was making a very diffuse statement as to the details, when I said, " At all events they were given to Mr. Froude, so that the property passed to him." She said, " Yes." The wording therefore was mine and not hers, though she accepted and never disclaimed it. No dispute had arisen at this time, nor did I expect any, but I thought her statement important and took it down.

'The " Reminiscences " were published soon afterwards. The MS. notebook containing the Sketch was on May 3 returned to Mrs. A. Carlyle (see her letter to Mr. Ouvry dated May 11). It was regarded as a part of the " imperfect copy and original letters " bequeathed to her by Mr. Carlyle. Mrs. Alexander

Carlyle was apparently much offended at the publication in the " Reminiscences " of the Sketch, and a controversy between you and her in the *Times* newspaper followed. She accused you (May 5, 1881) of violating Mr. Carlyle's express directions in publishing the Sketch. You replied (May 6) that the direction written in 1866 was revoked by the will made in 1873, which gave you absolute discretion as to publication, and you added that Mr. Carlyle was in his lifetime made aware of your intention to publish these papers. You have often told me in conversation how this was: that his mind was much exercised on the question whether the publication should take place or not; that he appeared to you to wish that it should, but that he wished the decision to be yours and not his; that you, thinking the publication proper, and wishing also to set his mind at rest, told him you meant to publish; that he said 'very well,' seemed relieved and satisfied, and never afterwards returned to the subject. Substantially the same statement is made in the last volume of his biography, pp. 466–7.

'Mrs. Alexander Carlyle wrote (May 7) to suggest that you should " surrender the papers now to be examined and decided upon by three friends of Mr. Carlyle." You (May 9) refused this suggestion, and said, " The remaining letters (*i.e.* the materials for the biography), which I was directed to return to Mrs. Carlyle so soon as I had done with them, I will restore at once to any responsible person whom she will empower to receive them from me. I have reason to complain of the position in which I have been placed with respect to these MSS. They were sent to me at intervals without inventory or even a memorial list. I was told that the more I burnt of them the better, and they were for several years in my possession before I was aware that they were not my own. Happily I have destroyed none of them, and Mrs. Carlyle may have them all when she pleases."

You afterwards considered yourself entitled, and I entirely agreed with you, to refuse to carry out the intention thus expressed. It had no legal validity. It was a mere statement of your intention, and was at the most a voluntary promise, founded on no consideration, made in a moment of irritation, and which did not in any degree alter Mrs. Alexander Carlyle's position. If a man made an unqualified promise to leave all his property to another, he would, I think, be entitled to withdraw it at any time before it had affected the plans in life of the person to whom it was made.

'To have given up the papers would have been to waste the labour of seven or eight years of your life, and to fail in carrying out the wish of Mr. Carlyle, that you should write his life, and your promise to him to do so.

'Quite apart from this a further question arose. You discovered soon after writing the letter of May 9 that you had no right to give the papers up without my consent. We were advised by counsel, on May 13, 1881, and upon a case which embodied your statement of the facts, that the papers in question belonged not to you personally but to Mr. Carlyle's executors, and that Mr. Carlyle's direction to give them up to Mrs. Alexander Carlyle when you had done with them was "an attempted verbal testamentary disposition, which has no legal authority." You could not therefore have given them up without my consent, and I never gave, or would have given, it.

'I saw Mrs. Alexander Carlyle, and heard from her several times upon this matter. I have only a general recollection of these interviews, which took place nearly six years ago. Mrs. A. Carlyle appears to have written me a letter of some importance, February 26 or 27, 1881, but I have not got it and do not remember its contents. On May 29, 1881, however, she wrote me a letter, in which she says,

"I should like very much to accept your offer to talk the matter over with my solicitor, but, strictly speaking, I have at present no solicitor of my own entirely acquainted with the case. Messrs. —— act for me; but, as it appeared to friends of mine who have taken a very kind interest in the case that they had nothing practical to suggest, these friends, with my permission, have stated the facts to their solicitor, who is drawing up a case for an opinion of counsel. I have given them copies of the most important papers in my possession relating to the subject, and have told them all the facts I know, some of which have only lately come to my knowledge, and of the importance of most of which I was not myself aware." It is obvious from this that, till she talked over the matter with the friends referred to, she was not aware of the importance of her conversation with Mr. Carlyle in 1875.

'On May 31 I received a letter from Mr. Benson, the gentleman referred to as the solicitor of Mrs. Alexander Carlyle's friends. It states that he is drawing up a case, and the case itself must, from further letters, have been sent to me early in June, though I cannot give the exact date. The case was returned to Mrs. Alexander Carlyle's solicitor, and I have no copy of it, but I well recollect its principal statement, and my recollection is confirmed by references to it in subsequent letters in the hands of Mr. Farrer. The effect of it was that in the year 1875 Mr. Carlyle had made a present verbally of all his papers to Mrs. Alexander Carlyle, and had given her the keys of the receptacles which contained them. I had never heard a hint of this before; it appeared to me to be extremely difficult to reconcile with the delivery of the MSS. to you, though I did not then know at what precise time it had taken place, and it seemed inconsistent with the statement which she made to me, as recorded in my memorandum of February 21.

You were afterwards able to state positively that the papers said to have been given by Mr. Carlyle to Mrs. Alexander Carlyle, in 1875, were delivered to you not later than the very beginning of 1874, and probably in 1873. Your reason was that you remembered observations made by your late wife, who died in February 1874, on matters of personal interest to her contained in the papers. Of course, if the documents were put into your possession in 1873, with directions to burn what you pleased, it was difficult to believe that in 1875 they were comprehended in a verbal gift made to Mrs. Alexander Carlyle, of which gift no notice was given to you. If in 1873 they were, as Mrs. Alexander Carlyle told me in February 1881, given to you " so as to pass the property in them," they were not Mr. Carlyle's to give in 1875. Besides, it is a rule of law that a claim upon a dead man's estate cannot be admitted upon the uncorroborated statement of the claimant, and it appeared to me that there was no corroboration here. Several circumstances were mentioned in the case which, as Mrs. Alexander Carlyle's advisers contended, supplied the necessary corroboration, but I could not accept them as such. On June 10, 1881, I wrote to her solicitor, Mr. Benson, saying that I could not " consent to the recognition of Mrs. Alexander Carlyle's claim as against the residuary legatees, unless and until it was duly established in a court of law," and that you, as my co-executor, put yourself in my hands.

'I expressed at the same time the opinion that, as between her and you, the matter might be easily settled. In order to explain what I proposed, I must go back a little. Whatever might have been the exact understanding between Mrs. Alexander Carlyle and yourself as to the proceeds of the " Reminiscences," you had long been prepared to let her have the whole of them except 300*l*., which was to be reserved on account of your having edited the book, and of the fact that it included the sketch of Jane Welsh Carlyle, which was your property by the will. These profits amounted at that time, "after the deduction of 300*l*.," to 1,500*l*. and upwards, and subsequently reached 1,630*l*. You had paid about 1,500*l*. to Mr. Ouvry in May—namely, 1,400*l*. from the English edition and 100*l*. from an American edition. He had put it on deposit at Coutt's Bank in May (see his letter of May 13, 1881, to Mrs. A. Carlyle), but about that time I raised the question of the rights of the executors on behalf of the residuary legatees, and it remained at the bank at interest.

'Again, it was clear that, whoever might be the actual proprietor of the papers used as materials for the biography, it was Mr. Carlyle's intention that you should use them until the biography was written, and that when it was written you should return them to Mrs. Alexander Carlyle. I therefore proposed that a deed should be drawn, to which the residuary legatees were to be parties, reciting all these facts and settling all questions by declaring that Mrs. A. Carlyle should have all the past and future profits of the "Reminiscences" except 300*l*., you retaining the literary control over the work; that you should keep the materials of the biography till you had done with them, and that you should then return them to Mrs. Alexander Carlyle, and that the residuary legatees and executors should consent.

'Much discussion followed. In the course of it the residuary legatees consented to our settling the matter as we thought fit, but Mrs. A. Carlyle refused to consent, on the ground that the compromise gave her nothing but what she was entitled to apart from your letter to *The Times* of May 9, and apart from the alleged gift to her, said to have been made in 1875, and that it practically recognised your right to withdraw your letter of May 9, already referred to. Her counter-offer was that you should give up the papers and not complete your book, and that you should, on the other hand, take the 1,500*l*. profits on the "Reminiscences." We wholly refused this offer. She afterwards proposed that the papers should be returned to her, but that you should have access to them at her house, and this also was refused. This discussion lasted till the autumn of 1881.

'At last, after many letters and several interviews, Mr. Farrer wrote to Mr. Benson on October 15, 1881, the following letter:

"66 Lincoln's Inn Fields, London, W.C.,
October 15, 1881.

"*Carlyle's Executors.*

"DEAR SIR,—The executors have written to me to say that they have fully considered the matter, and are not disposed to modify the views which Sir James Stephen expressed to Mr. Benson at our office, that further discussion seems likely to lead to no good result, and that the offer then made must be accepted before November 1 or refused; and unless it is accepted as made, it will be considered as wholly withdrawn on that day. In that event Mr. Froude will withdraw every promise of every description he has made to Mrs. Carlyle, and will leave her to enforce any legal rights she may have. That there may be no misconception, I repeat the terms proposed by the executors.

"1. Mr. Froude offers to make over to Mrs. Carlyle all the proceeds of the 'Reminiscences,' past or future, subject to a deduction of 300*l*. Mr. Froude is to retain the literary control over the book. Mrs. Carlyle's right to these proceeds is to be considered as arising solely from this agreement.

"2. Mrs. Carlyle agrees that Mr. Froude shall keep the papers now in his possession as materials for the life of Mr. Carlyle until that work is completed, and that he shall use them as materials for that work. She also renounces all claim upon the copyright.

" Mr. Froude agrees that the papers shall be given to Mrs. Carlyle when the work is completed or on his death.

" It is understood on both sides that this does not apply to the Letters and Memorials of Jane Welsh Carlyle given by Mr. Carlyle to Mr. Froude in 1870 or 1871, and bequeathed to him by Mr. Carlyle's will.

" 3. If Mr. Froude and Mrs. Carlyle come to this agreement, the executors will not press their claim either to the MSS. or to the proceeds of the 'Reminiscences.'

" I may add that the Letters and Memorials of J. W. Carlyle bequeathed to Mr. F. by Mr. Carlyle's will were given to him in 1870 or 1871 by Mr. Carlyle, and consist of a large number of letters, all numbered, annotated, and with autobiographical matter prefixed and interspersed. Mr. Froude considers that these are his absolute property. With reference to the papers given to him in 1875 [1873], he considers not only that they are his property by Mr. Carlyle's gift, but that under the will he has a right to such of them as are illustrative of the Letters and Memorials of J. W. C.

" Yours truly,
" (Signed) FREDK. WILLIS FARRER."

'I quote this letter at length because it expresses the position which we took up, and from which neither of us receded. It was followed by a long correspondence which lasted till August 3, 1882, and in which a great variety of matters were discussed. There was at first a prospect of an administration suit, and no express comprehensive settlement was ever made. Long letters were written, and proposals and counter-proposals were made. Our principal difficulty was to arrange for the payment of the 1,500*l.* without admitting Mrs. A. Carlyle's claim to the papers on which she founded her claim to the money. There was also a great deal of discussion as to the length of time during which you were to keep the papers, the steps by which they were to be delivered over to Mrs. A. Carlyle, and the making of an inventory of them. These matters were settled by degrees, and I think I may say on the terms which were stated in Mr. Farrer's letter of October 15, 1881. The stipulation that Mrs. Carlyle should admit that her rights to the proceeds should be considered as arising from the agreement only, was, however, not insisted on.

'On June 29, 1882, Mr. Benson, Mrs. A. Carlyle's solicitor, signed a receipt for four bundles of letters connected with the first part of the Biography of Carlyle, which was published in 1882. You had then done with these papers.

'On August 3, 1882, Mr. Benson gave a receipt for Messrs. Farrer's cheque for the sum of 1,544*l.* 3*s.* 8*d.* being the then proceeds of the "Reminiscences," less 300*l.* Mrs. A. Carlyle's receipt I have not seen, but I believe she gave one. No doubt she duly received the money. You afterwards paid her two sums of 120*l.* and 10*l.*, which you received from America, I think in 1882 and 1883.

'There was never, so far as I know, any acknowledgment, written or otherwise, as to the terms on which the money was given or received. You always considered that from first to last the whole was voluntary generosity on your part. This also was and is my own opinion. She persistently claimed it as a right. This is, no doubt, the explanation of an apparent contradiction between Mrs. A. Carlyle and yourself in letters relating to Mr. Norton's publication about Mr. Carlyle. You said you had given her the proceeds of the "Reminiscences." She said

(November 4, 1886), " The assertion that I received the proceeds of the ' Reminiscences ' as a gift from Mr. Froude I simply deny, and can, if necessary, produce my lawyer's statement on the point." Mrs. Carlyle has a right to her own opinion. Mine is that you paid the money voluntarily, and she received it as a right. She never sued for it, and I do not believe she could have recovered it if she had ; for she could have claimed it as her own only on the ground that the MSS. were hers by virtue of a gift of Mr. Carlyle, a claim which I think no court would have acted upon on her uncorroborated assertion, especially if it were proved, as it could have been, that the papers were deposited with you more than a year before, as she said, they were given to her. It was my whole object throughout to prevent a lawsuit for the determination of what I felt was a merely speculative question, and to defeat the attempt made to prevent you from writing Mr. Carlyle's life, and I am happy to say I succeeded.

' You finished the biography and published the two remaining volumes in 1884.

' A long correspondence took place between your solicitor, Mr. Leman, and Mrs. A. Carlyle's solicitor, Mr. Benson, as to the delivery to her of the papers. There were various delays, owing to your absence abroad, to your wish to make some final corrections, etc., but on December 5, 1884, your solicitor handed the papers in two boxes to Mrs. Carlyle and took her receipt for them.

' On March 28, 1885, Mr. Benson told Mr. Leman that she was " much pleased at the contents of the boxes," and Mr. Leman adds in his letter to you : " It appears that they contained more papers than she had expected to find in them." There was subsequent correspondence about a particular MS. which had been accidentally mislaid.

' In 1885 a further correspondence took place

about the assignment to Mrs. Carlyle of the copyright of the " Reminiscences." It ended by your assigning the copyright to her last June, protesting at the same time that you were under no contract to do so.

'I have told the story at full length in order to put upon record the particulars of your conduct in all this matter. You appear to me to have acted throughout quite straightforwardly. You carried out precisely what from the first you acknowledged to be your moral obligations. Indeed, where only your own interests were concerned, you went beyond them ; for you accepted Mrs. A. Carlyle's recollection of the arrangement about the profits of the " Reminiscences " instead of your own, and you gave up the claim to retain the literary control of that work —which you admittedly possessed—for the sake of peace. On the other hand, where your duty to Mr. Carlyle was in question you stood firm, and performed your promise to write his life and to use the materials which he had provided for that purpose, notwithstanding Mrs. A. Carlyle's attempts to prevent you from doing so, and in opposition to claims which she did not attempt to enforce by law. You returned the papers to Mrs. A. Carlyle when you had done with them, according to her uncle's wish, though you were advised that it was not legally binding. You gave Mrs. A. Carlyle above 1,600*l*., which she could not have compelled you to give her, as your original promise was made voluntarily. No doubt she had a moral claim to a part of it, but to a large part of it she had no moral claim, except upon the supposition, which you accepted, that her recollection of conversations which took place about two years before was right and your own wrong. You were provoked into writing a hasty letter to *The Times*, which you afterwards withdrew. It was a letter which imposed no legal obligation, and, as I think, no moral obligation, and you could not have fulfilled the intention which you there expressed without wasting the labour of eight years of your life, breaking a pledge to Mr. Carlyle to write his life, and violating a legal duty of which, when you wrote the letter, you were not aware. In a word, in your whole conduct I see nothing to regret, and I wish to add that I was just as much responsible for it morally as you were, though your letters were written independently of me.

'Of Mrs. Alexander Carlyle, I will say only that she took a view of the publication of the "Reminiscences" which many people do take, and tried to stop the publication of the biography on what she believed to be valid legal grounds. I think she was erroneously advised; but the question is one of mere curiosity, which can never now be decided in an authoritative way.

'I know you have suffered much worry and annoyance from all this matter, and this is the main reason why I have gone over it so fully. After a close intimacy of nearly thirty years, it would be impossible to me to believe that your conduct had fallen short of the highest standard of truth and honour. The whole difficulty in this matter arose from the feebleness and indecision, natural enough in extreme old age, which prevented Mr. Carlyle from making up his mind conclusively as to what he wished to be done about his papers, and having his decision put into writing. The paralysis which latterly disabled his hand from writing was no doubt a partial explanation of this. His sending his papers to you was inconclusive; whatever he said to Mrs. Alexander Carlyle in 1875 was inconclusive; so much so that she seems not to have appreciated its importance till her friends pointed it out to her some months after his death, and after she had conveyed a totally different impression to my mind of the state of affairs. Lastly, the conversations about the profits of the "Reminiscences" were even more inconclusive and difficult to ascertain precisely than the rest. This, however, was no fault of his. The natural result of leaving such matters in such an ill-defined position was to cause the difficulties which subsequently arose.

'I should like to add one further remark. People will of course differ as to the way in which you exercised the most painful discretion which Mr. Carlyle, in order to save himself the pain of a decision which he wished you to make for him, chose to impose upon you. I can bear testimony which throws light on the motives which influenced you in writing as you did. I believe them to be stated with absolute truth in your prefaces to the first volume of each of the two parts of his biography, and in a few words in a letter to Mr. Farrer of May 12, 1881, which I think he must have sent to Mrs. A. Carlyle: "Carlyle's memory is as dear to me as it can possibly be to Mrs. A. Carlyle. I honoured and loved him above all men that I ever knew or shall know. It is my duty to show him as he was, and no life known to me, taken as a whole, will bear a more severe scrutiny. But he wished, especially wished, his faults to be known. They are nothing, amount to nothing, in the great balance of his qualities. But such as they were they must be described. Surely this is no unfriendly hand." I believe this to be the truth, the whole truth, and nothing but the truth.

'For about fifteen years I was the intimate friend and constant companion of both of you, and never in my life did I see any one man so much devoted to any other as you were to him during the whole of that period of time. The most affectionate son could not have acted better to the most venerated father. You cared for him, soothed him, protected him as a guide might protect a weak old man down a steep and painful path. The admiration you habitually expressed for him both morally and intellectually was unqualified. You never said to me one ill-natured word about him down to this day. It is to me wholly incredible that anything but a severe regard for truth, learnt to a great extent from his teaching, could ever have led you to embody in your portrait of him a delineation of the faults and weaknesses which mixed with his great qualities.

'Of him I will make only one remark in justice to you. He did not use you well. He threw upon you the responsibility of a decision which he ought to have taken himself in a plain, unmistakable way. He considered himself bound to expiate the wrongs which he had done to his wife. If he had done this himself it would have been a courageous thing ; but he did not do it himself. He did not even decide for himself that it should be done after his death. If any courage was shown in the matter, it was shown by you, and not by him. You took the responsibility of deciding for him that it ought to be done. You took the odium of doing it, of avowing to the world the faults and weaknesses of one whom you regarded as your teacher and master. In order to present to the world a true picture of him as he really was, you, well knowing what you were about, stepped into a pillory in which you were charged with treachery, violation of confidence, and every imaginable base motive, when you were in fact guilty of no other fault than that of practising Mr. Carlyle's great doctrine that men ought to tell the truth.

'Make any use you like of this, and give it any degree of publicity which you think desirable.

'I am ever, my dear Froude,
'Most sincerely yours,
'J. F. STEPHEN.'

XX*

LEMAN TO MESSRS. BENSON

51 Lincoln's Inn Fields,
February 12, 1890.

'Dear Sirs,—Mr. Froude writes to me that another edition of his life of Mr. Carlyle is called for. As the accuracy of some of his extracts from Mr. Carlyle's letters has been challenged, he would like to have an opportunity of verifying them with the originals once more, and requests therefore that Mrs. M. Carlyle will give him the means of doing so by some competent person to be nominated by him. He does not propose to do this himself. I shall be glad if you will communicate with Mrs. Carlyle and let me know what arrangement she can make with reference to this matter. Believe me,

'Yours very faithfully,
'J. Curtis Leman.

'Messrs. Benson,
'1 Clement's Inn, W.C.'

XXI*

MARY CARLYLE TO MR. BENSON

23 Rudall Crescent, Hampstead,
February 21, 1890.

'My dear Sir,—I am obliged by your letter enclosing a copy of Mr. Leman's to you.

'I wish to consult Professor Norton before asking you to reply to Mr. Leman's letter more specifically than to assure him that I shall be most willing to have all relevant manuscripts of Mr. Carlyle in my possession examined by two competent men of letters (with an umpire if necessary), one to be named by Mr. Froude, the other by Professor Norton. I think that the remuneration of these nominees should be liberal, so as to ensure a thorough examination and a decision as to Mr. Froude's accuracy or otherwise which may be regarded as final. I should of course require an undertaking that Mr. Froude will act upon the conclusions of fact arrived at by the nominees so far as not to republish as manuscript of Mr. Carlyle anything that they consider an incorrect rendering of the original.

'Mr. Froude will no doubt consider it fair that he should provide for the expense of this examination, unless, indeed, the result of it should prove that the extracts given in his "Life of Carlyle" are substantially correct, in which case I will myself bear the whole expense of the investigation.

'I am,

'Yours very truly,

'MARY CARLYLE.'

XXII*

LEMAN TO BENSON

51 Lincoln's Inn Fields,
London, W.C.,
February 1890.

'DEAR SIR,

'*Carlyle.*

'I have submitted to Mr. Froude Mrs. Carlyle's letter. He had no intention, when he instructed me to write to you, of entering into any such arrangement as that suggested by Mrs. Carlyle. He desired merely to have the opportunity for his own satisfaction of verifying his extracts from the letters, the verbal accuracy of which has been impugned, and of ascertaining if there are any further corrections to be made than those (neither many nor material, as he tells me) which he has already noted, and he desired to employ some other person to do this mainly owing to his own eyesight being now not so good as heretofore ; but it was most remote from his purpose to constitute a sort of tribunal of appeal in the matter of the volumes generally. If this were done, as Mrs. Carlyle proposes, the enquiry would be one into the general accuracy of Mr. Froude's volumes which might involve entering into other particulars which there is no present occasion to make public, and upon an examination of other documents in Mr. Froude's own possession. As regards Mr. Froude's request, Mrs. Carlyle would have nothing to do with the payment of any person employed by Mr. Froude, which is entirely his affair ; if she require to have any other person present during the examination, to safeguard the papers, this on the other hand is her affair and Mr. Froude has nothing to do with it.

'Mr. Froude adds in his letter to me that perhaps Mrs. Carlyle has a list of the misprints and inaccuracies alleged, and if so perhaps she would let Mr. Froude have a copy which might save some trouble in the matter to both parties.'

XXIII *

LEMAN TO FROUDE

51 Lincoln's Inn Fields,
London, W.C.,
March 17, 1890.

'My dear Mr. Froude,—I am not sure whether I have correctly understood your intention, but please see if the enclosed conveys your ideas accurately. I do not like you to commit yourself absolutely to the proposition that you will *adopt* any alterations, even mere verbal alterations, that Mrs. Carlyle may send. It seems to me that your original proposal was reasonable enough. Mrs. Carlyle has rejoined by an elaborate proposal of referees and a covert suggestion that you or your representatives are not to be trusted with the papers. As you had them for so many years in your own hands, the proposition requires only to be so stated to show the absurdity of it. I think Mrs. Carlyle's elaborate proposal about the payment of referees, umpires, etc., shows she is making difficulties in complying with your request.

'Believe me,
'Yours very sincerely,
'J. Curtis Leman.

'I was unable to write on Saturday, so please return draft letter [that is, the letter which had been submitted for Froude's approval] by my son, the bearer of this.

'J. A. Froude, Esq.'

XXIV *

LEMAN TO BENSON

51 Lincoln's Inn Fields,
London, W.C.,
March 20, 1890.

'Dear Sir,

'*Carlyle*.

'Mr. Froude does not require any referee with regard to this matter, but if Mrs. Carlyle will furnish him with her list of corrections of alleged misprints, he is prepared to accept them, and will note them as derived from her, unless in those cases where they correspond with what he has already noted.

'He adds also that any further remarks, or any additional information on matters of fact which Mrs. Carlyle may be willing to communicate to him shall be carefully considered by him, if she will put them in writing to him or if she wishes to communicate verbally with any representative on Mr. Froude's behalf, he will send his son to call upon her.

'I have been delayed in replying to your last letter owing to Mr. Froude being out of town.

'Believe me,

'Yours very faithfully,

'J. Curtis Leman.

'J. B. Benson Esq.,
'1 Clement's Inn, London.'

XXV †

THOMAS CARLYLE TO JANE WELSH

Hoddam Hill,
July 29, 1825.

'My Dearest,—Your letter reached me but a few hours ago. I was doubly shocked on reading it a second time to find it dated Sunday. What a week you must have had. It were inhuman to keep you another moment in uncertainty.

'You exaggerate this matter greatly. It is an evil, but it may be borne : we must bear it *together*. What else can we do ? Much of the annoyance it occasions to me proceeds from selfish sources of a poor enough description. This is unworthy of our notice. Let it go to strengthen the schoolings of experience. Let it be another chastisement to vanity : perhaps she needs it ; and if not who is *She* that I should take thought of her ?

'Nor is the other more serious part of the mischief half so heinous in my eyes as it seems to be in yours.

There was a want of firmness in withholding an avowal which you thought might give me pain. There must have been suffering in the concealments and reservations it imposed on you. But there is a heroism in your present frankness, a fund of truth and probity which ought to cancel all that went before. You say it was not voluntary. So much the more difficult. I honour it the more. You ask me to forgive you, you stand humbled and weeping before me. No more of this for God's sake. Forgiveness! Where is the living man that dare look steadfastly into his "painted sepulchre" of a heart, and say I have lived one year without committing fifty faults of a deeper dye than this! My dear Jane, my best Jane, your soul is of a more ethereal temper than befits this very despicable world. You love truth and nobleness. You are forced to love them and you know not how they may be reached. Oh God! what a heartless slave were I if I discouraged you for any paltry momentary interests of my own in the sacred object you are aiming at! Believe me, my Dearest, this struggling of a pure soul to escape from the contaminations that encircle it, is but more touching to me that its success is incomplete. It is human nature in the loveliest aspect our poor Earth admits of, flesh and spirit, the clay of the ground made living by the breath of the Almighty.

'Oh, love truth, my dearest: prize it beyond all fame and power and happiness. Continue to love it fearlessly through good and bad report: it is the day-star from on high that shines to us in this gloomy wilderness of existence: There is still hope of him who knows and venerates its light and dares determine to hold fast by it to the death. Help me too to love it: I can talk more largely of it than you, but many an hour I could say with Brutus "Virtue, have I worshipped thee as a substance and found thee an empty shadow?" It is not so. By the majestic Universe, by the Mysterious Soul of man, it is not so. There is a worth in goodness which defies all chance. The *happy* man was never yet created: the virtuous man, though clothed in rags and sinking under pain, *is* the jewel of the earth, however I may doubt it or deny it in my bitterness of heart. Oh! never let me forget it! Teach me, tell me when the fiend of suffering and the base spirit of the world are ready to prevail against me and to drive me from this last stronghold.

'You feel grateful to me that I have "forgiven" you? You thank me and say I treat you generously? Alas, alas, I deserve no gratitude. What have I done? Assured you that my affection is still yours, that you are even dearer to me for this painful circumstance. But do you know the worth of that affection? Have you ever seen me and my condition in the naked eye of your reason? You have not; you do not know me: the affection you rejoice in is worse than worthless. It is hurtful. It may be your ruin. What is my love of you or of anyone? A wild peal through the desolate chambers of my soul, forcing perhaps a bitter tear into my eyes and then giving place to silence and death. You know me not: no living mortal knows me, seems to know me. I can no longer love. My heart has been steeped in solitary bitterness till the life of it is gone. The heaven of two confiding souls that live but for each other, encircled with glad affection, enlightened by the sun of worldly blessings and suitable activity is a thing I contemplated as from a far distance, without the hope, sometimes without even the wish of reaching it. Am I not poor and sick and helpless and estranged from all men? I lie upon the thorny couch of pain. My pillow is the iron pillow of despair. I can rest on them in silence, but that is all that I can do. Think of it, Jane! I can never make you happy. Leave me then. Why should I destroy you? It is but one bold step and it is done. We shall suffer, suffer to the heart, but we shall have obeyed the voice of reason, and time will teach us to endure it. *Verschmerzen werden wirs: denn was verschmerzte nicht der Mensch*? No affection is unalterable or eternal; we ourselves with all our passions sink to dust and are speedily consumed.

'I know your generous heart. You say, I will not leave this poor true-hearted brother. He *is* my brother and faithful to me, though sinking in the waves of destiny. I will clasp him to my heart and save him or perish with him. Alas, you know not what you do. You cannot save me: it is Fate alone that can save me if I am to be saved at all. You do not know me: believe me, you would be wretched with me in a week. "Save me!" "Make me happy!" I smile to hear the recipe of our kind Mrs. Montagu. "Exorcism" with a vengeance. *Ach du lieber Gott*!

'These things have long, for years, more or less distinctly lain upon my heart. I have told you them, that I might imitate the sincerity you have so nobly set before me as a pattern. If you say they are "blue devils," vapours of sickness, I shall be sorry: for it will but show me you have not understood or believed: If you think them merely the weak querulous wailings of a distempered mind you will do me some injustice: if you think they are pretexts and that I have ceased to love you, you will do injustice both to yourself and to me. Oh Jane! But what use is it to talk? I could write forty quires on that subject and yet not make it clear to you. You are young, you know not life, know not yourself. Secluded all your days from the native country of your spirit you have grasped at every semblance of it: first the rude smoky fire of Edward Irving seemed to you a star of Heaven; next the quivering *ignis fatuus* of a soul that dwells in me. The world has a thousand noble hearts in it that you do not dream of and you think that you will never meet another. What am I, or what is my father's house, that you should sacrifice yourself for me ?

'I know not whether it was good to write these things, for a spoken word is more dangerous than a whetted sword. They assume a thousand forms in my thoughts. This, as near as I could paint it, is a glimpse of their general aspect. At least therefore they are true. They seem to demand *your* solemn calm deliberation, and the speedier the decision it may be the better for us both. Again and again I repeat it, you do not know me ! Come and see and determine. Let me hear you and do you hear me. As I am take me or refuse me, but not as I am not, for this cannot and will not come to good. God help us both and show us both the way we ought to walk in. When will you come ? You are forever dear to me, in spite of all I say and feel. God bless you.

'I am always and wholly yours,

'TH. CARLYLE.'

XXVI

PROFESSIONAL CONFIDENCE

'From the earliest times of Medicine, the absolute necessity for preserving the strictest secrecy concerning personal matters which have become known to them in the course of their professional duties has been inculcated on all practitioners of the Art ; and it is needless to say that this rule has been so carefully and honourably fulfilled that it is almost proverbial how sacred such confidential knowledge is considered by medical men. In other countries, indeed, in which

Law governs everything, the State has incorporated in the legal code special rules providing for professional secrecy; and not only enjoining such confidence on the part of practitioners, but also safeguarding them to a certain degree from penalties if they refuse to divulge information thus confidentially obtained. In this country, such legal measures have never been considered necessary, with the one exception that it is now laid down as part of our "judges' law" that a medical man under oath to speak the truth, the whole truth, and nothing but the truth, in a court of justice cannot claim any privilege or exemption, but must, if the judge holds the question to be relevant, answer and give information which has only been communicated to him in professional confidence. It will be a bad day for the medical profession if this rule were ever extended, because it is a matter of common knowledge that many facts are entrusted to a medical practitioner in simple and absolute trust that they will be held as secret as in the confessional of the Roman Church.

'In view of this almost basic principle of medical practice, it is easy to understand the painful feelings which have been aroused in the medical world by the present controversy concerning the life of Carlyle. It has brought about more or less divulgence of facts which could only have been regarded as absolutely confidential, and the flame of controversy has unhappily been fanned by the wild incursion into the matter of perhaps the most injudicious writer of the present day. He may have been actuated by feelings of personal friendship, but he has certainly employed his medical knowledge in dissecting and exposing personal matters which cannot be regarded as of the slightest professional interest; and, considering that they relate to a man and woman who have been buried for many years, cannot even be regarded as of public interest. Unfortunately, these unsavoury details have been published at length in the columns of a medical contemporary. We are informed that this article has caused extreme surprise among leading writers in the lay press, who are almost unanimous in considering that this particular controversy should never have been opened ; and, secondly, that in the form to which it has now attained it is almost an outrage on public decency. Unfortunately, however, the *cacoëthes scribendi* is a powerful perverter of common sense ; and, especially in this age when self-advertisement seems in certain minds to be the chief end to be attained, it is difficult to foresee to what further lengths this controversy may go. But, as we believe the present occasion is one of the first upon which a medical man of any standing has imported purely medical details concerning a dead and gone celebrity into a public controversy, we take an immediate opportunity of expressing our opinion that such a proceeding cannot be deemed for the advantage either of the public or the medical profession. There are newspapers even in this country which revel in garbage so long as it is of a personal nature ; but such papers are wanting in reputation, and are probably extremely limited in their circulation ; but a serious feature of the present-day craze for personalities, as evinced, for example, in the scandal to which we particularly allude, is the precedent now set for malignant, not to say indecent, vilification of the characters of long deceased celebrities, and which may be, in future, adopted by any scurrilous scribbler who desires to obtain a wide advertisement for himself at whatever cost to the reputation of the dead, to the happiness of the living, or to the cause of public decency. We therefore earnestly join in the protest made by the leading papers of the country against the present wantonly indecent controversy concerning the sexual capabilities of Thomas Carlyle and his wife.

'And especially do we deprecate and regret the

fact that any medical man should, in support of his side of the contest, consider it advisable to resuscitate and publicly discuss, from a medical point of view, rumours which were probably almost entirely forgotten.'—*The Medical Times and Hospital Gazette*, July 4, 1903.

FROUDE AND CARLYLE

'We have received several letters relative to the article by Sir James Crichton-Browne on Froude and Carlyle which appeared in the *British Medical Journal* of June 27. We have elsewhere expressed our own opinion on this unsavoury quarrel over dead men's graves, and thought it right to give Sir J. Crichton-Browne an opportunity of setting out the evidence in his possession; but we do not think the particular matter here in dispute of sufficient medical importance to justify the allotment of any further space to it in the *Journal*. In order, however, to show the trend of opinion among our readers on the subject, we give abstracts of the more important letters received.

'Sir William Thomson, C.B., Ex-President of the Royal College of Surgeons in Ireland, and Direct Representative for Ireland on the General Medical Council, writes:

"In the course of the article which Sir James Crichton-Browne has contributed to the *Journal* on the disgusting Froude-Carlyle controversy he says: 'Sir Richard (then Dr.) Quain was professionally consulted by Mrs. Carlyle, treated her for a number of years and gave her death certificate, and was not, as Chairman of the General Medical Council, likely to commit an act infamous in a professional respect by divulging a secret confided to him by a patient in his professional capacity.' Of course not: but in another part of the same article he makes the following extraordinary suggestion: 'Nor did he (Froude) think fit to test Miss Jewsbury's statement in any way, although he regarded it as not a mere bit of idle talk, but as of vital importance, and made it the keynote of his whole biography. Carlyle was alive: *many medical men who had attended Mrs. Carlyle were accessible*; judicious friends of hers like Mrs. Russell, of Thornhill, who had been in far more confidential relations with her than Miss Jewsbury, might have been appealed to: but no step did Froude take to apply the touchstones which lay ready at hand.' I have put one of these clauses in italics because it should be read in the light of what the writer says regarding a possible offence by Sir Richard Quain. What does he mean by referring to the medical men who were 'accessible'? Does he mean that Froude should have gone to these men, who knew her 'professional secrets,' have 'applied the touchstones'; have invited them to divulge 'a secret confided to (them) by a patient in (their) professional capacity'—'an act infamous in a professional respect?'

"I cannot help saying that the whole of these discussions are an impudent intrusion into matters which do not concern any one of the living public. They are an outrage on the memory of a great man and a great woman. May one appeal to the noisy disputants to cease from furnishing us with the ugly details of the marital relations of the Carlyles, and all the unpleasant garnishing with which these details are served up?"

'Lieutenant-Colonel Nathaniel Alcock, Army Medical Staff, writes in defence of Froude. He says:

"Sir J. Crichton-Browne under his own hand proves himself to be in his present frenzied state not much less neurotic than the late Miss Jewsbury or Mrs. Carlyle herself, and consequently by no means a safe guide."

'In reply to the opening words of Sir James

Crichton-Browne's article ("Mr. J. A. Froude has fitly crowned the column of calumny, etc.") he quotes the preface to "My Relations with Carlyle," in which Froude's children say, "In making facts public on which Mr. Froude had after long and anxious consideration *decided to be silent*, we are fully aware of the responsibility, etc.," and asks :

"Is it not sad to see a heated controversialist thrusting words into the silent mouth of one long dead which he had determined never to utter, and which were only found after his death written in pencil in a notebook and had been shown to no one ?"

'In regard to the question of virility, Lieutenant-Colonel Alcock holds that had Froude made, as is suggested by Sir J. Crichton-Browne, an appeal to some of Mrs. Carlyle's lady friends, his conduct would have deserved to be characterised as "filthy," "scurrilous," etc. Finally, Lieutenant-Colonel Alcock retorts on Sir James Crichton-Browne the charge which he brings against Froude of introducing into his books on Carlyle contentious matter that added largely to their piquancy and increased the sales.

'Dr. G. N. W. Thomas, of Cardiff, who treats the allegation of impotence as a "charge" against Carlyle, complains that Froude took no steps to corroborate Miss Jewsbury's statement :

"In such a charge as this, surely Carlyle's medical attendant would have been one of the first to be consulted (!)"

'While he holds that as medical men we must come to the conclusion that the statement that Carlyle was impotent is certainly "not proven," yet he thinks that Sir James Crichton-Browne "has not given us any proof that he was not impotent, though he has endeavoured to do so." Dr. Thomas continues :

"Sir J. Crichton-Browne has, after much trouble, and with the conspicuous ability we should expect from him, done his best to clear Carlyle of the imputation ; but, on the other hand, I do not consider he is at all justified in charging Mrs. Carlyle with sterility simply because she was born prematurely with a nervous temperament and delicate constitution."

'Dr. T. Parry Wilson expresses disapproval of the publication of such details as Sir James Crichton-Browne has gone into. He adds :

"If it were the case that Sir Richard Quain imparted to Mrs. Venturi the communication he is stated to have done in the article in question, one can only think it was a peculiar and exceptional measure to take—using a third party, and that a lady, as the medium of a most private and personal matter. Should one not have rather expected him to have waited to see Carlyle himself, or have written him a private note on the subject ? It seems still more curious, however, that Sir James Crichton-Browne should have thought fit to repeat it in public. In any case, it proves nothing either way."

'Pax also protests against the public discussion of a question which is of no public or scientific interest, and only concerns the persons actually involved.

"Had there arisen any question of the legitimacy of children then an entirely new aspect would have presented itself, but this does not arise."

'He concludes :

"Surely these two dead people are entitled to be left alone, and their personal and domestic characteristics forgotten in the beauty of their public work."

'A lady correspondent who signs herself "Mrs. Carlyle's Sympathiser," thinks that "whether Carlyle had a genital defect or not cannot in any way take away from him being 'one of the noblest and best of his species.' . . . Carlyle was created for higher and nobler ends than the mere propagation of his kind." She goes on to ask :

" Is there not a marriage on a higher plane where mind meets mind and soul meets soul, and are knit together by a bond stronger than any earthly bond? If Carlyle's pretty love letter to his young wife breathed only passion as Sir J. Crichton-Browne would have us believe, and not that diviner, purer love which Mrs. Carlyle's letters and life surely showed she craved for, would that not cause some clouds in their sky? The woman who had believed she was receiving from so grand a man a divine love, to find it but an earthly passion. What a fall from Heaven to earth!"

'For the following interesting communication we are indebted to Dr. D. A. Alexander of Clifton:

" Readers of Froude will remember in the present controversy another excursion by him into the secret history and morbid experiences of the great. It is the relations of a royal pair which he is discussing—Henry VIII and Anne Boleyn. Having vindicated the moral character of the King, and accepted the evidence of the charges upon which his consort suffered, he proceeds to remark: 'Historians, to make their narrative coherent, assume an intimate acquaintance with the motives for each man's or woman's actions. Facts may be difficult to ascertain, but motives, which cannot be ascertained at all unless when acknowledged, they are able to discern by intuition. . . . I pretend to no intuition myself. . . . In this instance I hazard a conjecture—a conjecture merely—which occurred to me long ago as an explanation of some of the disasters of Henry's marriages, and which the words, alleged to have been used by Anne . . . tend, *pro tanto*, to confirm (" *Que le Roy n'estoit habille en cas de copuler avec femme, et qu'il n'avoit ni vertu ni puissance.*") Henry was already showing signs of the disorder which eventually killed him. Infirmities in his constitution made it doubtful, both to others and himself, whether healthy children,

or any children at all, would in future be born to him. It is possible—I do not say more—that Anne, feeling that her own precarious position could only be made secure if she became the mother of a prince, had turned elsewhere 'for assistance.'" The passage is taken from the 'Divorce of Catherine of Aragon.'"
—*British Medical Journal*, July 4, 1903.

THE FROUDE-CARLYLE CONTROVERSY

'Reference has already been made in the *British Medical Journal* to the unedifying controversy which has been rekindled by the publication of a book, entitled "New Letters and Memorials of Jane Welsh Carlyle," with an introduction by Sir James Crichton-Browne. Sir James, in the ardour of his championship of Carlyle, cursed the memory of Froude with a vigour and a wealth of vocabulary which Ernulphus might have envied. Mr. Ashley Froude and Miss Margaret Froude retorted by publishing a private record by Froude himself of his relations with Carlyle not intended by him to see the light. They cannot fairly be blamed for seeking to vindicate the character of their father; it is deplorable, however, that the publication of such a document should have been judged to be necessary. It consists of notes written by Froude in pencil, unrevised, and never seen by anyone till after his death. These notes show how keenly he felt the storm of criticism which broke over his head after the publication of his "Life of Carlyle." The special interest of the book from our point of view lies in the fact that it contains a statement in plain terms of what is obscurely hinted at in the biography—namely, that the secret of Carlyle's life was that "he was one of those persons who ought never to have married." In the last issue of the *British Medical Journal* Sir James Crichton-Browne came forward in defence of Carlyle against this " cruel imputation." He swings his controversial Excalibur with such might that he speedily reduces an adversary to the " doleful dumps " of the hero in the ballad. Had Mr. Froude been still alive he might perhaps have " fought upon his stumps," but being dead he has not a leg to stand upon.

'We do not propose to go into the details of the question at issue. Sir James Crichton-Browne says that Froude " trusted entirely to rumour," and he certainly shows that the witness on whose testimony he appears mainly to have relied was quite untrustworthy. The evidence of Sir Richard Quain is not so entirely convincing to us as it is to Sir James Crichton-Browne ; but we are heartily glad that the discreditable story as to the examination of Mrs. Carlyle's body after death in St. George's Hospital is now shown to be utterly false.

'If Froude trusted entirely to rumour, it is only fair to say that Sir James Crichton-Browne seems to trust largely to gossip—some of which, as for instance the remarks attributed to the late Dr. Maclagan, seems irrelevant. On both sides it is a case of " what the soldier said," and that, as we know from the pronouncement of Mr. Justice Stareleigh, is not evidence. Sir James complains that Froude did not test Miss Jewsbury's statement, and points out that " many medical men who had attended Mrs. Carlyle were accessible." This strikes us as a somewhat remarkable suggestion from a writer who a little further on makes a fine display of indignation at the mere thought of Sir Richard Quain having committed an act infamous in a professional respect by divulging a secret confided to him by a patient. We take this opportunity of making a strong protest against the notion that seems to exist in the public mind that medical advisers are at liberty to tell everything they know about a patient who happens to be a man or woman of genius. One satisfactory feature in this wretched business is that the rumours and tattlings about the Carlyle *ménage* cannot be traced to the medical men who at various times attended the distinguished couple.

'The fact is, there is no conclusive evidence either way as to Carlyle's physical condition. Sir James Crichton-Browne says that Froude has done his best to "brand Carlyle as a Narses." With all respect we submit that Froude did no such thing. Narses was a eunuch, and we have seen no suggestion that Carlyle presented any physical deficiency or anomaly. The evidence of trussmakers, etc., is really nothing to the purpose. There is a psychical as well as a physical impotence, and it is precisely men absorbed in brain-work, as Carlyle was, who are most likely to be the victims of the spell expressed in the old French phrase *nouer l'aiguillette*. Many a strong man has been bewitched in this way; some never recover from the mental effects of an initial failure. It has been hinted that this is just what happened to Carlyle, but no one can now know the truth about the matter; nor is it of the slightest importance to mankind or to the memory of the dead that it should be known.

'Of Froude's statement we may say as the lisping French philosopher said of the existence of a deity: *Zolie hypothèse! Ça explique bien des choses.* We would point out, however, that this pretty hypothesis in no way touches the moral character or intellectual greatness of Carlyle. Therefore, to speak of the allegation as a "vile imputation," a "foul falsehood," etc., as if impotence were a heinous crime, shows a want of the sense of humour which Carlyle himself displayed in regard to this very matter. Who that has read it can have forgotten his account of the squire of dames who was wounded in a duel and lived many years afterwards, doubtless breaking many commandments but keeping *one* with inflexible rigour?

'We earnestly hope that this unseemly controversy will now be allowed to come to an end. By us, at any rate, the matter will not be again referred to, nor can we allow it to be discussed further in these columns.'—*British Medical Journal*, July 4, 1903.

THE MARRIED LIFE OF THE CARLYLES

'It is little less than sacrilege to draw aside the curtain which should ever veil the joys and sorrows of domestic life, and it is a relic of barbarism which allows the ruthless stripping of all-sacred draperies from the sanctity of marriage. But the sexual concerns of the Carlyles have become subject for common gossip, and the relations of Thomas Carlyle and Jane Welsh now afford matter for jest as well as for profound sorrow. We consider a very grave responsibility has been undertaken by those who, presumably in the interests of biographical truth, have dragged into the unprotected gaze of a selfish public physiological and psychological conditions which might well have been treated with such respect and reticence as has always characterised the procedure of the medical profession in regard to such matters. In a recent number we referred to Froude's contention that the only true explanation of the differences and misunderstandings which arose between these two exceptionally gifted souls was to be found in the impotence of the master man. Sir James Crichton-Browne has now issued a peculiarly bitter and in many ways unfortunate and unsatisfactory reply to Froude's imputation, in which the charge is, as he calls it, "considered medically." He certainly succeeds in showing that there is strong circumstantial evidence that Carlyle was not the subject of any disability, as has been suggested. It is clear, however, that the childless state of the Carlyle home accounts for much in the wide separation of these two lives, sundered far though lived together. Sir James, in the introduction to the recent volume of letters of Mrs. Carlyle, and in his last effort to wipe all mud of slander and filth of false accusation from his much-beloved master, has hardly granted that charity which would protect Jane Welsh Carlyle from abuse. Indeed, much of his argument seems based upon a determined effort to glorify the man by despising and degrading the woman. The discussion is not creditable to the literary spirit of to-day. Such subjects must of necessity come within the scope of serious medical inquiry, and no physician desirous of serving his day and generation can afford to neglect a careful study of the psychological and physical states influencing or deranging sexual functions ; but we think the reckless exposure of these matters in all their nudity to an ignorant and oftentimes lewd public opinion will be shown to be ill-advised and useless, and will bring shame and a measure of disgrace to all concerned in such exposure.'—*Medical Press* (London), July 8, 1903.

XXVII

TEXTUAL VARIATIONS

The following quotations are from the memoir of Jane Welsh Carlyle in Carlyle's 'Reminiscences' as given in the edition indicated. Where more is not needed, only a portion of the context is given.

'It broke her health for the next two or three years, and in a sense almost broke her heart.' Froude, ii. 94.

'It broke her health, permanently, within the next two or three years ; and, in a sense, almost broke her heart.' Norton, i. 72.

'. . . but her filial heart repelled the notion.' Froude, ii. 195.

'. . . but *her* filial heart abhorred the notion.' Norton, i. 122.

'In 1849, after an interval.' Froude, ii. 198.

'In 1850, after an interval.' Norton, i. 125.

'Chapman (hard-fisted cautious bibliographer).' Froude, ii. 199.

'Chapman (hard-fisted cautious Bibliopole).' Norton, i. 126.

'In 1845, late autumn.' Froude, ii. 201.

'In 1844, late Autumn.' Norton, i. 128.

'. . . discourse of ten or thirteen minutes.' Froude, ii. 204.

'. . . discourse of ten or fifteen minutes.' Norton, i. 131.

'But I intend to put down something about her parentage now, and what of reminiscence must live with me on that head.' Froude, ii. 101.

'Intend to put down something about her Parentage etc., *now* ;—and what of reminiscence most lives with me on that head.' Norton, i. 132–133.

'Within one year, February 16, 1774, these Hunters had married him to their eldest girl (about sixteen, four months younger than himself), and his schooldays were suddenly completed !' Froude, ii. 107.

'Within one year, 16th February 1774, these Hunters had married him to their eldest Girl (about sixteen, three months *younger* than himself), and his schooldays were suddenly completed !' Norton, i. 137–138.

'For chief or almost sole intimate he had the neighbouring (biggish) laird, " old Hoggan of Waterside," almost close by Penfillan, whose peremptory ways and angularities of mind and conduct are still remembered in that region.' Froude, ii. 109.

'For chief or almost sole intimate he had the neighbouring (biggish) Laird, "old Hogan of Waterside," almost close by Penfillan, whose peremptory ways and regularities of mind and conduct are still remembered in that region.' Norton, i. 139.

'Went first, I clearly find, as Regimental Surgeon, August 16, 1796.' Froude, ii. 113.

'[Went first, I clearly find, as Regimental Surgeon, 10th August 1796.' Norton, i. 142.

'. . . if especially a touch of hypocrisy and perfect admiration were superadded.' Froude, ii. 121.

'. . . if especially a touch of hypocrisy and perfect assentation were superadded.' Norton i. 148–149.

'He was serious, pensive, not more, or sad, in those old times.' Froude, ii. 126.

'He was serious, pensive, not morose or sad, in these old times.' Norton, i. 153.

'. . . the good "Larry" faring us.' Froude, ii. 139.

'. . . the good "Harry" *faring* us.' Norton, i. 163.

'. . . and the poor old cotter woman.' Froude, ii. 141.

'. . . and the poor old Cowar-woman.' Norton, i. 165.

'. . . a young peasant woman, pulling potatoes by the brink.' Froude, ii. 146.

'. . . a young peasant woman, peeling potatoes by the brink.' Norton, i. 169.

'She read the first two volumes of "Friedrich," much of it in printer's sheets (while on visit to the aged Misses Donaldson at Haddington); her blame was unerringly straight upon the blot, her applause (should not I collect her fine notekins and reposit them here?) was beautiful and as sunlight to me, for I knew it was sincere withal, however exaggerated by her great love of me.' Froude, ii. 243.

'She *read* the first two volumes of "Friedrich," much of it in printer's sheets (while on visit to the aged Misses Donaldson at Haddington); her applause (should not I collect her fine Notekins and reposit them here?) was beautiful and as sunlight to me,—for I knew it was sincere withal, and unerringly straight upon the blot, however exaggerated by her great love of me.' Norton, i. 203.

'. . . an artificial champagne cask.' Froude, ii. 259.

'. . . an artificial *champagne-cork*.' Norton, i. 216.

The following are from the memoir of James Carlyle in Carlyle's 'Reminiscences,' as given in the edition indicated.

'Jan. 26, 1832.' Froude, i. 3.

'January the 24th, 1832.' Norton, i. 1.

'Even at every new parting.' Froude, i. 5.

'Ever at every new parting.' Norton, i. 3.

'My mind is calm enough to do it deliberately, and to do it truly. The thought of that pale earnest face which even now lies stiffened into death in that bed at Scotsbrig, with the Infinite all of worlds looking down on it, will certainly impel me.' Froude, i. 6–7.

'My mind is calm enough to do it deliberately; and to do it truly the thought of that pale earnest face which even now lies stiffened into Death in that bed at Scotsbrig, with the infinite All of Worlds looking down on it,—will *certainly* impel me.' Norton, i. 4.

'It is good to know how a true spirit will vindicate itself with truth and freedom.' Froude, i. 7.

'It is good to know how a true spirit will vindicate itself into truth and freedom.' Norton, i. 4.

'There looked honestly through those clear earnest eyes a sincerity that compelled belief and regard.' Froude, i. 13.

'There looked *honesty* through those clear earnest eyes; a sincerity that compelled belief and regard.' Norton, i. 9.

'... rending asunder official sophisms.' Froude i. 13.

'... rending asunder official sophistries.' Norton, i. 9.

'... when working in Springhill.' Froude, i. 16.

'... when working at Springkell.' Norton, i. 11.

'I knew Robert Burns, and I knew my father.' Froude, i. 18.

'I know Robert Burns, and I knew my father;' Norton, i. 13.

'... saw the Highlanders come through Ecclefechan over the Border heights.' Froude, i. 30.

'... saw the Highlanders come through Ecclefechan (over the Cowden-heights).' Norton, i. 23.

'... about 1720.' Froude, i. 35.

'... about 1727.' Norton, i. 27.

'Wylie Hill.' Froude, i. 38.

'Wylie-hole.' Norton, i. 30.

'... at all events married his eldest daughter's child.' Froude, i. 41.

'... at all events married his eldest daughter and child.' Norton, i. 32.

'... fond of genealogies, old historic poems.' Froude, i. 43.

'... fond of genealogies, old histories, poems.' Norton, i. 34.

'They were (consciously).' Froude, i. 44.

'... they were (censoriously).' Norton, i. 34.

'Perhaps my father was William Brown's first apprentice. Somewhere about his sixteenth year, early in the course of the engagement, work grew scarce in Annandale. The two "slung their tools" (mallets and irons hung in two equipoised masses over the shoulder), and crossed the hills into Nithsdale to Auldgarth, where a bridge was building.' Froude, i. 45.

'Perhaps my Father was William Brown's first Apprentice: somewhere about his sixteenth year. Early in the course of the engagement, work grew scarce in Annandale: the two "slung their tools" (mallets and irons hung in two equipoised masses over the shoulders), and crossed the Hills into Nithsdale, to Auldgarth, where a Bridge was building.' Norton, i. 35.

'A flood once carried off all the centres and woodwork.' Froude, i. 46.

'A flood once carried off all the cinctures and woodwork.' Norton, i. 36.

'Our country was all altered; browsing knowes were become seed-fields;' Froude, i. 46.

'The country was all altered; broomy knowes were become seed-fields;' Norton, i. 36.

'He lives with more or less impetuosity.' Froude, i. 48.

'... he tries with more or less impetuosity.' Norton, i. 38.

'. . . which showed impressively through his stout decision and somewhat cross-grained deeds and words.' Froude, i. 51.

'. . . which shone impressively through his stout decisive, and somewhat cross-grained deeds and words.' Norton, i. 40.

'. . . and otherwise produced me far higher benefit.' Froude, i. 51.

'. . . and otherwise procured me far higher benefits.' Norton, i. 40.

'. . . but long time suspected to be none of the most perfect.' Froude, i. 52.

'. . . but long since suspected to be none of the most perfect.' Norton, i. 41.

'We were all particularly taught.' Froude, i. 55.

'We were all practically taught.' Norton, i. 44.

'. . . and to me full of movement.' Froude, i. 58.

'. . . and to me full of moment.' Norton, i. 46.

'I read aloud to a little circle twice weekly.' Froude, i. 60.

'I read aloud to a little circle thrice weekly.' Norton, i. 48.

XXVIII

The following material became available upon the publication of 'Life and Letters of George Jacob Holyoake,' by Joseph McCabe. (Watts & Co. 1908). The passages are from vol. ii., pp. 126–127. For a copy of this material I am indebted to my friend and former colleague, Mr. Norman Macdonald.

'More interesting was a correspondence with Froude that grew out of his [Holyoake's] American visit. Readers of "Sixty Years" will remember that, when in Canada in 1882, he visited Carlyle's sister (Janet) Mrs. Hanning, at Hamilton. It seems that during his earlier visit he got some document from Mrs. Hanning, through Mr. Charlton, and sent it to Froude, who was then in the heat of the controversy over the Carlyle letters. Froude answered :

'Dear Mr. Holyoake,—I am sincerely grateful to you for sending me Mr. Charlton's letter and its enclosure. There is nothing in the letter with which I was not acquainted. It shows only that Mrs. Hanning's memory is a good one. My own difficulties have arisen rather from the excess of material than the absence of it. I am glad to have succeeded in interesting you in *Mrs.* Carlyle. *She* is my special legacy from Carlyle. His chief desire was that her portrait should be accurately drawn. Both characters were essentially magnificent. But she had a bitter tongue, and he was irritable, and in fact men and women of genius find or make an uneasy time of it in this world.

'I am glad to have been brought thus accidentally into correspondence with you. You have fought a brave battle for many years ; and if others now find the road more easy to travel, you were one of the pioneers when it lay through thorns and brambles. I never saw you or heard your voice, but I have not watched your action with the less interest.

'Yours faithfully,

'J. A. Froude.'

In thanking him Holyoake observed :

'A single sentence in your letter enables me to better understand Mr. and Mrs. Carlyle than what else I have read from their friends. I was among those who thought you should have omitted parts of the "Reminiscences," but the portions of his life you have published satisfied me that you were right. I regarded him as the greatest ruffian in literature since Dr. Johnson, but since he wished to be described as he was, I recognised in that the daring and sense of self-justice which redeemed Johnson and restore respect for Carlyle. The passages in the "Reminiscences" relating to his wife I knew to be a wail of remorse rather than of love. All great thinkers, being mostly unconscious of the claims of others, act as though their absorption was selfishness, which it is not, though it so appears to others.'

When Holyoake returned from Canada in 1882, he wrote to tell Froude that he had visited Mrs. Hanning. She told him :

'A paper was sent to me by the family to sign against Mr. Froude. I said I did not wish to sign it. Mr. Froude was my brother's friend. He always spoke of Mr. Froude with great regard. My brother trusted him, and I think the family ought. I said I wanted nothing artificial said about him. My brother was always for the truth, and so am I.'

Froude wrote in reply to his report of this :

'You are most kind in writing to me. I do not wonder that some members of Carlyle's family and that the world generally are perplexed and angry. It is so unusual in these days that a man who is conscious that he has fallen short in an important part of his duty should wish to make a public reparation that such an interpretation is the last which would occur to him. Yet this is what Carlyle felt, and he trusted to me as a friend on whom he could rely to execute his desire. I considered his retention of these letters and preparation of them for publication to be the finest act of his very noble life. I could not dissuade him from it—for it was really needed—and hereafter men will understand and honour him for his courage and truthfulness. I can do nothing at present but let the storm rage on.'

INDEX

The arrangement of material in this volume, as a reference to the table of contents will show, affords almost sufficient guidance to the reader. In this index an attempt is made to list only the more important names and topics. A complete catalogue of references to those chiefly concerned in the controversy would include almost every page in the text.

INDEX

INDEX

Printed in England at The Ballantyne Press
Spottiswoode, Ballantyne & Co. Ltd.
Colchester, London & Eton